Every
Pilgrim's Guide to
England's Holy Places

Other titles in the *Every Pilgrim's Guide* series:

Every Pilgrim's Guide to Assisi

Judith Dean

Every Pilgrim's Guide to Celtic Britain and Ireland

Andrew Jones

Every Pilgrim's Guide to the Holy Land

Norman Wareham and Jill Gill

Every Pilgrim's Guide to the Journeys of the Apostles

Michael Counsell

Every Pilgrim's Guide to Oberammergau

Michael Counsell

Other books by Michael Counsell:

Prayers for Sundays (HarperCollins*Religious*)

More Prayers for Sundays (HarperCollins*Religious*)

Kieu by Nguyen Du, bilingual edition (Thé Giói Press, Hanoi)

Two Thousand Years of Prayer (Canterbury Press and Morehouse Publishing)

All through the Night (Canterbury Press and Westminster John Knox Press)

The Little Book of Heavenly Humour (Syd Little, with Chris Gidney and Michael Counsell; Canterbury Press)

Every Pilgrim's Guide to England's Holy Places

MICHAEL COUNSELL

with illustrations by
JILL BENTLEY

CANTERBURY
PRESS
Norwich

First published in 2003 by the Canterbury Press Norwich
(a publishing imprint of Hymns Ancient & Modern Limited,
a registered charity)
St Mary's Works, St Mary's Plain,
Norwich, Norfolk, NR3 3BH

www.scm-canterburypress.co.uk

British Library Cataloguing in Publication data

A catalogue record for this book is available
from the British Library

ISBN 1-85311-522-3

Typeset by Regent Typesetting, London
Printed and bound by
Bookmarque Ltd, Croydon, Surrey

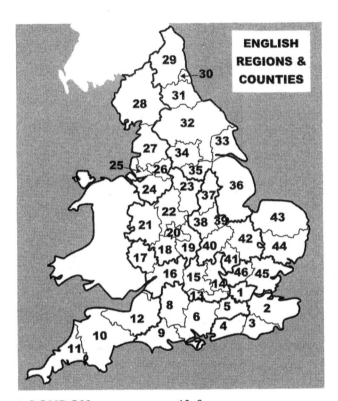

ENGLISH
REGIONS &
COUNTIES

1. LONDON

THE SOUTH-EAST
2. Kent
3. East Sussex
4. West Sussex

THE SOUTH COAST
5. Surrey
6. Hampshire
7. The Isle of Wight
8. Wiltshire
9. Dorset

THE WEST COUNTRY
10. Devon
11. Cornwall

12. Somerset

WEST OF LONDON
13. Berkshire
14. Buckinghamshire
15. Oxfordshire
16. Gloucestershire
17. Herefordshire

**THE WESTERN
MIDLANDS**
18. Worcestershire
19. Warwickshire
20. West Midlands
21. Shropshire
22. Staffordshire
23. Derbyshire

THE NORTH-WEST
24. Cheshire
25. Merseyside
26. Greater Manchester
27. Lancashire
28. Cumbria

THE NORTH-EAST
29. Northumbria
30. Tyne and Wear
31. County Durham
32. North Yorkshire
33. East Riding of Yorkshire
34. West Yorkshire
35. South Yorkshire
36. Lincolnshire

THE EAST MIDLANDS
37. Nottinghamshire
38. Leicestershire
39. Rutland
40. Northamptonshire
41. Bedfordshire
42. Cambridgeshire

EAST ANGLIA
43. Norfolk
44. Suffolk

NORTH OF LONDON
45. Essex
46. Hertfordshire

Contents

Preface   xii

Practical Details   1
A Time Line of English History   4

LONDON   6
  Westminster Abbey   6
  St Paul's Cathedral   8
  Hampton Court Palace   10
  Chelsea   12
  The Brompton Road   12
  Westminster Cathedral   13
  Tyburn   13
  Covent Garden   14
  Piccadilly   15
  Trafalgar Square   15
  Whitehall   16
  Holborn; The Strand; Fleet Street   17
  The Inns of Court   19
  The City of London   19
  The Tower of London   22
  South London   22
  Greenwich   25

THE SOUTH-EAST   30
  Canterbury (Kent)   30
  Rochester (Kent)   35
  Aylesford (Kent)   37
  Chichester (West Sussex)   37
  Stone; Lullingstone (Kent)   39
  Minster-in-Thanet; Barfreston; Dover (Kent)   40
  Winchelsea (East Sussex)   41
  Battle (East Sussex)   42
  Ditchling (East Sussex)   42
  Arundel (West Sussex)   43
  Didling (West Sussex)   45

THE SOUTH COAST   46
  Winchester (Hampshire)   46
  Salisbury (Wiltshire)   50
  Bemerton (Wiltshire)   52

Contents

Guildford (Surrey)   52
Chawton (Hampshire)   54
Wellow (Hampshire)   54
The Isle of Wight   54
Malmesbury (Wiltshire)   57
Bradford on Avon; Edington (Wiltshire)   58
Shaftesbury (Dorset)   59
Sherborne (Dorset)   59
Christchurch (Dorset)   60
Bournemouth (Dorset)   60
Wimborne (Dorset)   61
Wareham (Dorset)   61
Corfe Castle (Dorset)   62
Bere Regis; Milton Abbas (Dorset)   62
Dorchester (Dorset)   64
Whitchurch Canonicorum (Dorset)   64

THE WEST COUNTRY   66
Exeter (Devon)   66
Buckfast Abbey (Devon)   67
St Michael's Mount (Cornwall)   68
Glastonbury (Somerset)   69
Wells (Somerset)   71
Crediton (Devon)   74
Plymouth; Buckland Abbey (Devon)   74
Parracombe (Devon)   76
St Clether; Altarnun; Trewint; St Neot (Cornwall)   77
Bodmin (Cornwall)   79
Truro (Cornwall)   79
Trebetherick (Cornwall)   81
Tintagel (Cornwall)   82
Isle Abbots (Somerset)   84
Burrington Combe (Somerset)   84
Bath (Somerset)   84
Bristol (County Borough)   86

WEST OF LONDON   89
Windsor; Eton (Berkshire)   89
Oxford (Oxfordshire)   91
Dorchester-on-Thames (Oxfordshire)   99
Tewkesbury (Gloucestershire)   101
Gloucester (Gloucestershire)   101
Hereford (Herefordshire)   103
Kilpeck (Herefordshire)   105
Cookham (Berkshire)   106
Olney (Buckinghamshire)   106

Wing; North Marston (Buckinghamshire)   107
Chalfont St Giles; Stoke Poges (Buckinghamshire)   108
Littlemore (Oxfordshire)   110
Abingdon (Oxfordshire)   110
Fairford (Gloucestershire)   111
Cirencester (Gloucestershire)   112
Hailes Abbey (Gloucestershire)   112
Prinknash (Gloucestershire)   113
Deerhurst (Gloucestershire)   113
Abbey Dore (Herefordshire)   114
Shobdon (Herefordshire)   115

THE WESTERN MIDLANDS   116
Worcester (Worcestershire)   116
Coventry (West Midlands)   118
Lichfield (Staffordshire)   120
Kidderminster; Great Witley (Worcestershire)   123
Great Malvern; Pershore; Evesham (Worcestershire)   125
Stratford-upon-Avon (Warwickshire)   127
Warwick (Warwickshire)   128
Polesworth (Warwickshire)   129
Birmingham (West Midlands)   129
Shrewsbury (Shropshire)   132
Ludlow (Shropshire)   133
Oswestry (Shropshire)   134
Hoar Cross (Staffordshire)   135
Cheadle (Staffordshire)   136
Eyam; Tissington (Derbyshire)   136
Ashbourne (Derbyshire)   137
Melbourne (Derbyshire)   138

THE NORTH-WEST   139
Liverpool (Merseyside)   139
Mow Cop (Cheshire)   143
Chester (Cheshire)   144
Manchester (Greater Manchester)   145
Stonyhurst College (Lancashire)   145
Lancaster; Heysham (Lancashire)   146
Cartmel (Cumbria)   147
Swarthmoor Hall (Cumbria)   148
Furness Abbey (Cumbria)   149
St Bees (Cumbria)   150
Keswick (Cumbria)   151
Carlisle; Wreay (Cumbria)   151

Contents

THE NORTH-EAST   153

Durham (County Durham)   153
Fountains Abbey; Studley Royal (North Yorkshire)   157
York (North Yorkshire)   159
Lincoln (Lincolnshire)   162
Vindolanda; Corbridge; Hexham (Northumbria)   166
Lindisfarne (Northumbria)   168
Jarrow (Tyne and Wear)   170
Escomb (County Durham)   171
Whitby (North Yorkshire)   172
Mount Grace (North Yorkshire)   174
Rievaulx (North Yorkshire)   174
Ripon Cathedral (North Yorkshire)   175
Bridlington (East Riding of Yorkshire)   176
Beverley (East Riding of Yorkshire)   177
Kingston-upon-Hull (East Riding of Yorkshire)   178
Leeds (West Yorkshire)   179
Haworth (West Yorkshire)   180
Sheffield (South Yorkshire)   181
Epworth (Lincolnshire)   183
Stow-in-Lindsey (Lincolnshire)   185
Brant Broughton; Heckington; Boston (Lincolnshire)   185
Grantham (Lincolnshire)   187
Crowland (Lincolnshire)   187

THE EAST MIDLANDS   189

Little Gidding (Cambridgeshire)   190
Cambridge (Cambridgeshire)   190
Ely (Cambridgeshire)   197
Newark-on-Trent; Southwell (Nottinghamshire)   200
Staunton Harold; Mount Saint Bernard; Lutterworth
(Leicestershire)   201
King's Cliffe (Northamptonshire)   204
Northampton (Northamptonshire)   204
Brixworth; Earls Barton (Northamptonshire)   205
Bedford (Bedfordshire)   206
Barnack; Castor (Cambridgeshire)   208
Peterborough (Cambridgeshire)   209
Huntingdon (Cambridgeshire)   210

EAST ANGLIA   211

Walsingham (Norfolk)   212
Norwich (Norfolk)   214
Walpole St Peter (Norfolk)   216
King's Lynn (Norfolk)   217
North Elmham; Salle; Weston Longville (Norfolk)   218

Wymondham (Norfolk) 219
Mildenhall (Suffolk) 219
Bury St Edmund's (Suffolk) 220
Flatford Mill; Nayland; Sudbury (Suffolk) 221
Lavenham; Kedington (Suffolk) 222

NORTH OF LONDON 223
St Alban's (Hertfordshire) 223
Thaxted; Copford (Essex) 224
Waltham Abbey (Essex) 226
Hatfield House (Hertfordshire) 227

Further Reading 229

Glossary 230

Index 235

Preface

Cathedrals and parish churches, hilltops and ruins, private houses and stately homes – what makes a place holy? Pilgrims have travelled to sites associated with some great saint, where they felt a sense of awe that moved them to prayer. Today we also visit places where great writers, poets, artists or musicians found their inspiration. Down the ages worshippers have felt that God's house should be more splendid than any human dwelling, and have given of their best in money and skills to create beautiful churches and cathedrals, and we visit them today to share in their 'worship in stone'. Or it may simply be the knowledge that many prayers have been offered in these places that gives a sense of the closeness of God.

The English, and English-speakers everywhere, have a particular attitude to the world, which is formed by the events of English history. There is far too much in England to see in the course of one holiday, and this book may take readers to places they had never thought of visiting before.

The book is divided into regions; it is convenient to arrange the material as though a pilgrim were touring round England in a clockwise direction, starting in London, but you can choose whatever route you wish to visit a small selection of the sites at one time. Each section begins with some of the 'must see' places; these are followed by a number of places that you could call in at on the way, or that are worth a small diversion. I hope my readers will visit those places listed here not only as tourists but also as worshippers and pilgrims, and that they will be enriched by the experience.

My thanks to the many guidebooks, clergy and volunteers who have helped me have such fun compiling this book.

Michael Counsell
2003

Practical Details

Admission Charges, Opening Times, Service Times

The Church of England receives no financial assistance from the State. The interest on its investments is less than enough to pay the pensions of its retired clergy. Something like one-sixth of all the money offered in church collections for religious purposes is spent on maintaining and repairing the hundreds of ancient churches that are our heritage from the past, so any contribution that visitors and tourists can make is very welcome. A few cathedrals have recently imposed an admission charge; many others announce a 'recommended donation'. However, if you enjoy visiting old churches it is kind to look for a collection box and make a generous donation to help those who sacrificially support these beautiful and expensive buildings.

Sadly many churches have to be locked when there is nobody to watch against theft and vandalism. The notice board should give details of where the key can be obtained. Every effort has been made to give the correct opening times and service times at the time of writing, but they can change without notice, and there are often special arrangements at Christmas and Easter. Where no times are given, you can usually find a church open between about 09.00 and 17.00. When numbers such as (1, 3, 5) appear after a Sunday service time at a particular church, it means that the service is only at that time on the first, third and fifth Sunday of the month, etc. 1 January, Good Friday, Easter Monday, the first and last Mondays in May, the last Monday in August, and 25 and 26 December are public 'Bank Holidays', shown as 'BH' in this book. You can link to many church websites through **http://www.church-search. com** and **http://www.cofe. anglican.org**

The British Tourist Authority

The British Tourist Authority is at Britain Visitor Centre, 1 Regent Street, London SW1Y 4XT; **http://www. visitbritain.com** with offices in many cities around the world. It publishes free factfiles, which give basic facts for visitors. You can also buy, for about £1.40, a map of Britain with postal and internet addresses of all the local tourist information centres. Online maps and information about accommodation, attractions and leisure are at http://www.visitmap.com

Emergencies

For the emergency services, telephone 999, and when the operator answers say whether you want police, fire or ambulance and answer questions about your present location.

English Heritage

If you visit several English Heritage sites, you will save money by becoming a member; your membership card gives you free admission. An Overseas Visitors Pass gives unlimited admission for one or two weeks. Obtain either at any English Heritage site, or write to English Heritage, 23 Savile Row, London W1X 1AB. Alternatively call Customer Services 08700 3331181, or visit http://www.english-heritage.org.uk

The National Churches Tourism Group

This group encourages local churches to grasp the opportunities of tourism for faith sharing. Contact Rosemary Watts, Church House, The Old Palace, Lincoln LN2 1PU. Tel. 01522 529241; email church.tourism@lincoln.anglican.org; http://www.geocities.com/nctg_uk

The National Trust

If you visit several National Trust sites, you will save money by becoming a member; your membership card gives you free admission. Join at any National Trust site, or write to The National Trust, PO Box 39, Bromley, Kent BR1 3XL. Tel. 0870 4584000. Full details of all sites are included in the National Trust's handbook, free for members. For enquiries contact enquiries@thenationaltrust.org.uk; http://www.nationaltrust.org.uk or for US residents contact the American arm of the English National Trust: The Royal Oak Foundation, 26 Broadway Suite 950, New York, NY 10004, USA. Tel. 1-800-913-6565. Email general@royal-oak.org; http://www.royal-oak.org

Retreats

The Association for Promoting Retreats publishes an annual magazine, *Retreats*, listing over 200 retreat houses and how to contact them, with the types of retreats they offer and the

dates available. Write to
256 Bermondsey Street,
London SE1 3UJ.

Tel. 020 7357 7736.
Fax. 020 7357 7724.
Email apr@retreats.org.uk

A Time Line of English History

BC (or BCE)

6000	Formation of English Channel
5000	New Stone Age
2700	Beaker People arrive; Iron and Bronze workers
1800	Construction of Stonehenge, etc.
700	Celts arrive
55	Julius Caesar lands

AD (or CE)

42	Roman invasion
61	Queen Boudicca leads a revolt against the Romans
122	Construction of Hadrian's Wall
314	British bishops attend the Council of Arles
410	Roman Legions withdraw
449	Angles, Saxons and Jutes begin invasion
597	St Augustine of Canterbury arrives
627	St Aidan comes from Iona to Northumbria
664	Synod of Whitby
731	Venerable Bede writes *Ecclesiastical History of the English People*
851	Viking invasion of Eastern England begins
871–99	Reign of King Alfred the Great
876	Danes occupy York
978–1016	King Ethelred the Unready
1016–35	King Canute
1042–66	King Edward the Confessor
1066	Battle of Hastings; Norman rulers
1154	Henry II, first Plantagenet king
1170	Archbishop Becket murdered
1189–99	Richard I the Lionheart; Crusades begin
1215	Magna Carta
1348	Black Death
1455–61	Wars of the Roses
1485–1509	King Henry VII, first Tudor king
1509–47	King Henry VIII
1533	Henry VIII's divorce and Act of Royal Supremacy
1536–39	Dissolution of the Monasteries
1547–53	King Edward VI

4

1549	First *Book of Common Prayer*
1553–58	Queen Mary I
1558–1603	Queen Elizabeth I
1588	Drake defeats Spanish Armada
1603–25	King James I of England and VI of Scotland, first Stuart king
1605	Gunpowder Plot
1625–49	King Charles I
1642–49	Civil War
1649–60	Commonwealth, Oliver Cromwell Lord Protector
1651	King Charles II crowned, defeated at Worcester, flees to France
1660–85	Restoration of the Monarchy
1665	Great Plague
1666	Great Fire of London
1672	Declaration of Indulgence relaxes penalties against Roman Catholics and Dissenters
1673	Test Act excludes Roman Catholics and Non-conformists from public office
1685–88	King James II
1685	Monmouth Rebellion
1688	King William of Orange; James II exiled to France
1702–14	Queen Anne
1714–27	George I, first Hanoverian king
1807	Abolition of the slave trade
1829	Catholic Emancipation Act
1837–1901	Queen Victoria
1901–10	King Edward VII
1910–36	King George V
1914–18	First World War
1936	King Edward VIII accedes to the throne and abdicates
1936–52	King George VI
1939–45	Second World War
1952	Accession of Queen Elizabeth II

London

Londinium was founded by the Romans in 43 AD, and now with a population of over seven million it is Europe's largest city. Traffic moves slowly through the crowded streets, so the Underground (sometimes called 'the Tube') and the buses are the best way to get around. Enquire at the railway and underground ticket offices about maps and travel cards, covering multiple journeys after 09.30. Important buildings are signs of the legacy of religious life.

WESTMINSTER ABBEY

One of the most holy places in London is Westminster Abbey. A community of monks lived on Thorney Island, situated to the west of London, from the eighth century, and it became known as the West Minster. Edward the Confessor, the last of the Saxon kings, rebuilt the Abbey church in Romanesque style; William the Conqueror, the first of the Norman rulers, was crowned there in 1066. Since then every English monarch except two has been crowned there, and from Henry III to George II almost all were buried there. It was rebuilt by Henry III in 1220 in Gothic style. When Henry VII completed his chapel around 1503–1519, architecture had moved into the Perpendicular style, and the **fan-vaulting with pendants** of the chapel is a superb example. At the Dissolution of the Monasteries (see p. 43) the community of monks was disbanded, but Queen Elizabeth I gave a charter replacing them with a Dean and twelve canons, and the College of St Peter, now known as **Westminster School**.

The **west towers** of the Abbey were designed by Christopher Wren and Nicholas Hawksmoor in the seventeenth and eighteenth centuries but retaining the Gothic style. Entering through the **north transept**, known as the statesmen's aisle because of the monuments to politicians, we come to the **Lady Chapel** at the east end, which is Henry VII's Perpendicular masterpiece and his burial place; it contains the banners of those who have been made Knights Grand Cross of the Order of the Bath (KCB). Beneath the **Battle of Britain window**, which commemorates airmen who died defending England against enemy attack in

LONDON

1940, a plaque marks where Oliver Cromwell was buried until the Restoration of the Monarchy, when his body was disinterred, hanged at Tyburn and beheaded. In the aisle north of this chapel **Queen Elizabeth I** and **Queen Mary** are buried. In the **Chapel of Edward the Confessor** his shrine is surrounded by the tombs of five kings and three queens. Against a carved stone screen dated to 1441, the wooden **Coronation Chair** dates from around 1300. In the **south transept** is **Poets' Corner.** Geoffrey Chaucer was the first poet to be buried there; since then the transept has been filled with memorials to most of the great English poets, though many of them are buried elsewhere. The sculpture of the four 'censing angels' in the south transept is one of the most beautiful medieval sculptures in the world. Through the south choir aisle visitors can reach the **Great Cloisters**, rebuilt in

---

St Edward the Confessor (c. 1002–66)

Edward, who reigned from 1042, was a weak king but a saintly Christian. He was brought up at the court of the Dukes of Normandy, and preferred Norman ways to English customs. He became absorbed in religion, and the building of Westminster Abbey, and neglected his kingdom. Whether Edward ever promised the throne of England to William of Normandy remains doubtful, but the life of Edward paved the way for Norman culture, and his death was the cue for the Norman Conquest. His reputation for sanctity led to his description as a 'Confessor'. He was made a saint in 1161.

Queens and Poets

Queen Mary (1516–58) was the daughter of Henry VIII and his first wife Catherine of Aragon. She retained her Roman Catholic faith, and married the future Philip II of Spain, son of the Holy Roman Emperor Charles V. She became known as Bloody Mary because she ordered around 300 Protestants to be burned at the stake, leading to centuries of suspicion between English Catholics and Protestants. Her half-sister, Queen Elizabeth I (1533–1603), the daughter of Henry by Anne Boleyn, succeeded her in 1558, and although some Catholics were persecuted in her reign, as they had been under Henry, she sought to establish a balance between Papist and Puritan. It is ironic and at the same time touching that Mary and Elizabeth should be buried side by side in Westminster Abbey, in a gesture of reconciliation beyond the grave. Poets' Corner contains monuments to poets of many persuasions: Robert Browning, Geoffrey Chaucer, William Shakespeare, Alfred Lord Tennyson, T.S. Eliot, and many others.

1298 and now leading to a shop and a brass-rubbing centre. At the east end of the cloister are the octagonal **Chapter House**, where the House of Commons met from 1257 until it moved to the Palace of Westminster; the **Pyx Chamber**, where the Abbey's silver and gold plate is displayed; and the Norman **Undercroft Museum** with a collection of royal death masks. Returning to the **nave**, which is 30 metres (more than 100 feet) high and the tallest in England, we leave by the west door, passing the **Tomb of the Unknown Soldier**. With three million visitors each year, the Abbey is the most visited church in Britain.

ST PAUL'S CATHEDRAL

On the site at the top of Ludgate Hill where St Augustine of Canterbury's colleague Birinus, the first Bishop of London, established his cathedral, stands the fourth or fifth building on the site. The dome of St Paul's still dominates the city. When Old St Paul's was destroyed in the Great Fire of London (1666), Sir Christopher Wren immediately submitted plans for the new building, and was then commissioned to lay out the whole city around it, with designs for 50 other churches. The foundation stone was laid in 1675; in 1708 he saw his son lay the topmost stone in the lantern,

111 metres (365 feet) high. The **dome** was influenced by that of St Peter's in Rome, though it is not as large. A **statue of St Paul** surmounts the pediment at the west end, and another is on **'Paul's Cross'** in the churchyard. The Cathedral is in the shape of a cross. In the north aisle of the nave is a huge monument to the **Duke of Wellington,** victor of the Battle of Waterloo. The north transept has a font,

and one of several copies of *The Light of the World,* by Holman Hunt, showing Christ knocking at the weed-covered door of our hearts; the original is in the chapel of Keble College, Oxford. In the apse behind the high altar is the **American Chapel,** dedicated to the memory of 28,000 North American servicemen who died in the Second World War. In the south transept is a statue of **Lord Nelson,** the victor of

---

John Donne (1571/2–1631)

By the seventeenth century Anglicanism was gaining in self-confidence and thinking out a distinctive theology. In the reigns of Charles I and Charles II eloquent preachers and writers arose who, because they emphasized the Church as the creation of God, were called High Churchmen. These 'Caroline Divines' all showed holiness of life, simplicity and discipline in prayer, and devotion to scholarship and poetry.

John Donne was born the son of a Roman Catholic ironmonger in London, studied at Oxford and Cambridge, and took up law. He served as secretary to Sir Thomas Egerton, but was dismissed in disgrace and thrown into prison after secretly marrying his patron's niece, Ann More. During the second part of his life, when he had left the Roman Catholic Church but was not yet convinced of the truth of Anglicanism, he wrote passionate and erotic verse. But he was beginning to write religious poetry also, and after a long struggle with his conscience he was persuaded by King James I to seek ordination in the Church of England, and in 1621 was made Dean of St Paul's. The passion that he had previously expended on the flesh he now converted into love for God. This is shown in some of his greatest poems, his brilliant sermons, and his *Devotions upon an Emergent Occasion,* when he was lying sick in bed and expected to die, from which comes the famous quotation 'Ask not for whom the bell tolls...'

Sir Christopher Wren (1632–1723)

Christopher Wren was the son of the Dean of Windsor, and at court, among the intellectuals surrounding King Charles I, he developed an interest in mathematics. During the Civil War the Wren family had to flee from Windsor, and he lived with his brother-in-law, who helped him to experiment in astronomy. Educated at Westminster School and Oxford, he was appointed Professor of Astronomy at Gresham College, London, and was one of the founder members of what became the Royal Society. After designing the chapel of Pembroke College, Cambridge, he began to be in demand as an architect. He is buried in the crypt of St Paul's Cathedral, and the simple Latin inscription means 'If you wish for a monument, look around you'.

Trafalgar. The choir is furnished with finely carved, dark oak **choir stalls**, the work of Wren's carver Grinling Gibbons. There is a sculpture of the Virgin and Child (1984) by **Henry Moore** in the north choir aisle, and a statue of **John Donne**, standing up in his burial shroud, in the south choir aisle, one of the few things in the cathedral to survive the Great Fire.

Climbing inside the dome, 259 steps take you to the **Whispering Gallery**, where words whispered against the wall on one side can be clearly heard on the opposite side. Then a total of 543 steps take you to the **Golden Gallery**, directly below the golden ball and cross – Christ ruling over the globe – which is on top of the dome, with one of the best views in London. Going down to the **crypt**, the tombs of many military figures are found; immediately on your right is **Artists' Corner** with tombs of many great painters and architects, including Sir Christopher Wren himself. In open-air processions round the cathedral the monks used to recite the Lord's Prayer, beginning at **Paternoster Row** and finishing at **Amen Corner**.

There are many other holy and historical places in London that are well worth a visit; for convenience I have grouped them geographically from west to east.

HAMPTON COURT PALACE

Hampton Court Palace is beside the River Thames and the A3 west of Kingston-upon-Thames; it is the finest Tudor palace in England. It was first built between 1514 and 1529 by Cardinal Wolsey, and after his disgrace appropriated by King Henry VIII for his own use. Henry enlarged and transformed the palace, redesigning the chapel, adding on the wings, and building a **Great Hall** with a splendid hammerbeam roof. The **astronomical clock** in Clock Court was made for Henry, originally for St James's Palace, and was brought here in the nineteenth century. William and Mary planned to alter Hampton Court, but the work was eventually carried out under Sir Christopher Wren in 1688. The **east and south fronts** were rebuilt, together with the **State apartments** and the smaller **royal apartments.** They were given ceilings painted by Verrio, and carvings by Grinling Gibbons. They are filled with a wonderful collection of furniture and paintings. The **Chapel Royal** was originally built for Cardinal Wolsey, and enlarged and embellished for Henry VIII, then William and Mary, and later for Queen Anne; it is served by a chaplain and a full-time choir. The reredos was planned for Whitehall Palace by Sir Christopher Wren and carved by Grinling Gibbons, but after Whitehall burnt down it was adapted for Hampton Court. The royal pew is in the west gallery. The **kitchens, wine cellars** and the **King's beer cellar** have been restored to their

---

Cardinal Thomas Wolsey (c.1474–1530)

Son of an Ipswich butcher, Wolsey rose to be the Archbishop of York, and the Lord Chancellor, which was the top office in the ministry of the Church and the service of the King. He tried to make England the arbiter between the King of France and the Holy Roman Emperor, but made many enemies by his ruthless taxation to pay for the war with France. He failed to persuade the Pope to allow him to decide King Henry VIII's application for the annulment of his marriage with Catherine of Aragon, and was disgraced in 1529. The office of Lord Chancellor was taken away and all his property handed over to the King, but his archbishopric was restored to him. He spent his last months caring for his diocese and in works of charity, but he died a year later saying, 'Had I but served God as diligently as I have served the King, he would not have given me over in my grey hairs.' The colleges he had founded at Ipswich and Oxford were suppressed, but the latter was re-founded as Christ Church College.

original appearance. The **gardens** were laid out in the reigns of several monarchs, especially Charles II and William III. The triangular **maze** was planted in 1690, and the **Great Vine** was planted by the landscape designer Capability Brown in 1768 for George III; it now produces 500–600 bunches of grapes each year from August to September. The easiest way to get to Hampton Court is by train from Waterloo Station.

CHELSEA

Taking a number 11 bus from Victoria Station down the King's Road, then walking down Old Church Road, brings us to Cheyne Walk (pronounced CHAIN-ee), and **Chelsea Old Church**. It is a fine old Norman church, reconstructed in the 1950s following extensive damage in the Second World War. Sir Thomas More, who lived nearby, built the south chapel in 1528 as his family's place of worship, and this chapel alone survives undamaged; there is a modern statue of him outside facing the River Thames.

THE BROMPTON ROAD

Travelling north through Chelsea and South Kensington brings us to Brompton Road. Where the Cromwell Road from the South Kensington museums joins it, stands **Brompton**

Sir Thomas More (1478–1535)

A thorough education in the classics and in law led Thomas More to become a barrister and then a Member of Parliament. He thought of becoming a monk, but decided he was not called to celibacy. His house at Chelsea was visited by all the great minds of Europe. While he was acting as an envoy for Henry VIII in Flanders he wrote *Utopia*, describing an ideal society living in natural obedience to God's laws. His was a contradictory character: his letters to his family were full of simple affection, yet he wrote against Martin Luther, and in favour of the veneration of saints and images and the punishment of heretics; he is suspected of having organized the execution of the Bible translator William Tyndale. In 1529 he was made Lord Chancellor, but he opposed the King's divorce, and he was imprisoned in the Tower of London for 15 months, using it as an opportunity for prayer and penance and to write devotional books. He was beheaded on Tower Hill on 6 July 1535.

Frederick William Faber (1814–63)

Faber was an Evangelical who was influenced by Pusey and the other 'Tractarians' while an undergraduate at Oxford. He was ordained in the Church of England, but followed Newman into the Roman Catholic Church, and joined Newman's Oratory in Birmingham. He was sent to London to start a branch house, and the Brompton Oratory became extremely popular, mainly as a result of Father Faber's preaching and his devotional books. His hymns, such as 'Hark! hark, my soul! Angelic songs are swelling', are redolent with the emotionalism of Victorian times, and he had a deep love for God and for people, especially the poor: 'There's a wideness in God's mercy', he wrote, 'like the wideness of the sea'.

Oratory. Father Faber was sent to London to form a branch house of the Birmingham Oratory. It was so successful that a large Italianate building was erected in the late nineteenth century, containing marble statues of the apostles from Siena Cathedral. The Anglican church behind the oratory is **Holy Trinity, Brompton**, famous as 'HTB', the centre of charismatic worship in the Church of England, and of the 'Alpha Courses', a series of training courses used by all denominations to welcome newcomers to faith and encourage Christians to claim the gifts of the Spirit.

WESTMINSTER CATHEDRAL

Take the Underground from Sloane Square to Victoria. In Victoria Street, the Piazza is on your right, and behind that is the Roman Catholic Cathedral. It was begun in 1895, in a neo-Byzantine style, in alternate stripes of Portland stone and terracotta-coloured bricks. The interior was intended to be covered in marble, but this has only been completed in the side chapels, decorated with over 100 different types. The campanile is 274 feet high; there is a lift to the viewing platform. It was a great source of pride to Roman Catholics when it was opened in 1903, for after centuries of discrimination they could at last have an impressive church of their own.

TYBURN

On the northeast corner of Hyde Park, Marble Arch was erected in 1828 to form a triumphal entrance for Buckingham Palace, but now it is stranded in the middle of

---

Tyburn Martyrs

St Edmund Campion (1540–81)

During the Reformation both sides considered it a Christian action to put their opponents to death for their beliefs. Roman Catholics can boast of many glorious martyrs. Edmund Campion was a deacon in the Church of England and a fellow of St John's College, Oxford. He gave up his fellowship when he joined the Roman Catholic Church in France, in 1571. He studied at Douai, and joined the Society of Jesus (Jesuits). He came back to England in disguise in 1580, but was soon arrested and charged with treason. He was tortured on the rack, and then hanged at Tyburn. He was made a saint in 1970.

Robert Southwell (1561?–95)

Southwell was born near Norwich, and educated at Douai and Rome. He became a Jesuit priest, and was prefect of the English College in Rome. He also wrote some moving poetry. In spite of the dangers he returned to England in 1584. He spent most of his time in disguise or in hiding, but made many converts. In 1592 he was betrayed, tortured and thrown into the Tower of London. Three years later he was condemned for high treason, hanged and quartered at Tyburn.

> 'The Nativity of Christ'
> Behold the father is his daughter's son,
> The bird that built the nest is hatch'd therein,
> The old of years an hour hath not outrun,
> Eternal life to live doth now begin,
> The word is dumb, the mirth of heaven doth weep,
> Might feeble is, and force doth faintly creep.

---

a traffic island. Nearby is the site of **Tyburn Gallows,** where many Christian martyrs were executed.

COVENT GARDEN

North of the Strand up Southampton Street lies the area originally called the Convent Garden. On the site of the vegetable garden of a convent of nuns, Inigo Jones laid out London's oldest planned square in the 1630s. At first it was fashionable, but soon it was taken over as London's fruit, flower and vegetable market. The Royal Opera House was built in 1858 by Sir Edward Barry, and restored in the 1990s. Several interesting museums have opened around the square recently, and now

Lord Shaftesbury (1801–85)

Anthony Ashley Cooper, seventh Earl of Shaftesbury, entered Parliament as a member of the Conservative Party and devoted himself to caring for the working classes. After visiting the London slums for himself, he had the Ten Hours' Bill and the Factory Act passed by Parliament. He fought for protection for women and children working in the coal mines, and for the boy chimney sweeps for whom he introduced the Climbing Boys Act. Among the many Evangelical societies he supported was the British and Foreign Bible Society, whose president he was for many years.

that the fruit market has moved away, it is devoted to arts and crafts or food stalls and street theatre. The only remaining parts of Inigo Jones's plan are two rebuilt sections of the north side arcading, and **St Paul's Church**. The developer told him to make a simple building, 'not much better than a barn', to which Jones is alleged to have replied, 'You shall have the handsomest barn in Europe.' J.M.W. Turner the artist and W.S. Gilbert were baptized here, and Samuel Butler, Grinling Gibbons and Thomas Arne are buried in the churchyard. There are overhanging porticos at both ends; under the one that faces the square, George Bernard Shaw set the fictional first meeting of Eliza Doolittle with Professor Higgins (*Pygmalion*). Because it is close to so many West End theatres it contains monuments to many famous figures in the acting profession, and is called the Actors' Church.

PICCADILLY

Taking its name from the 'pickadills' or ruffs worn by the dandies who used to promenade here in the seventeenth century, Piccadilly has always been a fashionable area. In Piccadilly Circus is what is always called the **Statue of Eros**. In spite of the bow and arrow, it is not, however, the god of love, but 'The Angel of Christian Charity', and is a monument erected to the memory of the Earl of Shaftesbury.

TRAFALGAR SQUARE

Trafalgar Square was originally designed by John Nash in 1820, and named after the Battle of Trafalgar won by Admiral Lord Nelson, whose statue is on Nelson's column in the centre of the square. The statue of King Charles I on horseback, to the south of Nelson's column, was cast in 1633, and placed there soon after the Restoration of the Monarchy in 1660. It stands on the site of the original thirteenth-century Charing Cross, from which all distances from London were measured. The Victorian cross outside the nearby Charing Cross railway station is intended to commemorate the original but does not look much like it. When King Edward I's wife Queen Eleanor died near Lincoln in 1290, her coffin was brought to Westminster in procession, and at each place where it rested he erected a stone cross to mark his belief in the salvation brought by the cross of Jesus.

Northeast of Trafalgar Square stands the church of **St Martin-in-the-Fields**, designed by James Gibbs and completed in 1726. It boasts a Corinthian-style portico surmounted by a tower and steeple, an innovative design that has since been copied by many other churches around the world. It is the parish church of Buckingham Palace, and King George I was a churchwarden, the only reigning monarch to hold that office. The interior is simple but with elaborate Italian plasterwork on the barrel-vaulted ceiling. The organ installed in 1990 is one of the best in Europe. There are free lunchtime concerts, and a restaurant and brass-rubbing centre in the crypt.

WHITEHALL

Connecting Trafalgar Square with Parliament Square to the south, Whitehall is famous as the centre of the Civil Service. Whitehall Palace was the London home of the Archbishops of York until King Henry VIII confiscated it and moved in when the royal palace at Westminster was damaged by fire. It became the residence of the Kings and Queens of England during the sixteenth and seventeenth centuries until it in turn was destroyed by fire in 1698. The monarch moved to St James's Palace, but the **Banqueting House** survived the fire and may be visited today on the left-hand side of Whitehall as you walk towards Parliament Square, about halfway down. This was begun by Inigo Jones in 1619, and was the first building in England to be designed in the Palladian style. The upstairs room, now open to the public, has superb ceiling paintings by Rubens, glorifying the royal line of the Stuarts. They were commissioned by King Charles I, and in 1649 he stepped through the window of this room onto the scaffold, which had been

Sir Walter Raleigh (1552–1618)

A Devon man who interrupted his university education to fight for the Huguenots in France, he later fought against the Spanish and the Irish. Returning from unsuccessful expeditions seeking to found colonies in America, he introduced tobacco and potatoes to Britain. His place in Queen Elizabeth's favours was taken by the Earl of Essex and he was imprisoned in the Tower of London for his affair with Bessy Throckmorton, one of her maids of honour, whom he subsequently married. For three years he was a successful governor of the island of Jersey. He was falsely condemned following the intrigues at the end of Elizabeth's reign, and only when he reached the scaffold was his sentence suspended to perpetual imprisonment. He was released to lead an expedition up the Orinoco River, but because he burnt down a Spanish town, on his return the Spanish Ambassador demanded that the suspended sentence be carried out, and he was beheaded at Whitehall. His poetry, some of it written when he was a prisoner in the Tower, compares our life to the pilgrims who set off for the shrine of St James at Compostela (Spain) with a shell as their badge.

'The Passionate Man's Pilgrimage'
(supposed to be written by one at the point of death)
 Give me my scallop-shell of quiet;
 My staff of faith to walk upon;
 My scrip of joy, immortal diet;
 My bottle of salvation;
 My gown of glory (hope's true gage);
 And thus I'll take my pilgrimage . . .

erected outside, to be executed.

HOLBORN; THE STRAND; FLEET STREET

St Andrew's, Holborn (HOE-bun), is a Wren church of 1687 restored after wartime damage, with sculpted schoolboys from a charity school over the entrance, a green and gold ceiling, and a pulpit from 1752. Opposite is Ely Place, a short street which was the London residence of the bishops of Ely. In 1251 they built themselves a chapel, dedicated to **St Etheldreda**, with a cloister added in 1373. In 1793 a new church was built over the original crypt, and in 1874 the whole complex was acquired by a

> ### King Charles I (1600–49)
>
> King Charles was a saintly man but not a wise king. His
> dignity at the time of his trial and execution entitle him,
> however, to be numbered among the noble army of
> martyrs. After spending two hours in prayer, he remarked
> to Sir Thomas Herbert, the night before he died, 'Herbert,
> this is my second marriage day; I would be as trim today
> as may be; for before night I hope to be spoused to my
> blessed Jesus . . . I fear not death! Death is not terrible to
> me. I bless my God I am prepared.' In his speech from the
> scaffold he said, 'In troth, sirs, my conscience in religion I
> think is very well known to the world, and therefore I
> declare before you all, that I die a Christian according to
> the profession of the Church of England as I found it left
> me by my father . . . I have a good cause, and I have a
> gracious God. I will say no more . . . I shall say but very
> short prayers, and then thrust out my hands.'

Roman Catholic religious
order. They describe the
crypt as the only building of
the period in London, and
the only pre-Reformation
Roman Catholic church in
Britain.

South of Holborn is the
crescent called Aldwych,
leading into The Strand,
originally a beach along the
banks of the Thames. **St
Mary-le-Strand** is one of the
most beautiful Baroque
churches in England, dating
from 1714. Fortunately it
was undamaged during the
Second World War. The
ornate ceiling is strikingly
beautiful, and two paintings,
from 1785, in the sanctuary
are by the American artist
Mather Brown. **St Clement
Danes**, on a site where some
Danish settlers are alleged to
have built a church in the
ninth century, rebuilt by
William the Conqueror and
again in the Middle Ages,
was rebuilt by Sir
Christopher Wren in 1682;
the tower was added by
James Gibbs in 1719. Except
for the walls and the steeple
it was destroyed by enemy
action in 1941, and restored
in 1958 to the original
designs. It is now the church
of the Royal Air Force; the
organ was the gift of the
American Air Force, and
airmen of other nations are
commemorated in the crypt.
Together with other London
churches it gave rise to the
rhyme 'Oranges and lemons
say the bells of St Clement's',
which rings out from the
carillon at 09.00, 12.00,
15.00 and 18.00.

St Dunstan-in-the-West, Fleet Street, a Gothic-Revival octagonal church built from 1829 to 1833, was the last of the medieval London churches to be rebuilt, on a site that goes back to before the Norman Conquest. It escaped destruction during the Great Fire, but had become derelict and was pulled down in 1829. The high altar and reredos are Flemish woodwork surviving from the seventeenth century. Facing the road on the outside of the church is a statue of Queen Elizabeth I made in 1586 for Ludgate; and a famous clock with two giants who have been striking bells on the quarter-hours since 1671. The legendary Sweeney Todd, the demon barber of Fleet Street, is supposed to have disposed of the bones of his victims in the crypt of St Dunstan's. In 1966 a 100-year-old iconostasis was brought from Romania to be placed in St Dunstan's alongside altars from other Christian traditions so that the church could act as a focus of prayer for Christian unity.

St Bride's, Fleet Street, is dedicated to St Bridget of Ireland and was built by Wren in 1703 over a crypt with Roman and Saxon remains. An imaginative baker nearby copied the unique spire of St Bride's, with its layered pillars, as the model for the cake now almost universally used at weddings.

THE INNS OF COURT

South of Fleet Street are the traditional offices of London's lawyers, referred to as The Inns of Court, where the **Temple Church** stands at the centre of the Inner Temple courtyard. Temple Church, combining the Purbeck marble pillars of early Gothic with the round arches of Norman architecture, was built in 1185 by the Knights Templar, crusaders returning from Jerusalem. There they had seen the circular Church of the Holy Sepulchre, wrongly assumed that it was Solomon's Temple, and built circular churches all over Europe in imitation of it.

THE CITY OF LONDON

When Londoners talk about 'The City', they mean the small area originally enclosed by the walls from Roman times onwards. There were at one time numerous churches in and near to the City of London; those that have survived are of great interest – many of them are used for specialist ministry. South of St Paul's Cathedral is **St Benet's Welsh Anglican Church**, Paul's Wharf, Queen Victoria Street, built by Wren in 1677. Off Queen Victoria Street is **St Stephen,**

Walbrook. A Saxon church was built in the seventh century on the foundations of the **Temple of Mithras** (dated to the second century), in Queen Victoria Street, where the Roman soldiers of Londinium were initiated into the Mystery Religions before the good news of Jesus Christ reached Britain. This church was rebuilt in 1439 and then destroyed in the Great Fire. Sir Christopher Wren built a new church in 1672 on a site just round the corner, which was rebuilt after being damaged by bombs in 1941. Here in 1953 Revd Chad Varah founded The Samaritans, an international organization committed to answering telephone calls at all hours from those who are feeling depressed or suicidal (in Britain, 0845 790 9090). The rock-like altar was carved in 1987 by Henry Moore. **St Mary-le-Bow**, Cheapside, built by Wren over Saxon and Norman ruins, from which an eleventh-century crypt remains, was restored in 1964 after wartime bomb damage. It has a huge dragon weather vane (2.7 metres, nearly 9 foot long), and a hanging rood carved in Oberammergau as a symbol of reconciliation, and it is famous for Bow Bells (anyone born within the sound of Bow Bells is entitled to call themselves a Cockney;

Dick Whittington heard Bow Bells call him back to London to become Lord Mayor in 1397).

St Bartholomew the Great, Long Lane, Smithfield, was founded in 1123 by Prior Rahere, whose tomb is on the north side of the sanctuary, and who said that St Bartholomew had promised him, in a dream, that his church would be a place of healing; it was used for a long time as a hospital, which eventually became 'Bart's' hospital next door. The church is a breathtakingly beautiful Norman building, with a clerestory of 1405 and a tower of 1628. Outside is a memorial to the first Protestant martyrs, burnt at the stake here.

City Road is where **Wesley's House** is to be found. This is an eighteenth-century house in which John Wesley (see p. 183) lived for 12 years. It is now a museum containing many original items of furniture belonging to the founder of Methodism. Next door is a restored Methodist church built in 1778, with a pulpit from which Wesley preached. He died here and is buried in the churchyard. The church was built on the site of the Moorfields Foundery, where the Methodists first met; and the tiny Foundery Chapel contains benches from the

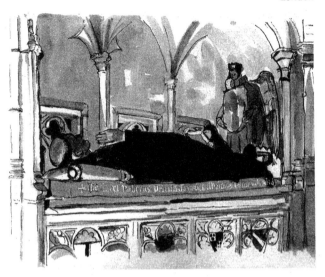

Prior Rahere's Tomb, St Bartholomew's, Smithfield, London

foundery and the organ that Charles Wesley played. Across the road is the Nonconformist cemetery of **Bunhill Fields,** where Susannah Wesley, Daniel Defoe, William Blake and John Bunyan are buried.

Travelling south from Liverpool Street Station you pass **St Botolph's without Bishopsgate,** on the corner of Bishopsgate Street and London Wall, which has Saxon foundations. The church was rebuilt in 1729, damaged by a terrorist bomb in 1993, and a modern window just inside the door marks its restoration in 1997. The Priory of St Mary of Bethlehem to the north of the church, after the Dissolution, was turned into the Bethlehem Hospital for Lunatics, whose name was corrupted into Bedlam. **St Ethelburga's, Bishopsgate,** on the other side of the street, was almost destroyed by the same bomb, but has been rebuilt and was reopened in November 2002 as a centre for reconciliation. **St Helen's,** which is in Great St Helen's Place off Bishopsgate, is a twelfth-century church with a seventeenth-century font and a Jacobean triple-decker pulpit, and more monuments than any other church in London; it was damaged by terrorist bombs in 1992 and 1993 and restored in 1995.

St Mary Woolnoth in Lombard Street, designed by Nicholas Hawksmoor (1661–1736) is where John Newton was Rector (see p. 107). **St Edmund, Lombard Street** is reopening in autumn 2004 as the London Centre for Spirituality.

THE TOWER OF LONDON

On the north bank of the River Thames, by Tower Bridge, at the eastern end of the city walls, stands the castle known as the Tower of London. King William the Conqueror built a wooden fort on this site in 1067, and replaced it with a stone one, now known as the White Tower, starting in 1077; it was completed in 1099. Later monarchs extended the courtyards and buildings. From 1300 to 1810 the Royal Mint, for manufacturing coins, was housed in the Tower; because it was so well defended it also became the storage place for the Crown Jewels and a large armoury. It was also a prison where many famous prisoners spent their last days, including King Henry VI, Thomas Cromwell, Anne Boleyn, Catherine Howard, Lady Jane Grey, and William Laud. There are two chapels within the Tower. **St John's Chapel** on the second floor of the White Tower was completed in 1080, and retains its original Norman simplicity of massive columns and round arches. In the Middle Ages the monarchs used to spend the night before their coronation in prayer in St John's Chapel. The other chapel, dedicated to **St Peter ad Vincula** (St Peter's Chains), was consecrated in the twelfth century and added to in the thirteenth and sixteenth centuries. Several royal dukes and two of Henry VIII's queens are buried there.

SOUTH LONDON

South of the River Thames, again moving from west to east, we start at **Clapham Common** (pronounced CLAP-um), a small open space in southwest London on the edge of the A3 and near to Clapham Junction on the railway. When John Venn (1759–1813) became the Rector of Clapham, the group of like-minded Evangelicals who gathered round him, including his father Henry Venn, William Wilberforce (see p. 179), and Hannah More, became known as the Clapham Sect.

The Metropolitan Tabernacle, usually known as Spurgeon's, is at the Elephant and Castle, an area named from the inn-sign; follow the signs through the pedestrian subways. The original Tabernacle was burnt down in 1898 and again in 1941, but the

Prisoners of the Tower

Lady Jane Grey (1537–54)

The great-granddaughter of King Henry VII, Lady Jane Grey was already fluent in Greek, Latin, Hebrew, French and Italian by the time she went to live with Queen Catherine Parr at the age of nine. During the final illness of King Edward VI, she was married against her will at the age of 15 to Lord Guildford Dudley as part of a plan to ensure a Protestant succession. When the King died she reigned as Queen of England for ten days, but was rapidly succeeded by the Roman Catholic Queen Mary and made a prisoner in the Tower of London. She wrote prayers of sincere devotion, but after a rebellion failed to restore her to the throne, she was beheaded on Tower Hill.

William Laud (1573–1645)

Laud was the son of a tailor of Reading, and rose to become Archbishop of Canterbury. He argued that the Roman Catholic Church and the Church of England are both parts of the same Catholic Church. He was, however, implacably opposed to the Puritans, and underestimated their popular support. He made the communion table rather than the pulpit the focus of the church, and ordered that it be surrounded by altar-rails to protect it against dogs. He wished to impose a general oath upholding the divine right of kings and swearing never to 'consent to alter the government of this Church by archbishops, deans and archdeacons, &c.'. This 'etcetera oath' exposed him to ridicule, and he was impeached by the Long Parliament in a travesty of a trial, imprisoned in the Tower of London and executed on Tower Hill. He wrote: 'Gracious Father, I humbly beseech thee for thy holy catholic church. Fill it with all truth, in all truth, with all peace. Where it is corrupt, purge it. Where it is in error, direct it. Where it is superstitious, rectify it. Where anything is amiss, reform it. Where it is right, strengthen and confirm it. Where it is in want, furnish it. Where it is divided and rent asunder, make up the breaches of it, O thou holy one of Israel.'

rebuilding retains the original portico and basement.

Travelling up Newington Causeway and Borough High Street brings us to **Southwark Cathedral** (SUTH-uk). The oldest part of the cathedral is a fragment of a Norman arch in the north wall. The choir was built as the Augustinian

Henry Venn (1725–97)

Henry Venn made a deep impression as Vicar of Huddersfield in Yorkshire, and by his book *The Complete Duty of Man* he influenced many to take a more earnest approach to Christian life. This was the beginning of the Evangelical Revival, and after he retired from Huddersfield, due to bad health, he took a living in Huntingdonshire, from where he was able to influence many at Cambridge University. His son, John, became the Rector of Clapham; together with the Clapham Sect they founded the Church Missionary Society and the British and Foreign Bible Society.

priory church of St Mary Overie in 1207 in the Early English style; it is the oldest and most complete Gothic building in London. There is a sumptuous stone altar screen dating from 1520, and an oak effigy of a knight from about 1275. The Harvard Chapel, commemorating John Harvard, benefactor of Harvard University, who was baptized in this church in 1607, is in the north choir aisle. There is a monument to William Shakespeare, whose reconstructed Globe Theatre is a short walk away down the south bank of the Thames. In the south choir aisle is the tomb of Bishop Lancelot Andrewes (see p. 49). The nave was rebuilt in 1897 to match the choir, and the chapel at the southwest corner is a monument to 51 people who died when the

Charles Haddon Spurgeon (1834–92)

Spurgeon was descended from generations of Independent ministers, but experienced a personal conversion, became a Baptist, and was given the appointment of Baptist pastor at Waterbeach at the age of 17. When he was 20 he went to Southwark, where in 1853 he took charge of a congregation that had been founded in 1650. His sermons attracted so many people that a new Metropolitan Tabernacle had to be built for him. He also founded a college to train others in preaching, now in Croydon. He led the congregation out of the Baptist Union as a protest against theological liberalism, and they are now known as Independent Baptists. His published sermons have been read by many for their shrewd common sense and humorous choice of illustrations.

William Booth (1829–1912)

Part-Jewish and born in Nottingham, William Booth
became a Methodist and had a conversion experience in
1844. He became a preacher, and in 1855 married
Catherine Mumford (1829–90). He left the Methodists in
1861 and founded the Salvation Army in Whitechapel; it
soon spread all over the world. He ministered especially to
the poor, by his preaching and by caring for their physical
needs. He had a particular concern to rescue victims of
alcohol, which is why there is no communion service in the
Salvation Army.

---

riverboat *Marchioness* sank
in 1989. The church was
made a cathedral in 1905,
to minister to London
churches south of the
Thames.

The massive **Salvation Army
College** is in Denmark Hill.
Visitors who want to
investigate the history of the
movement should telephone
in advance for an
appointment with the
Heritage Section.

GREENWICH

The charming suburb of
Greenwich (GRENN-itch)
lies at a bend in the River
Thames on the south bank,
accessible by train or
underground, or by the A2.
Greenwich was the outer
defence of London against
the invasions of the Danes: **St
Alfege**, the Archbishop of
Canterbury, attempted to
mediate in 1012 but was
mocked during one of their
feasts by the invaders, who
pelted him with meat bones,

culminating in a complete ox
head, the blow from which
killed him. A church was
built on the site of his
martyrdom, and a new
church built in around 1210;
Greenwich Parish Church,
the third on the site, was
designed by Hawksmoor and
dedicated in 1718. King
Henry VIII was baptized here
in 1491, and it was also the
church where the composer
of much wonderful church
music, **Thomas Tallis** (c.
1510–85), was an organist;
the keyboard of the organ he
used can be seen there.

Useful Addresses
British Visitor Centre 12 Regent
Street, London SW1Y 4NS. No
telephone enquiries.
http://www.visitbritain.com
London Tourist Board Glen
House, Stag Place, London
SW1E 5LT. No telephone
enquiries. Also at Victoria Station
forecourt, and Heathrow Airport.
http://www.LondonTown.com
London Travel Information 020
7222 1234. http://www.
transportforlondon.gov.uk

King Henry VIII (1491–1547)

King Henry was a tall, athletic, intelligent and cultured man, and it seems that all he needed was a wife who would bear him a son to succeed him on the throne. He could and did take mistresses, but their children would not be able to inherit. To form an alliance with Spain he was advised to marry Catherine of Aragon, his brother's widow. This was contrary to Church law, but for a suitable payment the Pope agreed to grant an exemption. Six miscarriages and one daughter – Mary – later, he decided that his misfortune was God's punishment for his illegal marriage, and so asked the Pope to rescind his decision. But the Pope was now in the power of Catherine's relations, and Henry had already fallen in love with Anne Boleyn. The tragic history of his six wives is summarized in the rhyme 'divorced – beheaded – died, divorced – beheaded – survived', but it seems that he was always driven by the need – as he perceived it – to have a male heir. To remove the control of a foreign pope over the law and finances of England was a popular move, but Henry did not see himself as starting a new church, and seems to have foreseen no change in the doctrines of the Church of England, even after he was excommunicated.

Opening Times and Service Times

Information on some London churches can be found at **http://www.london.anglican.org**, **http://www.cityoflondonchurches.com** and **http://www.londontourist.orgcity.html** All London telephone numbers begin with the area code 020.

Banqueting House, Whitehall

(Government functions permitting) Monday to Saturday 10.00–17.00; closed BH. Tel. 7930 4179 or 7839 8919

Brompton Oratory Services Sunday 07.00, 08.30, 10.00, 11.00, 12.30, 15.30, 16.30, 19.00; Monday to Friday 07.00, 10.00, 12.30, 18.00 (Latin); Tuesday to Friday 18.30; Saturday 07.00, 08.30, 10.00, 18.00. Tel. 7808 0900, Fax. 7584 1095. http://www.brompton-oratory.org.uk

Chelsea Old Church Monday to Saturday (also Sunday between services) 09.30–13.00, 14.00–17.00 (16.00 winter). Services Sunday 08.00, 10.00, 11.00, 12.15 (except 1), 18.00. Tel. 7352 7978, Fax. 5467. Email Chelsea@domini.org; http://www.domini.org/chelsea-old-church

Hampton Court April to October Tuesday to Sunday 09.30–18.00, Monday 10.15–18.00; November to March Tuesday to Sunday

09.30–16.30, Monday 10.15–16.30. **Gardens** close at 21.00 or dusk. **Chapel Royal** services Sunday 08.30, 11.00 (sung), 15.30 (sung); Monday to Wednesday, Friday 08.00, 08.30, 13.00. Tel. 0870 7537777. http://www.hrp.org.uk
Holy Trinity, Brompton Services Sunday 08.00, 09.30, 11.30, 17.00, 19.00; Thursday 12.30. Tel. 7581 8255, Fax. 7589 3390. Email reception@htb.org.uk; http://www.htb.org.uk **Alpha Courses** Tel. 7581 8255
Holy Trinity, Clapham Common Services Sunday 08.00, 10.00, 18.30; Wednesday 12.30. For opening times Tel. 7627 0941
Metropolitan Tabernacle (Spurgeon's) Services Sunday 11.00, 18.30. Tel. 7735 7076. Email enquiries@ MetropolitanTabernacle.org; http://www. MetropolitanTabernacle.org
Salvation Army College House 14, The William Booth College, Denmark Hill, London SE5 8BQ. Tuesday to Thursday 09.30–15.30. Tel. first 7332 8056. Email heritage@salvationarmy.org; http://www.salvationarmy.org/ history
St Alfege, Greenwich daily 10.00–16.00. Services Sunday 08.00, 09.30, 11.15, 18.30 (last); Friday 12.00 (3). Tel. 8853 2703. http://www.st-alfege.org
St Andrew's, Holborn Monday to Friday 08.00–17.00. Services Tuesday, Thursday 13.05; Wednesday 19.00; no services during holiday periods. Tel. 7353 3544. **Royal College of Organists** Monday to Friday 10.00–17.00

St Bartholomew the Great, Smithfield Tuesday to Friday 08.30–17.00; Saturday 10.30–13.30; Sunday 08.30–13.00, 14.30–20.00. Services Sunday 09.00, 11.00, 18.30; Tuesday 12.30; Thursday 08.30. Tel. 7606 5171. http://www.greatstbarts.com
St Benet's Welsh Anglican Church, Paul's Wharf Services Sunday 11.00, 15.30. Tel. 7723 3104
St Botolph's without Bishopsgate Monday to Friday 10.30–15.00. Services Wednesday 13.10; Thursday 12.10. Tel. 7588 3388/1053, Fax. 7638 1256. Email botolph.bgate@care4free.net; http://www.stbotolphs.org.uk
St Bride's, Fleet Street Monday to Saturday 08.00–17.00. Services Sunday 11.00, 18.30; Monday, Wednesday, Friday 08.30; Tuesday, Thursday 08.30; Thursday 13.15. Tel. 7427 0133. Email info@stbrides.com; http://www.stbrides.com
St Clement Danes, Strand Services Sunday 11.00; Wednesday, Friday 12.30. Tel. 7242 8282
St Dunstan-in-the-West Tuesday, Friday 09.00–15.00; Sunday 10.00–16.00. Services Tuesday, festivals 12.30. Tel. 7405 1929. Romanian Sunday 11.00. Tel. 7735 9515
St Edmund, Lombard Street opening autumn 2004
St Ethelburga's, Bishopsgate Tel. 7248 3177, Fax. 7638 1440. Email enquiries@ stethelburga's.org; http://www. stethelburga's.org
St Etheldreda's, Ely Place Monday to Friday 07.30–19.00. Services Sunday 09.00, 11.00

London

(Sung Latin); Monday to Friday
08.00, 13.00; Saturday 09.30.
Tel. 7405 1061, Fax. 7440
St Helen's, Bishopsgate
Services Sunday 10.15, 19.00;
Tuesday 12.35, 13.15. Tel. 7283
2231, Fax. 7626 8184.
http://www.st-helens.org.uk
St Martin-in-the-Fields daily
08.00–18.30. Services Sunday
08.00, 10.00, 12.00, 14.15
(Chinese), 17.00, 18.30; Monday
to Friday 08.00, 08.30, 17.30
(not Wednesday); Saturday
09.00 only; Wednesday also at
13.05, 17.00, 18.00. Tel. 7766
1100, Fax. 7839 5163. http:
//www.stmartin-in-the-fields.org
St Mary-le-Bow Monday to
Friday 06.30–18.15. Services
Monday, Wednesday to Friday
08.15, 13.05 (concert on
Thursday), 17.45 (not Friday);
Monday, Wednesday 13.05; Tue
07.30, 07.45, 13.05 (dialogue),
17.45; Wednesday, Friday
13.05; Thursday 17.30. Tel.
7248 5139, Fax. 0509.
http://www.stmarylebow.co.uk
St Mary-le-Strand Services
Sunday 11.00; Tuesday,
Thursday 13.05; Monday to
Thursday 17.15. Tel. 7836 3126
or 7405 1929
St Mary Woolnoth Monday to
Friday 09.30–16.30. Services
Tuesday, Friday 13.10, 20.00.
Tel. 7626 9701
St Paul's Cathedral Monday to
Saturday 08.30–16.00. Sunday
open for services only. **Galleries**
Monday to Saturday
09.30–16.00. Services Sunday
08.00, 10.15, 11.30, 15.15,
18.00; Monday to Saturday
07.30 (or Saturday 08.30),
08.00, 12.30, 17.00. The choir
sings at Sunday 10.15, 11.00,
15.15; Monday to Saturday

15.00. Tel. 7236 4128, Fax.
7248 3104. http://www.
stpaulscathedral.org.uk
St Paul's, Covent Garden
Monday to Friday 08.30–16.30.
Services Sunday 11.00, 16.00
(2); Monday to Friday 08.30;
Tuesday 12.30; Wednesday
13.10. Tel. 7836 5221.
http://www.covent-garden.
co.uk/Histories/stpaul.html
St Stephen, Walbrook Monday
to Friday 09.00–16.00. Services
Thursday 12.45, organ recital
Friday 12.30
Southwark Cathedral daily
08.00–18.00. Services Sunday
08.45, 09.00, 11.00, 15.00,
18.30; Monday to Friday 08.00,
08.15, 12.30, 12.45, 17.30;
Saturday, BH 09.00, 09.15,
16.00. Tel. 7367 6700, Fax.
6725. Email cathedral@dswark.
org; http://www.dswark.org/
cathedral
Temple Church Services
Sunday 08.30, 11.15 (no
services August to September).
For opening times Tel. 7353
3470, Fax. 1736
The Tower of London Monday
to Saturday 09.00–18.00;
Sunday 10.00–18.00; last
admission 1 hr before closing.
Chapel of St Peter ad Vincula
open for guided tour only and for
services on Sunday at 09.00
(except 1), 11.00; **St John's
Chapel** Services 09.00 (1). Tel.
7709 0765.
http://www.hrp.org.uk
**Wesley's House, Museum and
Church** Monday to Saturday
10.00–16.00, Sunday
12.00–14.00. Services Sunday
09.45 (except 1), 11.00;
Thursday 12.45. Tel. 7253 2262,
Fax. 7608 3825. Email
administration@wesleyschapel.

org.uk; http://www.forsaith-
oxon.demon.co.uk/
methodist-heritage/southern/
sites.html#city
Westminster Abbey Monday to
Friday 09.30–15.45; Wednesday
also 18.00–19.00; Saturday
09.30–14.45; except when
services are held, last admission
1 hr before closing time. Services
Sunday 08.00, 10.00, 11.15,
15.00, 18.30 (organ recital
17.45); Monday to Friday 07.30,
08.00, 12.30, 17.00 (choral
except Wednesday); Saturday,
BH 08.00, 09.00, 15.00
Saturday or 17.00 BH. Tel. 7222
5152, Fax. 7233 2072. http:
//www.westminster-abbey.org
Westminster Cathedral
Services Sunday 08.00, 09.00,

10.00, 10.30, 12.00, 15.30,
17.30, 21.00; Monday to Friday
07.00, 07.40, 08.00, 10.30,
12.30, 17.00, 17.30; Saturday
08.00, 09.00, 10.00, 10.30,
12.30, 17.30, 18.00; BH 08.00,
09.00, 10.00, 10.30, 12.30;
closes 17.30. Lift up the tower
daily April to October
09.00–17.00; November to
March Thursday to Sunday
09.00–17.00. Tel. 7798 9055,
Fax. 9090
Westminster Chapter House
(English Heritage) daily
10.00–17.30 (16.00 November
to March); subject to closure at
short notice on State occasions.
Ticket also valid for the Chapel of
the Pyx, Abbey Museum and
Jewel Tower. Tel. 7222 5897

The South-East

Pope Gregory's plans for the conversion of England began in the south-east, where most visitors – even then – first arrived in England, and this area therefore has a richness of holy places. Gregory sent his friend St Augustine of Canterbury – not to be confused with the teacher Augustine of Hippo – across Europe and he landed in Kent.

CANTERBURY (Kent)

Augustine landed at **Ebbsfleet** near Pegwell Bay in the Isle of Thanet, an area of the east Kent coast that is no longer an island. Augustine would not at first enter the pagan city of Canterbury, so he made a settlement where the ruins of **St Augustine's Abbey,** on Longport, now stand. An excellent English Heritage visitors' centre helps pilgrims to interpret the foundations of the Abbey buildings from the Norman period; there are also traces of Saxon burials and, to the east, of the sixth-century church of St Pancras,

originally a pagan temple and built of Roman bricks. In North Holmes Road, just off Longport, is **St Martin's Church,** one of England's oldest churches – the Venerable Bede (see p. 171) said it was built while the Romans were still there. It was built on the site of a Roman villa or temple and used by Queen Bertha and her chaplain; here King Ethelbert was baptized. There is Roman brickwork in the walls, and a Norman font.

Opening Times and Service Times
St Augustine's Abbey (English Heritage) daily April to

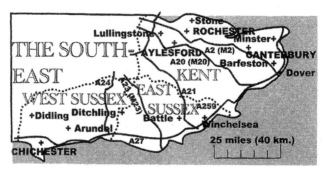

St Augustine of Canterbury (d. 604 or 605)

The young priest, Gregory, decided to become a missionary to the heathen English when he saw fair-haired boys for sale in the slave market in Rome and made the famous pun, 'Not Angles but Angels'. Being made Pope prevented him going in person, so in his place he sent his friend Augustine to Canterbury to convert the English, writing with very practical advice about how the worship in the new Ecclesia Anglicana was to be organized. The missionaries wanted to turn back when they heard what fierce savages the English were, but the Pope encouraged them. Augustine went first to the heathen king of Kent in his capital city of Canterbury. Queen Bertha was a French Christian, and had a bishop as her chaplain, but they had made no headway in converting the Anglo-Saxons until Augustine arrived. Soon King Ethelbert was baptized in St Martin's Church, and Augustine built the first cathedral inside the city.

September 10.00–18.00; October 10.00–dusk; November to March 10.00–16.00. Tel. 01227 767345
St Martin's Church temporarily closed except for services. Services Sunday 09.00, 18.30; Thursday 12.00. Keyholder Tel. 01227 402686 or 453469

Canterbury Cathedral

One of the most visited buildings in England, the Cathedral at Canterbury retains a friendly and welcoming atmosphere, and a sense of mystery and history. Once King Ethelbert had been converted, St Augustine set about building a church inside the walled city in around 602 AD. This church was enlarged in the eighth century, then destroyed in a fire in 1067, and the first Norman Archbishop of Canterbury, Lanfranc, set about building a larger one. Archbishop Anselm replaced Lanfranc's choir with a more ambitious structure. In 1170 Archbishop Thomas à Becket was murdered in the cathedral, and his tomb became the most important pilgrimage centre in Northern Europe. Only four years later, however, the cathedral, except for the crypt and the nave, was again destroyed by fire, so in the twelfth century, two architects, William of Sens and William the Englishman, built a magnificent new cathedral to honour the martyr's shrine. They introduced cream-coloured Caen stone, grey-black

Purbeck marble, and flying buttresses, in an early form of Gothic architecture that influenced the style of all later medieval English churches. The nave and most of the Great Cloister were rebuilt in the fourteenth century in the new Perpendicular style; the transepts and the southwest tower were built in the fifteenth century. The central tower, known as Bell Harry Tower, 76 metres (235 feet) high, was completed in 1505; the northwest tower was demolished in 1832 and replaced with a copy of the southwest tower.

You can enter the precincts from the town through **Christ Church Gate**, dating from 1517 and decorated with heraldic shields; the visitors' centre is on the right. The entrance to the cathedral is through the southwest porch, into the soaring **nave** built in the Perpendicular style from 1392 to 1404. The **great west window** on your left contains twelfth-century glass; Adam is digging in the Garden of Eden. On the opposite side of the nave near the north door is a seventeenth-century font with carvings of the writers of the four Gospels and the 12 apostles. The **north transept** is the site of Becket's martyrdom, which is marked by the Altar of the Sword's

Point, and a commemoration of the place where Pope John Paul II and Archbishop Robert Runcie prayed together for reconciliation in 1982. At this point visitors may go out into the **Great Cloister** (mostly fourteenth century but the north and west walls are one of the oldest parts of the cathedral, dating from Lanfranc's eleventh-century building). The twelfth-century barrel-vaulted **Chapter House**, opening off the cloister, is where the first performance of T.S. Eliot's play *Murder in the Cathedral* was given in 1935. Returning to the north transept, go down the steps into the Norman **crypt**. The centre of the crypt is dedicated as the **Chapel of Our Lady Undercroft**, with delicately carved Norman screens, and the witty and imaginative carvings on the capitals of the pillars form England's finest gallery of Norman sculpture. In the **north transept of the crypt** are altars to St Nicholas and St Mary Magdalene. The tomb of St Thomas à Becket was for the first 50 years in the centre of the eastern end of the crypt, in front of the **Jesus Chapel**. The **south transept of the crypt** was originally the **Black Prince's Chantry**; then when Huguenot Protestants fled to England from persecution in France they were invited to worship in this chapel, and

Archbishops of Canterbury

Among the hundred distinguished Archbishops of
Canterbury since St Augustine, there is only space to
mention a few:

Theodore of Tarsus (c. 602–690)

A native of Tarsus in modern Turkey, the birthplace of St
Paul, Theodore was consecrated seventh archbishop of
Canterbury in Rome in 668, and set out from there with a
number of companions including Benedict Biscop (see p.
170). He created an influential school in Canterbury,
where the Venerable Bede was among its pupils. In
cooperation with the kings, he achieved a high degree of
central control in the English Church, which brought him
into conflict with St Wilfrid of York, a dispute that ended
when Theodore apologized.

St Anselm (c.1033–1109)

A monk from the Abbey of Bec in Normandy, Anselm was
in frequent conflict with successive kings. He reasoned
carefully on what Jesus did on the cross – the doctrine of
the atonement – and on the ontological argument for the
existence of God. 'Credo ut intelligam', he wrote: 'I believe
in order to understand'.

St Thomas à Becket (1118–70)

Thomas's family were Norman merchants, and he became
a servant in the household of Archbishop Theobald of
Canterbury. He was sent to study law in Bologna and
Auxerre. He attracted the attention of King Henry, who
appointed him Chancellor of England, the apex of the
legal profession. Thomas's willingness to do the King's
bidding ended when he was made Archbishop of
Canterbury in 1162. He became an ardent defender of the
rights of the Church, and argued for the Church's
supremacy over the King. All 'clerks' – that is, not only
clergy but almost all who could read and write – could
claim the right to be tried for their crimes by ecclesiastical
courts; the King insisted that they must then be punished
by the King's courts. Becket refused to agree, and fled to
France. In 1170 Henry had his eldest son crowned as the
next king by the Archbishop of York, although this was
traditionally the function of Canterbury. Becket appealed
to the Pope and excommunicated the clergy who had

taken part. He returned to England after a partial reconciliation, but continued to punish those who had been involved in the illegal coronation. King Henry, in Normandy at the time, protested, 'Who will rid me of this turbulent priest?' Four knights who heard him sailed to England and murdered Becket in Canterbury Cathedral, claiming that these were the King's instructions. The Church claimed Thomas as a Christian martyr, and King Henry was forced to kneel before his tomb in Canterbury Cathedral, and allow the monks to scourge him there as an act of penance. Becket was canonized as a saint in 1173, and pilgrims who visited his shrine were promised a similar indulgence to those who travelled to Jerusalem.

William Temple (1881–1944)

Headmaster of Repton School, Bishop of Manchester, and Archbishop successively of York and Canterbury, William Temple's *Readings in St John's Gospel* reveal his deep learning and his devotional approach to Scripture; he was an advocate of social reform and of Christian unity.

services in French are still held here. Leaving the crypt by the southern stairs brings us back to the south transept; turning right into the **crossing**, we can admire the fan-vaulting under Bell Harry Tower, with coats of arms of donors on the bosses. Turning right again, under the fifteenth-century organ screen with figures of six kings, brings us into the fourteenth-century **choir**, with its thirteenth-century marble **St Augustine's Chair**, where Archbishops of Canterbury are enthroned, standing in its traditional position behind the high altar. The medieval **stained-glass** windows in the **Trinity Chapel** at the east end of the choir include a series,

probably made at Chartres, telling the story of Becket's life and death and the miracles attributed to him. This is where his shrine was placed from 1220 until the Reformation; only the **mosaic pavement** in front of it remains today. The stone stairs from the transepts up to the choir aisles show the wear from the feet of many pilgrims who came to pray here. The chapel at the extreme east end is known as the **Corona**; here is the thirteenth-century **Redemption Window**; the Corona is said to have held the top of Becket's skull. Notice also the **Tomb of the Black Prince**, who died in 1376; the **Tomb of King Henry IV**, who died in 1413;

Canterbury Pilgrims

When Geoffrey Chaucer wrote *The Canterbury Tales*, one
of the greatest literary works in the early English language,
he was describing a group of pilgrims who must have been
typical of those who journeyed to Canterbury. To
entertain themselves on the way, they took turns to tell
each other stories: some beautiful, some bawdy, all with
an insight into human nature. They travelled from the
Tabard Inn in Southwark, south London, to Canterbury,
along the old Roman Watling Street (now the A2). There
is no Tabard Inn now, though there is a Tabard Street in
Southwark, so modern pilgrims can start from the
galleried George Inn near Southwark Cathedral. The first
part of the journey will be along the busy Old Kent Road.
Near Dartford, walkers can strike off the main road onto
footpaths signposted and shown on large-scale maps as the
Pilgrim's Way. There is also the South Downs Way leading
from Winchester to Canterbury, which may have been
used by pilgrims.

and the **Chapel of St Anselm,**
in the southwest corner of
the Trinity Chapel, with a
twelfth-century wall painting
high up in the apse. The main
exit from the cathedral is
from the south transept.

Opening Times and Service Times

Canterbury Cathedral Monday
to Saturday 09.00–17.00 (16.30
in winter); Sunday 11.30–14.00,
16.30–17.30. **Crypt**
10.00–16.30 (17.30 Sunday).
Services Sunday 08.00, 09.30,
11.00, 15.15, 18.30; Monday to
Saturday 07.30 (Saturday 09.30),
08.00, 17.30 (Saturday 15.15);
Wednesday 11.00; Thursday
18.15. Huguenot service in
French Sunday 15.00. Tel.
01227 762862, Fax. 865222 or
762897. http://www.canterbury-
cathedral.org

ROCHESTER (Kent)

The Romans built a fortress
where Rochester Castle now
stands, and St Augustine of
Canterbury appointed
Ithamar, one of his
colleagues, to be the first
Bishop of Rochester, where
in about 609 he built
England's second oldest
cathedral. The position of the
Saxon apse is marked on the
floor at the northwest corner
of the present cathedral. In
1077 King William the
Conqueror instructed
Gundulf to rebuild **Rochester
Castle.** Gundulf had been the
architect of the White Tower
in the Tower of London, and
a strong castle was needed to
defend the approach to

London along the old Roman Watling Street through Rochester. King William also made Gundulf the Bishop of Rochester. Gundulf rebuilt **Rochester Cathedral**, and the west front, the nave and the crypt are largely Norman work. The west doorway and the tympanum above it are richly carved. In 1201 St William of Perth, a baker from Scotland, set off on a pilgrimage to the Holy Land, but he was robbed and murdered in Rochester. His tomb in the cathedral became a centre of pilgrimage, and was endowed by lavish gifts from the pilgrims. As the cathedral became richer in the thirteenth century, a programme of decoration with fine Purbeck marble columns in the Early English style began at the east end, but stopped abruptly halfway down the nave. There are some fine wall paintings on the walls of the choir, including half of a thirteenth-century image of the Wheel of Fortune represented as a treadmill. Rochester is noted as the place where St John Fisher was once the bishop.

Opening Times and Service Times

Rochester Cathedral daily summer 07.30–18.00; winter

St John Fisher (1469–1535)

John Fisher was appointed Bishop of Rochester in 1504, and influenced Lady Margaret Beaufort, mother of King Henry VII, to found Christ's College, Cambridge, in 1505, and also St John's College, Cambridge, though after her death he took over the task and established it himself in 1511. He wrote books attacking Lutheranism, which gave him a reputation as a theologian throughout Europe. In 1527 King Henry VIII and Cardinal Wolsey consulted Fisher about the validity of Henry's marriage to Catherine of Aragon. To the King's anger Fisher preached in defence of Catherine. He opposed the 1534 Act of Supremacy declaring the King, not the Pope, head of the temporal affairs of the Church of England. He and Sir Thomas More were imprisoned in the Tower of London for refusing to take the oath connected with this Act. At the end of the year an Act was passed by Parliament making such refusal treasonable, and the following May Pope Paul III made Fisher a Cardinal, effectively sealing his fate. Fisher refused to speak about the supremacy, but was reportedly tricked into admitting his opposition, was tried and condemned for treason, and beheaded on Tower Hill; he was made a saint in 1935.

07.30–17.00. Services Sunday
08.00, 09.45, 10.30, 15.15;
Monday to Saturday 07.30,
08.00, 17.30 (or Saturday
15.15), Thursday 13.00. Tel.
01634 401301, Fax. 401410.
http://www.cathedrals.org.uk

AYLESFORD
(Kent)

Aylesford Priory is a
Carmelite or 'Whitefriar'
friary founded in 1242, and
since 1949 again inhabited
by a Roman Catholic
Carmelite religious
community, who host
individual or group retreats
or conferences for all
denominations. The church
has been rebuilt as an open-
air arena; in the chapel are
the relics of St Simon Stock
who in 1251 received a
vision of the Virgin Mary
here. Follow the signposts to
'The Friars ✠' or simply to
'✠' from Junction 6 of the
M20.

Opening Times
Reception 08.30–19.00;
welcome centre 10.00–12.30,
13.30–17.00; **tea room** and
shop Monday to Saturday
10.00–17.00 (16.00 winter);
Sunday 11.00–17.00 (16.00
winter). Tel. 01622 717272, Fax.
715575

CHICHESTER
(West Sussex)

Chichester is the county
town of West Sussex. Work
was started on building
Chichester Cathedral in
1091, after the seat of the
Bishops of the West Saxons
had been moved from Selsey,
and completed in 1184; the
nave is mostly Norman, and
there are superb stone-carved
reliefs of Christ arriving at
Bethany and raising Lazarus,
dating from about 1140. But
there was a fire, after which
the remainder of the
cathedral was extensively
rebuilt. The porches,

The Retreat Movement

With a renewal of interest in the spiritual life in the
twentieth century came a rediscovery of the riches of the
Christian prayer tradition. Many local churches looked for
somewhere to take their members away for a quiet day or
a parish weekend. Many individuals sought a place apart
from the rush of daily life to be quiet, to think and to talk
to God. The Society for Promoting Retreats was founded,
with the slogan 'Retreat to Advance' (see p. 2). Retreat
centres all over Britain have facilities for individuals to
spend a time of prayer, alone or under the guidance of a
spiritual director, or to join a group retreat, either silent
with talks on prayer, or with artistic or other activities to
help the retreatants to discover God and to discover
themselves.

St Richard of Wyche (1197–1253)

Born at Droitwich, he became Chancellor of Canterbury under Archbishop Edmund Rich. King Henry III refused permission for Richard to be consecrated Bishop of Chichester until the Pope threatened to excommunicate the King. Richard was a deeply humble and spiritual man and an excellent administrator; he walked over most of his diocese on foot. 'The Prayer of St Richard of Chichester' is now one of the most popular in the English language: 'Praise to thee, Lord Jesus Christ, for all the benefits thou hast won for me, for all the pains and insults thou hast born for me. Most merciful redeemer, friend and brother, may I know thee more clearly, love thee more dearly, and follow thee more nearly, day by day. Amen.'

George Kennedy Allen Bell (1883–1958)

George Bell was made chaplain to the Archbishop of Canterbury in 1914, Dean of Canterbury in 1924, and then Bishop of Chichester in 1929. When Adolf Hitler came to power in Germany, Bishop Bell ensured that Jews and other non-Aryans fleeing from the Nazi regime could find asylum in England, and he formed links with the German Confessing Church which resisted Hitler. During the Second World War Bishop Bell was an outspoken opponent of saturation bombing, and afterwards of the British decision to make nuclear weapons; it is often said that his refusal to conform to the government line of the day was the reason he was never made an archbishop. He was prominent in movements seeking understanding and reunion between divided Christian denominations, and was chairman and president of the World Council of Churches.

retrochoir and clerestories are Early English; the tower, side chapels, and Lady Chapel are Decorated; and the cloisters are in the Perpendicular style. It has hardly been modified since about 1300, except for the unique free-standing, fifteenth-century bell-tower, now housing the cathedral shop, and the slender spire, rebuilt in 1861. Chichester is an example of Church sponsorship of the arts, and in the interior of the cathedral near to the tomb of St Richard is a huge altar-screen tapestry by John Piper, a painting by Graham

Sutherland, a stained-glass window by Marc Chagall, and the grave of the composer Gustav Holst. The American composer Leonard Bernstein wrote his *Chichester Psalms* to a commission from Chichester Cathedral.

Opening Times and Service Times

Chichester Cathedral daily October to March 07.15–18.00; April to September 07.15–19.00. Services Sunday 08.00, 10.00, 11.00, 15.30; Monday to Saturday 07.30, 08.00, 17.30; Wednesday 13.10; Thursday 10.30; Saturday 12.00. Tel. 01243 782595, Fax. 536190. http://www.chichester-cathedral.org.uk

STONE; LULLINGSTONE (Kent)

There are many other holy sites worth visiting in the South-East. Just east of Dartford on the A226 is the village of Stone, where St Mary's Church is believed to have been built about 1260 by masons who had been employed in the building of Westminster Abbey. As it was to serve as the chapel of the Bishop's Palace alongside, where distinguished pilgrims on their way to Canterbury were given hospitality, they built one of the most sumptuously decorated parish churches in the country.

Travelling south from Dartford on the A225 you come to the village of Eynsford, with signs to **Lullingstone Roman Villa,** half a mile south of Eynsford railway station. Many Romans settled down to farm in the English countryside, often after being discharged from the army, and built themselves a comfortable villa to live in. The foundations and floors of the one at Lullingstone are well preserved, and displayed under a weatherproof building; from them you can learn a lot about the way of life in the later Roman Empire. There is a cellar chapel to the pagan gods, but the rooms above it were destroyed in a fire. The plaster on the walls collapsed almost intact, and when the archaeologists pieced it together, they found that the room had been built as a Christian chapel. The pictures painted on the walls included the Chi-Ro symbol (XP, the first two letters of the word 'Christ' in the Greek alphabet), and pictures of members of the family with their arms raised in the distinctive Christian attitude of prayer. The first Christians used to meet in the existing rooms of private houses; the chapel at Lullingstone is the second oldest building in the world to be built specifically for Christian worship.

Christians in Roman Britain

The Romano-British inhabitants of what would later be called England included a number of Christians, and several traces of their faith remain. There are Chi-Ro badges dropped by Roman soldiers and travellers beside the Roman roads. There is the villa at Lullingstone. The mosaic face of Christ found in a villa at Hinton St Mary is now in the British Museum, and is interesting because it dates from before it became customary to portray him with a beard. The legends of King Arthur of Camelot are probably based on a tribal chieftain of a Celtic tribe near Queen's Camel in Somerset, who retained Roman culture and the Christian faith after the Roman legions had withdrawn from Britain. However, Christianity was driven into the Celtic west by the invasion of the Anglo-Saxons.

Opening Times and Service Times
St Mary's Church, Stone First Tel. 01322 382076; key at the Rectory. Services Sunday 10.00.
Lullingstone Roman Villa (English Heritage) daily April to September 10.00–18.00; October 10.00–17.00; November to March 10.00–16.00. Tel. 01322 863467

MINSTER-IN-THANET; BARFRESTON; DOVER (Kent)

St Mary's Church at Minster-in-Thanet is part of a convent that was founded in 670 by the great-granddaughter of King Ethelbert. **St Mildred's Priory**, a house of Benedictine nuns, can claim to be one of the oldest inhabited buildings in England.

Just off the A2 road from Canterbury to Dover, to the northeast, is the tiny village of **Barfreston**, where the twelfth-century church has superb Norman carvings of men, animals and angels on the inside walls and a figure of Christ in glory over the outside door, surrounded by animals playing musical instruments. Above this is a row of grimacing faces, probably the wittiest collection of Norman stone-carving in the country.

Dover has been England's first line of defence against invaders since before the Romans landed. In the heart of the sturdy castle is the church of **St Mary in Castro**. It has probably been a place of worship for 2000 years, for next to the Roman Pharos or lighthouse, which

---

Saxon Churches

Many of the churches that were built in England during the Anglo-Saxon period before the Norman Conquest were made of wood and have not survived; others have been so adapted and modified in later centuries that only traces of Saxon work remain. Small stone churches continued to be built, even after the Danish invasion, served by monks from nearby monasteries. They are distinguished by tiny windows, an apse, and certain distinctive masonry techniques. Examples mentioned in this book include Bradford on Avon, Dover Castle, Earl's Barton, Brixworth, Deerhurst, Escomb, St Benet's Cambridge, Heysham, Stow-in-Lindsey and Wing.

---

still stands on the summit of the hill, the Roman invaders probably built a temple, and the Saxons used Roman bricks in the arches and doorways of the church they built on the site in the seventh century. The church has been decorated and repaired several times, but the layout is still as it was in Saxon times.

Opening Times and Service Times

Barfreston church Services Sunday 09.00. Tel. 01304 830241

St Mary in Castro Services Sunday 10.00. Tel. 01304 211067, Fax. 214739

St Mary's, Minster-in-Thanet keyholder Tel. 01843 821250. Services Sunday 09.00, 10.00; Wednesday 10.30.

St Mildred's May to October 11.00–14.00, 14.30–16.00; November to April 11.00–14.00; closed Saturday afternoon and Sunday. Mass Sunday 08.30; Monday to Saturday 08.00. Daily

vespers 18.10; compline 19.45. Tel. 01843 821254

Dover Castle (English Heritage) daily April to September 10.00–18.00; October 10.00–17.00; November to March 10.00–16.00.

Kent Tourism: ask for the leaflet 'Kent, the Original Faith Zone', which lists 41 sites of special spiritual interest. Tel. 01622 696165. http://www. kenttourism.co.uk

WINCHELSEA (East Sussex)

When the old town was washed away in the great storm of 1287, Winchelsea, on the A259 between Rye and Hastings, built a large new church dedicated to St Thomas à Becket. However, French invaders destroyed the nave, so now we see the chancel, with fine tombs – some of them saved from the old church, some constructed soon after the new church was built; the whole building is an example of the Decorated style of architecture. There are also fragments of the ruined transepts. Nearby is **John Wesley's Chapel**, erected in 1785, where he preached in 1789. The next year, aged 87, he preached his last outdoor sermon in Winchelsea.

Opening Times and Service Times
St Thomas à Becket Church
Services Sunday 08.00, 10.30; Monday 18.00; Tuesday 07.30; Wednesday 09.30; Thursday 10.30; Saturday 09.30. Tel. 01797 226254
John Wesley's Chapel Tel. 01424 217804

BATTLE
(East Sussex)

William of Normandy, known as King William the Conqueror, landed at Pevensey Bay to the west of the town, and made Hastings his headquarters, before defeating King Harold's English army at Battle, 6 miles (10 km) northwest of Hastings in 1066. In thanksgiving for his victory he erected **Battle Abbey** in the new Norman style of architecture. It was occupied by a Benedictine community, and much altered down the ages, before being mostly destroyed at the Dissolution of the Monasteries. Apart from elements incorporated in the buildings of Battle

Abbey School, only some foundations and the monks' dormitory survive. The site of the church is outlined: the high altar marks the spot where Harold was killed. The large gatehouse, added in 1338, is the starting point for an audio-guided walk round the battlefield, including an audio-visual display on the events of 1066, which changed the course of the secular and religious history of England. Like the best modern interpreters they present both points of view and leave visitors free to choose.

Opening Times
Battle Abbey and battlefield
(English Heritage) daily April to September 10.00–18.00; October 10.00–17.00; November to March 10.00–16.00 or dusk. Tel. 01424 773792

DITCHLING
(East Sussex)

West of Lewes on the B2116, **Ditchling Museum** is full of wonderful creations by the Ditchling Guild of Catholic artists and craftsmen, including seminal figures such as Eric Gill and David Jones. There is a red brick **Old Meeting House**, dating from 1730, where Dissenters, those who would not accept the use of *The Book of Common Prayer*, gathered for worship. It is now used by Unitarians, who claim a

---

The Dissolution of the Monasteries (1536–39)

In Saxon and Norman times the English monasteries were at the forefront of the growth in faith, learning, the care of the sick, and agriculture. By the sixteenth century, on the one hand, they had become very wealthy, and owned a high proportion of the usable land. On the other hand, however, they were finding it increasingly difficult to recruit lay brothers to work the land, and were forced to rent it out. They were much criticized because of moral laxity in some places, and because they came under the ecclesiastical law and were exempt from the law of England. King Henry VIII, following his break with the Pope, was forced to begin preparations to defend England against a Crusade, which had been proposed in some countries. Desperate for cash, he suppressed 250 of the smaller monasteries in 1536 and confiscated their wealth; this was soon followed in the north of England by the protest known as the Pilgrimage of Grace, which was brutally crushed. Through the agency of Thomas Cromwell the remaining monasteries were suppressed in 1539. There was little resistance in the rest of the country: many of the monks became secular clergy, and much of the cash and land passed eventually to the local landowners. Some was used to establish six much-needed new bishoprics. While we may regret the loss of many beautiful buildings and works of art, we may ask from the opposite point of view how much longer a high proportion of the national wealth could have been devoted to maintaining such huge institutions, and whether the end of medieval monasticism was not in any case inevitable.

---

completely open religion, and exudes a palpable sense of peace.

Opening Times and Service Times
Museum, Church Lane Tel. and Fax. 01273 844744.
http://www.ditchling-museum.com
Old Meeting House, The Twitten keys at the cottage alongside. Services Sunday 11.00.

ARUNDEL
(West Sussex)

Arundel is 18 miles (29 km) west of Brighton on the A27. For seven centuries the Dukes of Norfolk have lived in **Arundel Castle**. The **Fitzalan Chapel**, rebuilt in 1380, is a curiosity in that half of the building belongs to the Roman Catholic Church and half to the Church of England. The

St Philip Howard (1557–95)

Philip was the eldest son of the fourth Duke of Norfolk, and inherited the earldom of Arundel on the death of his maternal grandfather. Although he was a Protestant, after his wife became a Roman Catholic in 1582 he was suspected of Catholic sympathies and involvement in Francis Throckmorton's plot. This was a plan to invade England with a French army, and to replace Queen Elizabeth I with her prisoner, Mary Queen of Scots. Howard was preparing to escape to Flanders when Queen Elizabeth herself visited him at his London home and ordered him to remain. In 1584 he became a Roman Catholic and made another attempt to flee the country. He was arrested and sentenced by the Star Chamber to life imprisonment. Nevertheless he was soon released, but then rearrested and charged with high treason and in 1589 condemned to death. Once again the sentence was never carried out, and he died in the Tower of London.

Roman Catholic half is entered from the castle, and is where the family of the Dukes of Norfolk, who have always been leading Roman Catholic laymen in England, are buried. But the western end of the building is the **Parish Church of St Nicholas**, and is entered from the town. In 1969 the stone dividing wall which had kept the two denominations apart was knocked down and replaced by a glass screen, which can be opened for joint services. Nearby is **Arundel Cathedral,** built in 1873 in French Gothic style for the Roman Catholics of the area by Joseph Hansom, the designer of the Hansom cab. The body of St Philip Howard was moved from the Fitzalan Chapel to the Cathedral at his canonization in 1970.

Opening Times and Service Times

Arundel Castle April to October Sunday to Friday 12.00–17.00 (16.00 last admission). Tel. 01903 883136 or 882173, Fax. 884581.
http://www.arundelcastle.org
Arundel Cathedral 09.00–dusk (winter); 09.00–18.00 (summer). Mass Sunday 08.00, 09.30, 11.00; Monday to Thursday 10.00; Friday 12.00; Saturday 10.00, 18.30. Tel. 01903 882297, Fax. 885335.
http://www.arundelcathedral.org
St Nicholas's daily till dusk. Services Sunday 08.00, 10.00; Tuesday 19.30; Wednesday 10.00; Friday 12.00. Tel. 01903 882262, Fax. 882201.
http://www.stnicholas-arundel.co.uk

DIDLING
(West Sussex)

St Andrew's Church,
Didling, known as 'The
Shepherds' Church', stands
in a fold of the South Downs,
reached down a narrow road
turning off the A286 at
Cocking, signposted to
Bepton. Going beyond
Bepton until you reach a sign
reading 'Didling Church',
you see a tiny building
isolated among the fields
where the sheep still graze.

There is a Saxon font, from
the Saxon church that once
stood here but was rebuilt in
about 1220. The rough
medieval benches, with
sockets for candles, contrast
with the beautifully turned
altar-rails from about 1640,
with balusters close enough
to stop the sheep-dogs from
entering the sanctuary.

Service Times
St Andrew's once a month
Sunday 10.30. Tel. 01730
825234

45

The South Coast

Before England was united, the Kingdom of Wessex saw the early development of English government in State and Church, and lives of heroic sanctity. There are many wonderful places to visit in this region.

WINCHESTER
(Hampshire)

Winchester was the capital of Wessex and then of England from the ninth century to the mid-twelfth century. Cenwall, a Saxon king of Wessex, built a church there in 648, and King Alfred the Great used Winchester for defence against the Danish invaders. The bones of Saxon kings are said to be in the iron caskets on top of the screens near the high altar of Winchester Cathedral, and in

Saxon times it was one of the first cathedrals in England to be combined with a monastery. Traces of the Saxon building were discovered in the 1960s. King William the Conqueror was crowned in Winchester as well as London, and built a castle and a new cathedral in 1079. The east end was reconstructed in 1202; in the early fourteenth century the Norman choir was rebuilt in the Perpendicular style; and between 1346 and 1404 the

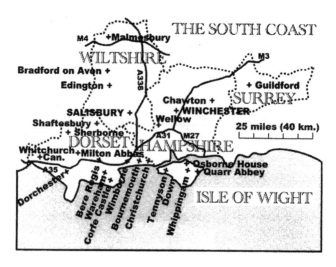

THE SOUTH COAST

M4 +Malmesbury

WILTSHIRE

M3

Bradford on Avon +

A338

Edington +

Chawton +

+ Guildford

SURREY

SALISBURY +

+ WINCHESTER

Shaftesbury +

Wellow

25 miles (40 km.)

+ Sherborne

A31 M27

DORSET HAMPSHIRE

Whitchurch + Milton Abbas

+ Can.

A35

+ Osborne House

+ Quarr Abbey

Dorchester

Bere Regis

Wareham

Corfe Castle

Wimborne

Bournemouth

Christchurch

Tennyson Down

Whippingham

ISLE OF WIGHT

View from the Dean Garnier garden, Winchester Cathedral

nave and west front were rebuilt. The work was completed between 1486 and 1528 by the remodelling of nave, Lady Chapel and chancel. In the Civil War the castle was largely destroyed and the cathedral damaged.

Winchester Cathedral

Winchester Cathedral is now one of the finest ecclesiastical buildings in the land, and the longest (169 metres, 556 feet) Gothic church in Europe. In the early twentieth century it was discovered that the east end had been built on a thirteenth-century raft of beech trees and was sinking into the marshy ground, causing cracks in the walls and parts of the ceiling to fall. So a diver, William Walker, working often under water from 1906 to 1912, replaced the rotting timbers with cement and saved the cathedral; there is a monument to him at the east end of the nave, and still the crypt is under water for much of the winter. Entering the **nave** you notice how the sturdy Norman pillars were decorated by Bishop William of Wykeham in the fourteenth century, with the slender lines of the Perpendicular arches and the 12 bays of the roof. Note the **west window**; the ornate **chantry** where prayers were said for the repose of the soul

---

King Alfred the Great of Wessex (849–99)

King Alfred defeated the Danish invaders; had he not, Christianity in England might not have survived. A considerable scholar himself, he wrote poetry, and with the help of his advisers he translated works of Gregory the Great, Boethius and St Augustine from Latin into English. He had some success in founding and reforming monasteries, and laid the foundations for the establishment of new dioceses. According to popular legend he was travelling in disguise and was told by a woman who gave him hospitality to watch her cakes, which were cooking by the fire. He was so busy thinking about his strategy against the Danes that he burnt the cakes, and received a severe scolding.

---

of William of Wykeham; **Jane Austen's grave,** window and brass in the north aisle of the nave; the richly carved **twelfth-century font** made of black Tournai marble, and the **Jacobean pulpit.** There are thirteenth-century wall paintings in the **Holy Sepulchre Chapel** in the north transept. The **tomb of King William Rufus** who died in 1100 is at the crossing; it is said that the original **tower** collapsed as a divine punishment for the burial of such an unholy man beneath it, and had to be replaced by a lower, stronger one. In the chancel, the **choir stalls** have fantastically carved misericords. There is a Tudor **ceiling** in the choir; the **stone reredos** is early sixteenth century. The thirteenth century saw the building of the **retro-choir,** in the Early English style, and the **Lady Chapel,** which has Tudor woodwork and wall paintings. From the south transept you can reach the twelfth-century **library,** with the richly illustrated **'Winchester Bible'** from the same period. Outside the cathedral, against the north wall, lines of bricks mark the site of the two **Saxon Minsters** that stood on the site.

St Cross Hospital

By walking for about a mile (2 km) south across the meadows, or driving down St Cross Street and turning down a drive next to the Bell Inn, you reach the oldest charitable institution in England. The St Cross Hospital was founded in 1136 by Bishop Henry de Blois, who built the magnificent Norman Transitional church and endowed almshouses for 13

St Swithin (d. 862)

It is said that Swithin (or Swithun), Saxon bishop of Winchester, was such a humble man that he left strict instructions that his grave was to be a plain one in the open air, where the rain of heaven could fall upon it. The Normans decided to build him a more elaborate shrine inside their new cathedral, and when his remains were 'translated' into their new resting place in a gorgeous ceremony on 15 July 1093, the humble saint was so angry that he caused it to rain for 40 days without stopping. Nowadays, the folklore says, if it rains on 15 July you can expect it to rain for 40 days afterwards.

William of Wykeham (1324–1404)

The bishop who modified the cathedral nave, and gave it its graceful Perpendicular lines, also built Winchester College, which stands on the other side of College Street from Cathedral Close. He established it in 1382 for the education of poor scholars, making it the oldest public school in England. Nowadays, by a quirk of English idiom, 'public schools' in England are in fact private, and charge fees. Former students of Winchester College are still referred to as Wykehamists, and the good bishop also founded New College in Oxford in 1379, which still reserves places for Wykehamists who pass the entrance examination.

Lancelot Andrewes (1555–1626)

A fellow of Pembroke Hall, Cambridge, Lancelot Andrewes went on to be Vicar of St Giles, Cripplegate, in London, and Prebendary of St Paul's Cathedral. Here his preaching attracted attention: Queen Elizabeth I offered him two bishoprics, which he declined, and he was made Dean of Westminster. Under James I he became successively Bishop of Chichester, Ely and Winchester. He was responsible for translating the Books of Moses and the Historical Books of the Old Testament in the Authorized or King James Version of the Bible. His was a classic Anglicanism which, reacting against the Puritanism of his youth, he decided should be reasonable, learned and catholic. Andrewes's *Preces Privatae* was compiled for his own use, and contains lists of people to pray for, with Greek and Latin quotations from the Bible; the original manuscript is 'slubbered all over with his pious hands and watered with his penitential tears'.

poor men, who wear black gowns. They were added to in 1445 by Cardinal Beaufort, who provided for another eight elderly men who wear mulberry-coloured gowns. The Brethren's Hall and the row of two-storey cottages for the residents date from the fifteenth century. *The Warden* by Anthony Trollope (1815–82), the first of the series of novels in which he portrays the loves and rivalries in the fictional cathedral city of Barchester, and enters, as no other novelist has, into the human passions of the Christian clergy, was based on a scandal at St Cross Hospital.

Opening Times and Service Times

Winchester Cathedral Monday to Saturday 08.30–18.00; Sunday 08.30–17.30. Services Sunday 08.00, 10.00, 11.15, 15.30; Monday to Saturday 07.30, 08.00, 17.30; Thursday 12.30. Tel. 01962 857200. http://www.winchester-cathedral.org.uk

St Cross Hospital April to October Monday to Saturday 09.30–17.00; November to March 10.30–15.30. Services Sunday 08.00, 10.30 (1, 2, 5), 11.15 (3, 4), 17.30; Monday to Saturday 10.00, 17.30. Tel. 01962 851375, Fax. 878221. http://www.stcrosshospital.co.uk

SALISBURY (Wiltshire)

An iron-age hill fort was built 2 miles (4 km) north of the present city of Salisbury, and altered by the Romans and Saxons. Now we call it **Old Sarum**. When the Normans took it over they built a fortress and moved the Bishopric of Sherborne here in 1075. They built two cathedrals: the first was built in 1078 but destroyed by lightning in 1099; the next building on the site lasted until the thirteenth century. By then, there was no longer any need for a hilltop fortress and the water supply was inadequate for the population, so they moved down to the river, taking many of the stones from the old cathedral with them to build a new one. Now only the ruins of the castle, inside the earthworks, and the plan of the cathedral beside them, can be seen beside the A345.

Salisbury Cathedral

Salisbury Cathedral points its slender spire towards heaven, seen in the view across flat, riverside fields immortalized in the paintings of John Constable. It has the tallest spire in England, at 123 metres (404 feet) high. It is the only ancient English cathedral to be built in a single style at one time. The **nave**, with an amazing sense

St Osmund (d. 1099)

Osmund came over as William the Conqueror's chaplain, and possibly his nephew. Unlike many Normans he sought friendship with the Saxons, and honoured the Saxon saints. He was made Chancellor of England from 1072 until he became Bishop of Salisbury in 1078. He completed and consecrated the cathedral at Old Sarum, arranging that it should be served by a group of clergy who were not monks; they were called secular canons and were formed into a cathedral chapter. This Norman pattern was then adopted by many other English cathedrals. He reorganized the worship of the cathedral, which became known as the Sarum Rite, and came into use in many parts of England. Osmund was made a saint in 1457; his remains were taken from Old Sarum and placed in the new Salisbury Cathedral.

Richard Poore (d. 1237)

Richard Poore was the illegitimate son of a civil servant. His brother Herbert was Bishop of Old Sarum and appointed him Dean. He succeeded his brother as bishop in 1215, and supervised the move from Old Sarum and the building of the new cathedral. He rose to be Bishop of Durham and Chancellor of England.

of space, height and light, represents the purest form of Early English Gothic, distinguished by pointed arches, lancet windows, and slender pillars of Purbeck marble, polished grey-black to contrast with the local silvery-grey limestone. Most of the building was done in the period from 1220 to 1265, but the **tower** was heightened and the **spire** built – in perfect harmony with the earlier style – a century later between 1334 and 1380. However the **piers at the crossing** have buckled slightly under the extra weight, and have been reinforced by internal and external buttresses and extra arches; at the eastern transepts there is an ingenious fifteenth-century arrangement of double arches in a scissors shape. The cathedral is still under constant study and repair. The oldest working **clock** in England, dating from about 1386, stands in the north aisle. The furnishings of the **St Laurence Chapel** are made from material used at the 1953 coronation of Queen Elizabeth II. The **Trinity Chapel** is dedicated to

Prisoners of Conscience around the world, with a blue window made in 1980 by Gabriel Loire, an artist-craftsman from Chartres. It is possible to take a fascinating tour of the **upper levels and roof** of the cathedral. In the **cloisters** is an octagonal **Chapter House**, with a frieze of scenes from the Old Testament on its walls, and the best of four surviving copies of **Magna Carta** from 1215, the foundation document of civil liberty. The spacious, grassy **close** surrounds the Cathedral.

Opening Times
Old Sarum (English Heritage) daily April to June, September 10.00–18.00; July to August 10.00–19.00; October 10.00–17.00; November to March 10.00–16.00. Tel. 01722 335398
Salisbury Cathedral daily September to May 07.15–18.15; June to August Monday to Saturday 07.15–20.15; Sunday 07.15–18.15. **Chapter House** November to February Monday to Saturday 10.00–17.15, Sunday 12.00–17.15; September to October, March to May Monday to Saturday 09.30–17.30, Sunday 12.00–17.30; June to August Monday to Saturday 09.30–19.45, Sunday 12.00–19.45. Tel. 01722 555100. Email visitors@salcath. co.uk; http://www. salisburycathedral.org.uk

BEMERTON (Wiltshire)

Follow the A36 from Salisbury towards Warminster, and just before the town boundary, after crossing a railway bridge, turn left into Church Lane, signposted 'Lower Bemerton'. Here on your left is **St Andrew's, Bemerton,** a small fourteenth-century church where the poet George Herbert was the parson.

Service Times
Bemerton St Andrew's Sunday 08.00; sometimes 18.30. Tel. 01722 333750. Limited parking on Lower Road, entered between the church and the Old Rectory

GUILDFORD (Surrey)

Southwest of London on the A3 is Guildford, the county town of Surrey. The **cathedral** is a modern one, consecrated in 1961; follow the signs past the railway station.

Opening Times and Service Times
Guildford Cathedral daily 08.30–17.30. Services Sunday 08.00, 09.45, 11.30, 18.30; Monday to Friday 08.40, 09.00, 17.30; Saturday 08.40, 09.00, 16.00. Tel. 01483 565287. http://www.guildford-cathedral.org

George Herbert (1593–1633)

George was made a fellow of Trinity College, Cambridge, on account of his classical learning and his musical ability; he played the lute and viol and sang. He was appointed Public Orator of the University, and seemed destined to shine as a courtier. The influence of his friend Nicholas Ferrar (see p. 190), however, turned his interest to religion, and in 1630 he was ordained a priest in the Church of England. William Laud persuaded him to become rector of the country parish of Fugglestone with Bemerton, near Salisbury, where he stayed for the rest of his life. In *The Country Parson* he gives simple and sage advice for the pastoral ministry. His poetry was written to be read at small gatherings of friends; on his deathbed he sent the collection known as *The Temple* to Nicholas Ferrar, leaving him to decide whether to burn or publish it. Yet many regard it as the greatest religious poetry in English: his deep faith was expressed in simple language. 'The God of love my shepherd is', 'Teach me, my God and king' and 'Let all the world in every corner sing' are hymns that speak directly to the heart of the worshipper.

Love bade me welcome: yet my soul drew back
Guilty of dust and sin.
But quick-eyed Love, observing me grow slack
From my first entrance in,
Drew nearer to me, sweetly questioning,
If I lacked any thing.
A guest, I answered, worthy to be here:
Love said, You shall be he.
I the unkind, ungrateful? Ah my dear,
I cannot look on thee.
Love took my hand, and smiling did reply,
Who made the eyes but I?
Truth Lord, but I have marred them: let my shame
Go where it doth deserve.
And know you not, says Love, who bore the blame?
My dear, then I will serve.
You must sit down, says Love, and taste my meat:
So I did sit and eat.

CHAWTON
(Hampshire)

Follow the sign at the roundabout where the A31 and A32 meet to the village of **Chawton**, where you can visit the house where the novelist Jane Austen lived.

Opening Times
Jane Austen house daily March to November; December to February Saturday to Sunday 11.00–16.30. Tel. 01420 83262. http://www.janeaustenmuseum.org.uk

WELLOW
(Hampshire)

From the A27 west of Romsey, follow the signs to 'The Wellows' or 'East Wellow', then to 'St Margaret's Church', to find **Wellow Church**, dating from 1215, with a wooden belfry. Here Florence Nightingale, the pioneer of modern nursing, is buried beneath a simple pillar, inscribed only with 'F.N.' and the dates of her birth and death, opposite the south door.

Service Times
Wellow Church Sunday 08.30 (1, 3, 5), 09.30 (all). Tel. 01794 323562

THE ISLE OF WIGHT

The Isle of Wight is roughly diamond shaped, and only 23 miles (36 km) wide. About a mile (2 km) southeast of East Cowes Queen Victoria established her home at **Osborne House**, built between 1845 and 1851 to designs by Prince Albert and Thomas Cubitt. When

---

Jane Austen (1775–1817)

Fifth of seven children of a Hampshire clergyman, Jane Austen published four of her six great novels anonymously, and the other two were not published until after she had died. She wrote almost in secret, hiding the paper under a folder if she heard the door creak as somebody entered the room. Yet her wit and amused tolerance of human behaviour made her a unique observer of the society of her time, and one of the world's greatest novelists. Her Christian faith is not so well known; she wrote: 'Incline us, O God, to think humbly of ourselves, to be saved only in the examination of our own conduct, to consider our fellow-creatures with kindness, and to judge of all they say and do with the charity which we would desire from them ourselves; through Jesus Christ our Lord. Amen.' Faith, for her, required both sense and sensibility: and neither cold reason nor hot emotion was allowed to override the other.

Florence Nightingale (1820–1910)

Florence was born to a well-to-do family and educated by her father. In 1837 she heard the voice of God calling her to a mission, but no hospital would give her nursing training. By studying Parliamentary reports she became an expert on public health and hospitals. Eventually a German Deaconess community trained her as a nurse. When the Crimean War broke out the Secretary of State for War put her in charge of the military hospital at Scutari in Turkey. She found the conditions appalling, and some of the nurses had to be sent home. By walking the wards alone at night she came to know most of the soldiers personally, winning her the affectionate nickname of 'The Lady with the Lamp'. She persuaded Queen Victoria to set up a Royal Commission on the health of the army, and used the money the public subscribed to establish at St Thomas's Hospital in London the world's first School of Nursing. She tried to reproduce the care for the sick shown by the nuns of the Middle Ages, which is why she used the titles of Sister and Matron. She created for nursing, for the first time, the status of a respected profession. When she was dying she refused the offer of a State funeral in Westminster Abbey and chose instead to be buried in the tiny village where her family had a country home.

the Prince Consort died, the inconsolable Queen spent most of her time at Osborne and died there in 1901. It has been kept almost exactly as it was in Albert's time.

One mile (2 km) to the south near the village of Whippingham, on a site which goes back to Norman and possibly to Saxon times, is the **Royal Church of St Mildred**, also designed by Prince Alfred, in the Gothic-Revival style; here the Battenbergs (who later changed their name to Mountbatten) have a family chapel.

Just off the A3054 between Fishbourne and Ryde, near the site of an abbey which was built in 1132, is **Quarr Abbey**. It is an impressive modern-Gothic church constructed between 1911 and 1912 in brick, by French Benedictine monks from Solesmes, famous for singing plainsong.

On the B3322 from Freshwater to the rocks called The Needles, you first

---

Alfred, Lord Tennyson (1809–92)

Alfred was the fourth son of a Lincolnshire rector; his first book of poetry was published when he was 21. Three years later he published early versions of *The Lotus Eaters* and *The Lady of Shallott*; he improved and republished them nine years later still. His college friend Arthur Hallam died young at this time and Tennyson began writing the elegies that he would later collect as *In Memoriam*; this explores optimistically the religious dilemma of the Victorians, confident in their civilization but uncertain because of the challenges that science was making to their faith. It was published in 1850, the year he married, was made Poet Laureate and moved to the Isle of Wight. He later wrote verse novels and drama, but it was the Arthurian *Idylls of the King* that made him a hero to all, especially to Queen Victoria. His last poem was an expression of confidence in the face of death: 'Crossing the Bar'.

---

pass the Farringford Hotel, formerly Farringford House, the home of the poet Tennyson. Then at the High Down Inn you turn up a narrow road from which you can walk to the Tennyson Memorial Cross on **Tennyson Down**. The poet found his inspiration walking up here; he said the fresh air was worth sixpence a pint!

Ferries

Wightlink Ferries PO Box 59, Portsmouth PO1 2XB. Tel. 08705 827744: Portsmouth to Ryde (catamaran, for foot passengers only); Portsmouth to Fishbourne car ferries; Lymington to Yarmouth car ferries. http://www.wightlink.co.uk
Hovertravel Quay Road, Ryde, Isle of Wight PO33 2HB. Tel. 023 9281 1000 or 01983 811000: Southsea to Ryde (hovercraft for foot passengers only).

http://www.hovertravel.co.uk
Red Funnel 12 Bugle Street, Southampton, SO14 2JY. Tel. 0870 444 8889: Southampton to East Cowes car ferries; Southampton to West Cowes (for foot passengers only). http://www.redfunnel.co.uk

Opening Times and Service Times
Osborne House and Gardens daily April to October 10.00–18.00; house closes at 17.00; last admission 16.00. For winter times Tel. 01983 200022, Fax. 281380
Quarr Abbey daily dawn–20.45; **shop** Monday to Saturday 10.00–12.45, 14.30–16.30; **tea room** Tuesday to Saturday 10.30–16.30. Services Sunday 10.00, 17.00, 20.30; Monday to Saturday 09.00, 17.00, 20.30. Tel. 01983 882420
St Mildred's, Whippingham: April, October daily 10.00–16.00;

May to September Monday to Friday 10.00–17.00. Services Sunday 11.15. Tel. 01983 884438

MALMESBURY
(Wiltshire)

Malmesbury Abbey (MARMS-bree), on the A429 in the extreme north of Wiltshire, is a fascinating collection of Norman fragments and flying buttresses, but also a living parish church. It was founded by St Anselm in 676, and King Athelstan was buried here in 941, but the earlier buildings were destroyed by fire in 1050. The present buildings were begun in the twelfth century, and by the fourteenth century were 98 metres (320 feet) long. Then in 1500 the tower and spire at the central crossing fell in a fierce storm, destroying the east end and transepts; in 1660 the west tower also collapsed, bringing with it the three westernmost bays of the nave. Six bays remain, and form the parish church. The south porch is a triumph of Norman architecture, with rare and beautiful carved figures of Christ and the apostles. On the south side of the nave is the watching loft, where those who could not attend the services could see over the chancel screen and watch them from there. There is a medieval stone screen at the end of the south aisle, forming the entrance to the chapel of St Aldhelm. A window commemorates Elmer the Flying Monk, whose attempt at flight from the top of the tower in 1010 took him for 230 metres (250 yards) through the air; he was convinced that he only crashed then because he had forgotten to provide himself with a tail.

Opening Times and Service Times
Malmesbury Abbey daily 10.00–17.00. Services Sunday 08.00, 10.30, 18.00. Tel. 01666 826666

St Aldhelm (639–709)

Educated at first at Malmesbury, which was under Irish Celtic influence, Aldhelm went on to study at Canterbury where he came into contact with continental European movements. He read Latin and Greek, and studied arithmetic and astronomy. When he was appointed Abbot of Malmesbury he busied himself building churches and founding monasteries, writing to other scholars, and writing poetry in Latin and Old English. He was made Bishop of Wessex and moved to Sherborne in 705, but returned to Malmesbury to be buried.

BRADFORD-ON-AVON; EDINGTON (Wiltshire)

On the A363 southeast of Bath is the delightful town of Bradford, on either bank of the River Avon. The river is spanned by an ancient nine-arched bridge which has an old prison cell in the centre of it, converted from a chapel. On Church Street stands one of the very few Saxon churches in the country to survive unaltered: the tiny **St Laurence Church**. It is a tall building, plain inside but decorated around the outside with blind arcading. Some say it dates from around 700 and was founded by St Aldhelm, though others say it was built beside St Aldhelm's church early in the eleventh century for the nuns of Shaftesbury, possibly to house the relics of King Edward the Martyr. It was wrecked by Viking invaders, used successively as a school, dwelling house and charnel house, but restored in 1856, when the dramatic carvings of angels were discovered over the chancel arch.

East of Westbury on the B3098 is the village of Edington. **Edington Priory** was built between 1351 and 1361, in the Transitional style between Decorated and Perpendicular, by William Edington (a local resident who went on to become Bishop of Winchester) for some Augustinian Canons who were known here as Bonhommes. In 1450 during 'Jack Cade's Rebellion' the Bishop of Salisbury was taken from the church by the mob and hanged on Edington Hill. The 1930s' reredos includes a figure of the poet George Herbert, who was married in this church in 1629. The tomb of Lady Anne Beauchamp shows her on a higher level than, and of equal height to, her less aristocratic husband; she had it carved when he died in 1630 and then worshipped within view of her own image when she survived him for 40 years. On the other side of the chancel is a delicate memorial carved by the great nineteenth-century sculptor Francis Chantry. There is an annual festival of church music, from which services are regularly broadcast on BBC Radio 3.

Opening Times and Service Times

St Laurence's, Bradford-on-Avon daily 10.00–19.00 (16.00 winter). Tel. 01225 865797

Edington Priory Temporarily closed on weekdays; keyholder Tel. 01380 830010 or 930374. Services Sunday 11.00, 18.30; Wednesday 09.30. **Festival of Music and Liturgy** for details Tel. 01380 830512

SHAFTESBURY
(Dorset)

Shaftesbury, on the A30 west of Salisbury, stands on top of a hill with fine views. Gold Hill is a much photographed steep and cobbled street with the old abbey wall along one side. Shaftesbury was once known as Shaston, which is also the name given to it in Thomas Hardy's Wessex novels. **Shaftesbury Abbey** was founded in 888 by King Alfred the Great for his daughter. The body of King Edward the Martyr (see p. 63) was brought here in 978, and pilgrims visiting his shrine and hoping that he would pray to God for them brought lavish gifts. It became the wealthiest convent in England, and in the sixteenth century there was a saying that if the Abbess of Shaston married the Abbot of Glaston – meaning Glastonbury – they would have more land than the King of England. Now only the ground plan of the original abbey, just off the main street, is visible, laid out as a garden with an award-winning museum. What were almost certainly the bones of King Edward were found here in 1931, and are now in the church of a Russian Orthodox group near Woking.

Opening Times
Shaftesbury Abbey daily April to October 10.00–17.00. Tel. 01747 852910. Email user@shaftesburyabbey.fsnet.co.uk

SHERBORNE
(Dorset)

Situated where the A352 meets the A30, the town of Sherborne, once the capital of the Kingdom of Wessex, is famous for its public school, its abbey and the two castles. The **Abbey** was founded in 705. St Aldhelm came here when he was made Bishop of Wessex in that year. King Alfred's two brothers, Ethelred and Ethelbert, are both buried in the northeast chapel of the Abbey. It was the Cathedral of the Diocese of Wessex until the see was moved to Old Sarum in 1075. Following a dispute between the Abbot and the town, the Abbey was burnt down in 1437. Most of what we see today is from the fifteenth-century rebuilding, when the townspeople were forced to pay for the costliest materials and workmanship, so it is counted one of the best examples of Perpendicular architecture in Britain, especially because of its delicate fan-vaulting. The misericords are particularly amusing. There is a famous peal of bells, with a tenor bell, 'Great Tom', presented to the Abbey by Cardinal Wolsey. Thomas Wyatt, the Elizabethan poet, is also buried in the northeast chapel.

To the southwest of the Abbey, across the Abbey Close, is the **Almshouse of St John the Baptist and St John the Evangelist**, founded in 1223, housed in buildings virtually unaltered since they were put up in 1437–45, apart from additions in 1864. The chapel contains fifteenth-century windows and a fifteenth-century triptych.

Sherborne School is housed in former monastic buildings to the north of the Abbey.

Opening Times and Service Times

Sherborne Abbey daily 08.30–18.00 (16.00 winter). Services Sunday 08.00, 09.30, 18.30 (or 17.00 winter); Monday to Friday 08.30 (except Wednesday), 17.30; Monday 09.00; Tuesday 12.00; Wednesday 10.30; Thursday 12.00; Friday to Saturday 09.00. Tel. 01935 812452. Email abbey@sherborne.netkonect.co.uk; http://www.sherborne-abbey.fsnet.co.uk
Almshouses of Saints John Tuesday, Thursday, Friday, Saturday 14.00–16.00 (summer). Service Friday 12.00

CHRISTCHURCH (Dorset)

On the A35 lies the town of Christchurch. **Christchurch Priory** is 95 metres (311 feet) long from end to end and is larger than some cathedrals. It was built on the site of a Saxon minster from 650, mostly in the Norman and, later, Perpendicular styles. While it was being built, a mysterious carpenter was seen working on the site who never collected his pay. One morning a beam, which had been too short the night before, was found miraculously raised and fitted in position. The workmen decided that it must have been the Carpenter of Nazareth, and the Priory was called Christchurch from then on. The north porch, with its fan-vaulting, is the largest in the country, and the view from the top of the high tower (34 metres; 112 feet) is magnificent.

Opening Times and Service Times

Christchurch Priory Monday to Saturday 09.30–17.00; Sunday 14.15–17.30. Services Sunday 08.00, 09.45, 11.15, 18.30; Monday to Friday 07.30, 08.00, 17.30; Thursday 11.00; Saturday 08.30, 09.00, 17.30. Tel. 01202 485804. http://www.christchurchpriory.org

BOURNEMOUTH (Dorset)

Further west on the A35, the large seaside resort of Bournemouth has two fine nineteenth-century churches: **St Stephen's Church**, St Stephen's Way, the work of J.L. Pearson; and **St Peter's Church**, in St Peter's Road, designed by the architect

G.E. Street. In the churchyard of St Peter's are buried Mary Shelley, the author of *Frankenstein*; her parents, both political writers; and the heart of her husband, the poet Percy Bysshe Shelley.

Opening Times and Service Times
St Peter's and St Stephen's
Monday to Friday 08.00–15.30; Saturday 09.00–15.30; Sunday 08.00–1530. Services St Peter's Sunday 08.00, 10.00, 16.00; Monday, Thursday 12.15. Services St Stephen's Sunday 08.00, 10.45; Tuesday 08.00; Wednesday, Saturday 10.00; Friday 07.45. Tel. 01202 554058 or 554355. Email admin@stp-office.fsnet.co.uk

WIMBORNE
(Dorset)

On the B3082 northwest of Bournemouth is Wimborne Minster. The twin-towered **Minster Church of St Cuthberga** dominates the town. Cuthberga died in 725; she was the widow of King Aldfrid of Northumbria; when she became a nun she founded the community at Wimborne. The Norman church was built on the site of her monastery, but later features have been added. On the west tower, which is in the Perpendicular style, a mechanical figure dressed as a grenadier of Napoleonic times strikes the quarter-hours on a bell. There used to be a spire, but it fell down in 1600, while people were worshipping in the church; the fact that nobody was injured is called 'the Wimborne miracle'. A fourteenth-century 'orrery clock', inside the west tower, marks the hours with an image of the sun, and the days of the month with the figure of the moon. The precious old books of the **Chained Library** are fixed to the shelves above the choir vestry, to prevent anyone taking them away – it dates from 1686.

Opening Times and Service Times
Wimborne Minster daily 09.30–17.30. Services Sunday 08.00, 09.45, 11.15 or 11.30, 18.30; Monday to Friday 17.30; Tuesday 08.00; Thursday 09.30; Saturday 09.15. **Chained Library** Monday to Friday 10.00–12.00, 14.00–16.00. Tel. 01202 884753, Fax. 842942. http://www.wimborneminster.org.uk

WAREHAM
(Dorset)

The streets of Wareham, which is off the A351 west of Bournemouth, are laid out on a grid pattern indicating the Saxon origin of the town, but the earth ramparts around it, known as The Walls, may be of even earlier origin. **St Martin's Church**, at the north end of the town on The Walls, has Saxon origins. There is a thirteenth-century wall painting in the sanctuary of St Martin, showing Martin in the days when he was a soldier before he became Bishop of Tours, dividing his cloak with a beggar who had none; later in a dream Martin was told that the beggar had been Jesus Christ in disguise. There is also a memorial to a very different hero: T.E. Lawrence, or Lawrence of Arabia. At the bottom end of the town by the river, **Lady St Mary's Church** is on the site of a wooden Saxon chapel where King Edward the Martyr was first buried, before his remains were removed to Shaftesbury.

Opening Times and Service Times

St Martin's Easter to October Monday to Saturday 10.00–16.00, Sunday 14.00–16.00. Keyholder 35 North Street. Services Sunday 11.15 (4); Wednesday 11.00 **Lady St Mary's** Services Sunday 08.00, 09.45, 11.30, 18.00; Wednesday 07.45, 19.00; Friday 07.45. Tel. 01202 552684

CORFE CASTLE
(Dorset)

Continuing south down the A351 we reach the peninsula known as the Isle of Purbeck, where the 'Purbeck Marble' was quarried to provide the dark columns which are such a feature of Early English

architecture. King Edward the Martyr was murdered in 978 near the village of Corfe Castle, though the castle was not built in stone until Norman times. The romantic ruins of the ancient stronghold rise up on a mound above the village. During the Civil War it was the home of Sir John Bankes, Attorney General to King Charles I, and was defended by Lady Bankes in her husband's absence against a siege by Cromwell's soldiers in 1643 and again for six weeks in 1645–6. Eventually one of her own men, Lt Col. Pitman, decided to let the enemy enter to save loss of life, and the Roundheads blew up the castle; but Lady Bankes was allowed to escape unharmed.

Opening Times

Corfe Castle (National Trust) daily March, October 10.00–17.00; April to September 10.00–18.00; November to February 10.00–16.00. Tel. and Fax. 01929 481294. Email corfecastle@ntrust.org.uk

BERE REGIS; MILTON ABBAS
(Dorset)

Bere Regis is situated on the A35 from Bournemouth, 11 miles (18 km) east of Dorchester. The interior of the roof of the Perpendicular-style **Church of St John the Baptist** is richly and imaginatively ornamented

King Edward the Martyr (c. 963–78)

Edward's father, King Edgar, who reigned from 959 to
975, was a strong supporter of the Christian monasteries,
but a faction grew up among his subjects who opposed the
amount of power which was being put in the hands of the
monks. When Edgar died in 975, an attempt was made to
claim the throne for his younger son Ethelred, but Edgar
was quickly elected King of England, although he was only
about 12 years old. It is doubtful whether he took sides on
the issue of the monasteries, but in 978 at Corfe Castle he
was murdered, at the age of 15 or 16. Ethelred became
King in his place, although it is not certain that he had
anything to do with the murder; he was an ineffective king
and was named Ethelred the Unready. Edward was
mourned as a Christian martyr, and was made a saint in
1001. His remains, which were said to produce miracles,
were transferred to Shaftesbury and venerated there until
the Reformation.

and coloured, with figures of
the 12 apostles, each more
than one metre (3 feet) long,
on the projecting beams.
There are twelfth-century
carved figures on the pillars
writhing in the agony of
toothache and a sore throat.
The monument to the
Turberville family inspired
Thomas Hardy's *Tess of the
d'Urbervilles*.

Milton Abbey has the most
charming situation, beside a
stately home built in the
eighteenth century, in
grounds laid out by
Capability Brown. When
Lord Milton, the Earl of
Dorchester, built the house,
he moved the village that had
stood there to another valley
a mile away. Back in 934
King Athelstan had camped

there, and received a vision
promising victory in a
forthcoming battle with the
Danes. When he won and
became King of Wessex, he
built a chapel in
thanksgiving, where the
present twelfth-century St
Catherine's Chapel now
stands on the hillside. A
Benedictine abbey was built
in the valley below, but it
was burnt down in 1309.
Rebuilding started at once,
but was stopped at the time
of the Black Death, and by
the time of the Dissolution
only the chancel and
transepts had been
completed. However, they
are enormous, with
impressive windows – now
filled with Pugin glass – and
coloured fan-vaulting. The
fifteenth-century reredos

would also have been coloured, but only the bottom tier retains traces of pigment. A rare fifteenth-century wooden hanging tabernacle, for holding the consecrated bread, has now been fixed to the wall. James Wyatt created a Lady Chapel in the south aisle; above the altar is a plaque to John Tregonwell giving thanks that he survived a fall from the abbey roof after his pantaloons filled with air forming a primitive parachute. Gilbert Scott restored the church in 1865 for Baron Hambro, whose tomb he designed. From the A354 follow signs to Milton Abbas, then to Milton Abbey, and park in the schoolyard.

Opening Times and Service Times

St John the Baptist, Bere Regis Services Sunday 08.00 (2, 4), 09.15 (1, 3, 5), 11.00 (2, 4), 18.00 (all); Monday, Wednesday 09.00. Tel. 01929 471262
Milton Abbey daily 10.00–17.30. Services Sunday in school terms 10.30. **House** Easter week and school summer holidays daily, 10.00–18.00. Tel. 01258 880489, Fax. 880310

DORCHESTER (Dorset)

Dorchester, the county town of Dorset – not to be confused with Dorchester-on-Thames in Oxfordshire – was first built by the Romans in about 70 AD on the London to Exeter road; it features as Casterbridge in the novels of Thomas Hardy (1840–1928). In High West Street stands **St Peter's Church**, rebuilt in 1420. When it was restored in 1856–7, Thomas Hardy, who was at that time a pupil of the architect, drew a careful plan of the church, a copy of which hangs in the South Chapel. There is an octagonal seventeenth-century pulpit. Outside is a statue of the Dorset dialect poet William Barnes (1801–86), who was churchwarden at St Peter's before his ordination.

Service Times
St Peter's Sunday 09.00, 10.30, 18.30; Monday to Friday 16.45; Thursday 10.00. Tel. 01305 268439

WHITCHURCH CANONICORUM (Dorset)

There is a thirteenth-century shrine in the north transept of **Whitchurch Canonicorum**, typical of the period, with a stone casket to hold the sacred relics, and three large openings below it for diseased limbs, or clothing belonging to the sick, to be inserted and experience the healing power of the saint. Apart from the shrine of Edward the Confessor in Westminster Abbey, this is the only one in

England that still contains the saint's bones. When the stone casket cracked in 1900, a lead casket was found inside, with the bones of a small woman aged about 40, and a Latin inscription stating that they were the remains of St Wite. Nobody knows for certain who she was, but it is believed she was probably a Saxon hermit who was killed by marauding Danes. Founded by King Alfred, and rebuilt during the eleventh to fifteenth centuries, the church of Wite, as its name suggests, belonged to the Canons of Salisbury, and was a popular place of pilgrimage both before and after the Reformation. It lies north of the A35 and northwest of Bridport.

Opening Times and Service Times

Whitchurch Canonicorum daily dawn–17.00. Services Sunday 08.00 (1, 3, 5), 10.45 (2), 11.00 (3, 4). Tel. 01297 489223

The West Country

With its rich brown soil and rocky coastline, the West country contains many ancient shrines of long-ago saints, tucked into narrow valleys and folds of the hills.

EXETER
(Devon)

Captured by the Romans, Exeter was re-founded by King Alfred the Great. By late Saxon times it had grown into one of the largest towns in England, so the seat of the Bishop, whose Diocese included Devon and Cornwall, was moved here from Crediton by Bishop Leofric in 1050. The two **Norman towers** on the transepts of **St Peter's Cathedral** are all that remain from that period, but between the arrival of Bishop Bromescombe in 1258 and the death of Bishop Grandisson in 1369 a major reconstruction was carried out, first seen in the elaborate carvings of the **west front**. It has three tiers of carved figures of angels, bishops and kings. The fourteenth-century **vaulted roof** of the nave, in the English Decorated style, with an uninterrupted vista of linking ribs like an avenue of palm trees, and gilded and coloured bosses where they meet, stretches for 91 metres (300 feet) and is the longest Gothic ceiling in the world.

One of the ceiling bosses shows the murder of St Thomas à Becket. The arches are supported by carved **corbels**, which are in turn each supported by pillars with clusters of 16 columns. The pulpit is a memorial to John Coleridge Pattison, a missionary to the Pacific islands who was martyred there in 1871. On the north side of the nave is a carved **minstrels' gallery**, with 14 stone angels playing on different medieval musical instruments; there is space behind them for the choir to sing at Christmas, their voices floating down as if from the mouths of the angels. The **choir** boasts an 18-metre high **bishop's throne** (60 feet), carved in oak in 1313–16, and **choir stalls** containing, under the seats, what may be the oldest complete set of **misericords** in the country. They have wooden carvings of fantastic variety from 1260 to 1280, including an elephant obviously carved by someone who had never seen one. The canopies over the choir stalls were designed by Sir Gilbert Scott in 1870–77. Above the

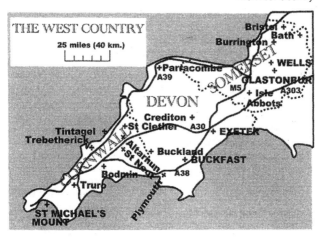

high altar there is much original stained glass in the late fourteenth-century **east window**. The Lady Chapel at the east end of the building, beyond the **ambulatory**, and the **Chapter House**, approached from the south transept, survive from the thirteenth century. In the north transept is a fifteenth-century **clock** showing the earth in the centre and the sun and moon revolving around it.

Opening Times and Service Times
St Peter's Cathedral daily 07.30–18.30 (17.00 Saturday). Services Sunday 08.00, 09.45, 11.15, 15.00, 18.30; Monday to Saturday 07.30, 07.45, 18.30 (except Saturday 15.00); Wednesday 13.15. Tel. 01392 255573 or 214219, Fax. 498769. Email admin@exeter-cathedral.org.uk;

http://www.exeter-cathedral.org.uk

BUCKFAST ABBEY (Devon)

Southwest of Exeter on the A38, above the town of Buckfastleigh and on the edge of wild and beautiful Dartmoor, stands **Buckfast Abbey**, home to a community of Roman Catholic monks. On the site of an abbey founded by the Danish King Canute in the eleventh century, it is a modern reproduction of the twelfth-century Cistercian Abbey, which was razed to the ground in 1535. The present-day Abbey was built by just six exiled French Benedictine monks over the course of 31 years and consecrated in 1932. There is an exhibition giving the history of the Abbey. The

67

entire east wall of the Blessed Sacrament Chapel is formed by a most moving modern stained-glass window of Christ with his arms open in welcome. Buckfast is a popular destination for a day-out for families and parish groups, with time to join in a period of prayer, admire the abbey church, and buy some of the wine that the monks make. There is a **Methodist Chapel** in the grounds of the Abbey.

Opening Times and Service Times

Buckfast Abbey daily May to October 09.00–17.30; November to April 10.00–16.00. Mass Sunday 09.00, 10.30; Monday to Saturday 08.00, 12.05. Monastic services Monday to Saturday 05.45, 06.45, 08.00, 13.00, 18.30 (Saturday 18.15), 21.00; Sunday 06.45, 07.45, 10.30, 13.00, 18.30, 21.00. Tel. 01364 642519
Buckfast Methodist Chapel Services Sunday 08.00, 10.00, 18.30

ST MICHAEL'S MOUNT (Cornwall)

On a coastal road off the A394 is the village of **Marazion**, its winding streets filled with tropical palm trees. A causeway leads to the romantic 91-metre-high (300 feet) island-fortress abbey of **St Michael's Mount**. In 495 Cornish fishermen reported seeing the Archangel Michael standing on the granite rock, and it became a popular place of pilgrimage. A Celtic monastery stood there from the eighth to the eleventh centuries. In about 1150, King Edward the Confessor built a Benedictine monastery, and handed it over to the Abbot of Mont-St-Michel, off the Normandy coast in France, on which it had been modelled. The library is the oldest part of the castle; the monks' refectory is now called the Chevy Chase room; and the Priory church, still used for services, is fourteenth century, later restored, with fifteenth-century windows. After the Dissolution of the Monasteries and the Civil War it was bought by Colonel John St Aubyn, who turned it into a private residence where the St Aubyn family still reside. In climbing the Pilgrims' Steps, and in the chapel, there remains a sense of holiness not completely overshadowed by its later use.

Opening Times and Service Times

St Michael's Mount (National Trust) across the causeway at low tide, or, in summer only, by boat from Marazion at high tide; April to October Monday to Friday 10.30–17.30 (16.45 last admission), and most weekends for charitable events; Sunday Interdenominational Services June to September 11.00. From November to March it is essential to telephone for information on

opening times. No dogs. Tel.
01736 710507, Fax. 711544.
Tide and ferry information Tel.
710265. Email mail@
stmichaelsmount.co.uk; http:
//www.stmichaelsmount.co.uk

GLASTONBURY
(Somerset)

For many people, and not
only Christians, Glastonbury
has a greater sense of
holiness than anywhere in
England. Glastonbury Tor
may well have been a high
place used by druids before
Christianity arrived.
Followers of New Age
religions claim to find
intersections of leylines at
Glastonbury, and meet there
frequently for their festivals.
Some Christians have
claimed that Joseph of
Arimathea came there with
the boy Jesus on one of his
trading expeditions to the
Roman lead mines in the
Mendip Hills, and returned
later to bury the Holy Grail,
the wine chalice used at the
last supper, near the Tor on
Chalice Hill, perhaps by
Chalice Well. Others say that
it was the Avalon of King
Arthur. Once it was one of
the largest monasteries in
England, of which only
romantic ruins remain. To
disentangle history from
legend is hard, and pilgrims
who are content not to
bother may simply enjoy the
atmosphere of sanctity.
Cynics, however, will point
out that many a monastery

became rich when it was
associated with a famous
saint. Whether the legends
are true or not, however, this
is a place where the sincere
prayers of many people have
been offered, and is holy on
that account.

There are traces of a Celtic
monastery, established by
Welsh or Irish monks in the
fourth or fifth century, below
the Tor. Stories were told of
both St David and St Patrick
visiting Glastonbury,
reorganizing the monastery
and being buried there, and
the bodies of St Aidan and St
Paulinus are said to have
been brought from the north
when the Danes invaded, and
reburied at Glastonbury. To
the south of the first church,
where the Lady Chapel ruins
are today, there grew up a
Christian cemetery. In the
seventh century, Somerset
was conquered by Christian
Saxons. According to the
history of Glastonbury
penned by William of
Malmesbury, the Saxon King
Ine of Wessex in 688, with
the guidance of St Aldhelm,
re-endowed the monastery
and built a new stone church,
which was situated at the
west end of where the nave
of the later Abbey church
stood. This was enlarged in
the eighth century and again
by St Dunstan in the tenth,
who introduced the concept
of the cloister here for the
first time in England. The

Saxon kings Edmund, Edgar and Edmund Ironside were buried here. A Norman church was built to the east of the Lady Chapel, to preserve the ancient cemetery there, and it had the longest nave of any known monastic church, at 177 metres (580 feet) long. In 1184 the whole Abbey and its treasures were destroyed by a fire, though the ruins were repaired and used until a new church was started, beginning from the old east end at the Lady Chapel, which now became the west end of the new church, which was completed in 1213. It became one of the richest Benedictine abbeys in the country, with a world-famous library. The monastery was dissolved in 1539, and many of the buildings in the town are built of stone stripped from the abbey, which was left in ruins.

Glastonbury lies at the intersection of the A39, from Junction 23 of the M5 to Wells, and the A361 to Shepton Mallet. **Glastonbury Tor**, 159 metres (521 feet) high, is on your right as you enter the town from the east, with the ruins of the fourteenth-century **St Michael's Tower** on the summit and a superb view. It was here that the last Abbot of Glastonbury was hanged.

Joseph of Arimathea

According to legend, Joseph of Arimathea, a rich Jew who provided for the burial of Jesus in his own tomb, was a relative of the Virgin Mary and owned a lead mine in the Mendip Hills in Britain. He brought the boy Jesus with him on one of his visits to his British property, a possibility which is referred to by William Blake (1757–1827) in his poem, usually known as 'Jerusalem', in the words, 'And did those feet in ancient time walk upon England's mountains green? And was the holy Lamb of God on England's pleasant pastures seen?' After the resurrection of Jesus, Joseph was rewarded for giving his own tomb at Golgotha by being allowed to take the wine cup or chalice which had been used at the last supper, known as the Holy Grail, and which had also been used to collect the blood from the wound in the side of Jesus at the crucifixion. He then brought it, together with the spear that pierced the side of Jesus, and buried them at Glastonbury. He planted his travelling staff, which blossomed as the Glastonbury thorn; it still blossoms, amazingly, every Christmas and again in May. He founded the Abbey and began the conversion of England to Christianity.

St Dunstan (c. 908–88)

A reforming Abbot of Glastonbury, in a time when monastic life had almost died out in England, Dunstan made it a centre of learning; he himself was a famous musician, metal worker and illuminator of manuscripts. He became minister to one king, was banished by the next, and under King Edgar was made Bishop of Worcester, then London, and subsequently Archbishop of Canterbury. King and Archbishop, together with Ethelwold, Bishop of Winchester, and Oswald, Archbishop of York, reformed both Church and State.

You can walk up the steep slopes as the medieval pilgrims did, taking the path from Wellhouse Lane which passes the **Chalice Well**, where the iron-red waters are supposed to have healing properties. The **Abbey Ruins** are entered from the High Street, and the **transept piers** and the shell of the **Lady Chapel**, with carvings of the Annunciation, the Visit of the Magi, and King Herod, are the most prominent remains. The **choir** is supposed to contain the tombs of **King Arthur and Queen Guinevere**. Two bodies, supposed to be theirs, were found in the cemetery in 1191 and re-buried here in 1278. Beyond this is the **Edgar Chapel** with the tombs of the Saxon kings. In the grounds is the fourteenth-century **Abbot's Kitchen**, still intact with four huge corner fireplaces and a central lantern in the roof. Behind the main entrance to the grounds is the **Glastonbury**

Thorn. The **Annual Pilgrimage** is on the second Saturday in July.

Opening Times
Abbey Ruins daily April to September 09.00–18.00; October 09.30–17.00; November 09.30–18.30; December to January 10.00–16.30; February 10.00–17.00; March 09.30–17.30. Tel. and Fax. 01458 832267. http://www. glastonburyabbey.com
Chalice Well daily April to October 10.00–18.00; November 09.00–17.00; December to February 12.00–15.00; March 12.00–18.00. Tel. 01458 831154, Fax. 835528. http://www.chalicewell.org.uk

WELLS (Somerset)

A few miles up the A39 northeast from Glastonbury brings you to Wells. Any town that contains a cathedral is counted as a city, and Wells is England's smallest city. The outline of a tiny Saxon church and a Norman one consecrated in 1148 can be traced in the Camery Garden reached from the cloisters. But the present **Wells Cathedral,** built mostly between about 1175 and 1508, was the first cathedral to be designed in the Early English architectural style. Its glory is the magnificent collection of over 300 thirteenth-century carved figures on the **west front,** half of them life size; originally they were coloured and gilded. The whole display is nearly 46 metres (150 feet) wide, and in the centre gable is a frieze of the 12 apostles, with *Christ in Majesty* – a modern sculpture by David Wynne for the twentieth-century restoration – flanked by six-winged cherubim. On the outside of the west wall of the north transept is a clock with what is called a **quarter-jack:** fifteenth-century mechanical figures of knights, which strike the bells with their pikes every quarter of an hour. The **north porch** has a twin doorway with thirteenth-century blind arcading. The magnificent Early English **nave,** completed in 1239, was strengthened in 1338 by three dramatic '**scissor-arches**'. In 1920 a great modern crucifixion scene was placed on the western arch, replacing the lost medieval

rood and dominating the nave. There is a stone **pulpit** dating from about 1547, and the nearby **Sugar Chantry** of 1489 has rich fan-vaulting and angel figures in the frieze. The **choir** contains a golden **Jesse-Tree** window of medieval glass (see Glossary), and twentieth-century embroidered backs to the canons' seats or stalls. There are interesting carved misericords. The vaulting is different in each part of the cathedral, reaching its climax in the octagonal star vault of the **Lady Chapel** east of the choir, where there is colourful stained glass dating from about 1315. The capitals and corbels in the **south transept** show imaginative carvings, including a man with toothache and two men caught 'scrumping' – stealing apples. The plain Saxon **font** here – it has been given a Jacobean font-cover – is the only item remaining from the first cathedral. The **north transept** contains an **astronomical clock** from 1390, where the time is shown by the sun and a star revolving around a 24-hour dial; the mechanical figures above represent a knights' tournament, where one knight is knocked down every quarter-hour, presided over by a figure called Jack Blandiver, high up on the right, who kicks a couple of bells on the quarters and

Thomas Ken, 1637–1711

Thomas Ken taught at Winchester College, where he wrote a manual of devotion to teach the boys how to pray, and the hymns 'Awake, my soul, and with the sun' and 'Glory to thee, my God, this night'. King Charles II made him Bishop of Bath and Wells, even though he refused to receive the royal mistress Nell Gwyn in his house. He was also critical of James II, but still regarded him as the true king, and refused to take the oath of allegiance to William and Mary. He was deposed, and lived in retirement, mostly at Longleat House, refusing to return to his bishopric when it was offered back to him. In his will he wrote: 'I die in the Holy Catholic and Apostolic Faith, professed by the whole Church, before the disunion of East and West: more particularly I die in the communion of the Church of England, as it stands distinguished from all Papal and Puritan innovations.'

strikes the bell in front of him on the hours. Opposite the clock, some worn steps dating from about 1290 lead up to the superb octagonal **Chapter House,** completed in 1306, with 32 ribs rising from a slender central pillar to form vaulting in the Decorated style. A recent Dean of Wells wrote the following advice to pilgrims: 'Walk around this Cathedral Church. Marvel at its beauty. Think of the faith which built it and sustains it still. It tells its own story as you talk quietly, walk softly and think deeply.'

South of the Cathedral, reached through the cloisters, is the 700-year-old **Bishop's Palace.** The Bishop of Bath and Wells fortified it in the fourteenth century for protection against the townsfolk, with whom he had had a quarrel. Here are the springs from which the city got its name, still producing about 180 litres (40 gallons) each second of pure water. In the moat that runs round the walls of the palace swim some tranquil swans, which are trained to pull a chain to ring for food when they are hungry.

Opening Times and Service Times

Wells Cathedral Monday to Saturday 07.30–18.00; Sunday 08.00–18.00. Services Sunday 08.00, 09.45, 11.30, 15.00; Monday to Saturday 07.30, 08.00, 17.15. Tel. 01749 674483, Fax. 832210. Email visits@wellscathedral.uk.net; http://www.wellscathedral. org.uk
Bishop's Palace April to

73

October Tuesday to Friday
10.30–18.00; Sunday
13.00–17.00. Tel. 01749 678691

CREDITON
(Devon)

There was a Saxon church, of which no trace remains, associated with St Boniface who was born here. In the tenth century Crediton became the seat of the bishop, replacing St German's, and a new cathedral was built. When the see was moved to Exeter in 1050, a Norman church was built in Crediton for a college of priests: the tower, crossing and Lady Chapel are all Norman. The Perpendicular **Church of the Holy Cross** we see today is the result of the fifteenth-century rebuilding.

The nave is dominated by a Gothic-Revival memorial to General Buller over the arch. There is a good modern sculpture of St Boniface by Witwold Kawalec, given in 1979. Crediton lies northwest of Exeter on the A377.

Service Times
Church of the Holy Cross
Sunday 08.00, 09.30; Friday 10.00. Tel. 01363 773226

PLYMOUTH;
BUCKLAND ABBEY
(Devon)

On the south coast of Devon is the naval town and port of Plymouth, from which the Devonian explorers and warriors Drake, Raleigh, Hawkins and Grenville,

---

St Boniface (680–754)

Born in Crediton and originally called Wynfrith, Boniface was renamed in honour of a Roman saint of that name. In 716 he travelled as a missionary to Frisia in Germany, but made few conversions until he went to Rome and was appointed by the Pope as Archbishop of Mainz in about 744, with eight dioceses. Thereafter he converted many pagans in Bavaria, Thuringia and Hesse, and bravely challenged their idolatry by chopping down the sacred oak of Thor in Geismar, near Fritzlar. He founded the famous Abbey of Fulda, where he was buried; he organized the Church in Germany and reformed the whole Church of the Frankish people. He resigned his archbishopric a few years after he was appointed, returned to the mission he had founded in Frisia, and there in Dokkum he met a martyr's death. In parts of Germany this Devon man is honoured more than he is in his home country; it has been said that he had more influence on world history than any other Englishman.

The Mayflower and the Pilgrim Fathers

'The Pilgrim Fathers' is a name first used in the nineteenth century for the 102 people who sailed from Plymouth in England in 1620 on the *Mayflower* to found the Plymouth plantation in America. The nucleus of the group were 'separatists', Christians whose conscience would not allow them to conform to the worship of *The Book of Common Prayer* and the government of the Church of England, and whose meetings for worship were therefore illegal. Some of them had fled from persecution in Scrooby in Nottinghamshire in 1608 to Holland. In 1618 they found a syndicate of London merchants who would finance them, and obtained permission to settle in Virginia. They were the first permanent settlers from Europe in the Massachusetts area.

Captain Cook and the Pilgrim Fathers all set sail. On the high ground on the edge of **Plymouth Sound** is **Plymouth Hoe**, with a dramatic view and a statue of Sir Francis Drake, who famously finished his game of bowls there before setting off to attack the Spanish Armada. East of this is the **Barbican,** with the **Mayflower Memorial** commemorating the sailing of the Pilgrim Fathers from this spot, and listing their names and their professions. These are repeated on the wall of the nearby Information Centre, and there is an interactive display at 'The Plymouth Mayflower Experience' opposite. Settlers in Canada, New Zealand and Australia are also commemorated at the Barbican.

St Andrew's Church is to the north of the Hoe on The Royal Parade; it was founded in 1050 and rebuilt in the fifteenth century, but firebombed in 1941; they worshipped in the garden from 1942 to 1949. The rebuilt church was consecrated in 1957, and has six colourful modern windows designed by John Piper (1904–92). There are interesting memorials, and contemporary graffiti celebrating Drake's voyage round the world.

Nine miles (15 km) north of Plymouth is **Buckland Abbey,** the last Cistercian Abbey built in England and Wales, founded in 1278. Sir Richard Grenville (1541–91), the famous Elizabethan naval commander, converted it into a mansion; then it was sold to his rival Sir Francis Drake. Since then it has been transformed into a Georgian family home, burnt, restored, and assigned to the National Trust; it is used as part of Plymouth City Museum and Art Gallery. There is a fourteenth-century Great Barn, showing how great was the wealth of the Cistercians at that time. The various galleries occupy what were formerly parts of the abbey, and the chapel was restored in 1917 on the site of the original high altar.

Opening Times and Service Times

Buckland Abbey (National Trust) April to October Friday to Wednesday 10.30–17.30; November to March Saturday to Sunday 14.00–17.00; last admission 45 min before closing time. Tel. 01822 853607, Fax. 855448

Plymouth Mayflower Experience daily April to October 10.00–18.00; November to March 10.00–17.00. Tel. 01752 306330, Fax. 600593. Email marketing@plymouth-mayflower.co.uk; http://www.plymouth-mayflower.co.uk

Plymouth St Andrew's daily 09.00–16.00. Services first Sunday of month 08.00, 10.00, 18.30; other Sundays 08.00, 09.30, 11.15, 18.30; Thursday 10.15. Tel. 01752 772139. Email office@standrewschurch.org.uk; http://www.standrewschurch.org.uk

PARRACOMBE (Devon)

When there were plans to demolish the mainly eleventh-century church of St Petroc in the nineteenth century, following the construction of a new church nearer the town, the architect John Ruskin led a protest. In consequence the old church was left untouched, and we have a rare example of

---

Sir Francis Drake (1540–96)

Drake was a Devon sailor, born near Tavistock, the first Englishman to see the Pacific Ocean and to circumnavigate the globe, in his ship *The Golden Hind*. He was knighted by Queen Elizabeth I, but died in an attack on Panama. Implacable foe of the Spanish Armada, he is said to have used this prayer on the day he sailed into Cadiz, in 1587: 'O Lord God, when thou givest to thy servants to endeavour any great matter, grant us also to know that it is not the beginning, but the continuing of the same, until it be thoroughly finished, which yieldeth the true glory; through him that for the finishing of thy work laid down his life, our Redeemer, Jesus Christ. Amen.'

---

eighteenth-century church furnishings, with a triple-decker pulpit (see Glossary), box pews, and the Lord's Prayer and the Ten Commandments taking the place of the crucifix on the rood screen. It is no longer used for worship, but is cared for by the Churches Conservation Trust. It is usually open in daylight, but a note in the porch gives the address of the keyholder. Look carefully for the signs 'Bridle Way to Parracombe and Ancient Church', just south of the northern turning to Parracombe on the A39.

ST CLETHER; ALTARNUN; TREWINT; ST NEOT (Cornwall)

St Clether is believed to have been a hermit who lived by the spring – springs in Christian tradition are always called wells – that bears his name, on the edge of Bodmin Moor, signposted from the A395. Beware, the lanes in the West Country are mostly single track with passing places. Any source of pure water is likely to have been venerated in ancient days, and some of the holy wells scattered around England could easily be pre-Christian; the early missionaries were probably wise enough to absorb them into Christian devotion. The chapel by the spring was used as the parish church

until the Normans built a new church nearby; this was where the present church, rebuilt after a fire in 1865, now stands. The water from the spring runs under the old chapel, and over a chamber made to hold the bones of the saint. The old chapel was renovated in the fifteenth century, and escaped destruction at the Reformation because it is so remote, but by the nineteenth century had become a ruin. The Revd Sabine Baring-Gould, the author of the hymn 'Onward, Christian Soldiers', restored it, and it is now one of the most impressive holy wells in the country. It is reached by a half-mile (1 km) grass track from the churchyard, and there is a plaque asking visitors to make a donation of three old pence!

Lanes south from St Clether lead to **Altarnun**; the name is derived from 'St Non's altar'; Non or Nonna was the mother of St David. The magnificent church is often called 'The Cathedral of the Moors'. There is nothing to see of the original Celtic church, though there is a fine Celtic cross by the gate of the churchyard, and little of the Norman one that followed it. The present church is fifteenth century, built of granite boulders found on the moors, and timber from the demolished mansion of the Trelawny family. It has three fine barrel-vaulted roofs and a wooden chancel screen, but its chief glories are the font and the bench ends. The font is Norman with four fierce faces, one at each corner, possibly of pagan origin and still showing traces of the original colouring. There are 79 bench ends, carved, signed and dated between 1510 and 1530, with an imaginative variety of subjects.

Leaving Altarnun by the road which, it is firmly stated, does *not* lead to the A30, in half a mile (1 km) you reach the hamlet of **Trewint**, where the tiny house of Digory and Elizabeth Isbell has been made a Methodist museum. In 1744 John Wesley stayed there, and for a while their house became a church. It was restored in 1950, together with Wesley's prayer room, described as the smallest Methodist preaching place in the world still used for services.

South of Trewint, and following signs from the A30, is the village of **St Neot** on the edge of Bodmin Moor. Its fifteenth-century parish church contains some of the best **stained-glass windows** in England, dating from the fifteenth and sixteenth centuries. The oldest is the fifteenth-century Creation window, at the east

Carved bench end, Altarnun, Cornwall

end of the south aisle, showing Adam and Eve in the Garden of Eden.

Opening Times and Service Times
Altarnun church; St Clether church daily 09.00–17.00. Services Altarnun 09.30 (1, 4), 11.00 (3), 18.30 (2); Wednesday 10.00. St Clether 11.00 (1), 18.30 (3). Tel. 01566 86108. http://www.bodminmoor.co.uk
St Neot church Services Sunday 08.00 (2, 3, 4), 11.00 (all), 18.30 (2)
Trewint museum daily except Christmas day 09.00–dusk. Service on Wesley Day. Email thesecretary@wesleycottage. fsbusiness.co.uk; http://www.lamc.org.uk

---

Wesley in Cornwall

John Wesley travelled on average 8000 miles (13,000 km) each year on horseback preaching the gospel. In Cornwall the established Church was very weak, with far too few clergy, and Wesley was sowing the seed of the Word, in effect, in virgin soil. A famous picture shows him addressing an open-air gathering at Gwennap Pit. Methodism met with an overwhelming welcome, and to this day the Methodists are the strongest denomination in some parts of Cornwall.

BODMIN
(Cornwall)

From Liskeard the A38 continues west to Bodmin, which is officially the county town of Cornwall, though most public offices are in Truro. At the end of Fore Street is **St Petroc's Church**, built between 1469 and 1472 on the site of earlier churches and with Norman masonry in the tower. It is the largest parish church in Cornwall, and contains an elaborately carved twelfth-century font, and, in the south wall, an ivory casket which is said to hold the bones of St Petroc. Many pilgrims have visited the shrine of Petroc over the centuries to ask for his prayers. He was originally buried in Bodmin, and King Edgar in 963 gave a gilded shrine to contain his remains; however, it was stolen in 1177 and taken to Brittany. King Henry II demanded that the remains be sent back with an apology, and they were returned in a casket made of ivory, shell and brass, with medallions made by Arab craftsmen in Sicily. It was hidden at the Reformation, and rediscovered during restoration work in the eighteenth century. At the foot of the steps leading up to the churchyard there is a sacred well, named after St Guron, a hermit who made himself a cell here soon after 500; there is also a ruined chantry in the churchyard.

Opening Times and Service Times

St Petroc's Church daily April to September 11.00–15.00. Services Sunday 08.00, 10.00, 18.00; Friday 10.30. Tel. 01208 73867

TRURO
(Cornwall)

Truro, a small city with Georgian houses demonstrating the prosperity that came with tin-mining in the early nineteenth century, lies at the junction of the A39 and A390. The nearest

Cornish Saints

On a tour round Cornwall you pass villages and churches named after many a saint whom you have never even heard of before. Some of them have been recorded as pioneer missionaries who brought the gospel to this part of the Celtic world; of others hardly anything is known, so that you begin to wonder whether some pre-Christian ancestor or hero has been baptized into popular legend. St Advent, St Day, St Endellion, St Erth, St Juliot, St Just, St Keri – Egloskerry means the Church of Keri – St Keyne, St Ladock, St Levan or Selevan, St Mawes, St Mawgan, St Minver, St Nectan – apart from late and imaginative legends, what do we know about them? **St Austell, St Mewan** and **St Samson** were all Welsh Christians who travelled through Cornwall establishing churches in the places that bear their names, but went on to evangelize in Brittany. **St Cleer** and **St Clethen** are probably the same Welsh hermit who settled in Cornwall in the sixth century. **St German** was probably Germanus (c. 378–448), Bishop of Auxerre in France, the teacher of St Patrick and St Illtud, who came to Britain in 429 to combat the heresy of Pelagianism. In 447 he came back and led the British to victory over the Picts and Saxons, teaching them to use 'Alleluia' as their battle cry. St Ives in Cambridgeshire is named after a seventh-century bishop; but the town of **St Ives** in Cornwall, pronounced Eve's, and the village of **St Ive,** seem to be dedicated to an otherwise unknown virgin called Ia, Hia or Iva. **St Mellane,** after whom the village of Mullion is named, is better known as the Breton St Malo, who may have come originally from Wales, and died in around 640 near the French port that is named after him. **St Neot** was a ninth-century Saxon monk of Glastonbury who became a hermit at the place named after him, St Neot in Cornwall. His relics may have been taken to St Neots in Cambridgeshire, or they may have been two different people. **St Perran,** Perin or Piran came to Cornwall from Ireland as a missionary in the sixth century, and gave his name to the village of Perranporth. **St Petroc,** also called Pedrog, Petrox and Perreux, lived at the end of the fifth century and the beginning of the sixth, and was the son of Glywys, a prince in mid-Wales. He was educated in Ireland, and returned in about 518, making his way to Cornwall, where he landed in Trebetherick. The monastery where he settled, founded originally by St

Wethinoc, became known as Petroc Stow or Padstow. After a 30-year ministry there, and a seven-year pilgrimage, possibly to Rome and Palestine, he settled in Bodmin and founded a religious community which continued to flourish after his death in 564.

Anglican bishop had for centuries been in far-off Exeter, so when Cornwall was made a diocese in 1880 the foundation stone of a new cathedral was laid, the first new Anglican cathedral in England since St Paul's in London. **Truro Cathedral** is in a Normandy Gothic style, completed in 1910. The baptistry is dedicated to the memory of Henry Martyn. The south choir aisle is formed from the remains of the parish church, consecrated in 1259 and restored during the sixteenth century, which stood on the site before the cathedral was built. A terracotta panel in the north choir aisle gives a lively and vivid picture of the Way of the Cross. A painting in the north aisle represents an aerial view of Cornwall as the 'Land of the Saints'.

Service Times
Truro Cathedral Sunday 08.00, 09.00, 10.00, 18.00; Monday to Saturday 07.30, 08.00, 17.30; Wednesday 13.00; Friday 11.00. Tel. 01503 276782. http://www.trurocathedral.org.uk

TREBETHERICK
(Cornwall)

Approached from Wadebridge and the B3314 is the tiny village of **Trebetherick** where Sir John Betjeman died, and down a narrow lane, and then by a path across the golf course, the church of **St Enodoc** where he is buried. The church may be on the site of

Henry Martyn (1781–1812)

Henry Martyn was born in Truro and became a fellow of St John's College in Cambridge. There he met Charles Simeon (see p. 195), and was inspired by him to seek ordination and go to Calcutta as a chaplain with the East India Company. Unlike some chaplains he did not limit his ministry to Europeans, but learnt local languages and shared the gospel with the Indian people. He translated the New Testament into Hindustani, Persian and Arabic, the Psalms into Persian and *The Book of Common Prayer* into Hindustani. He died at Tokat in Turkey on his way home and was buried by the Armenian clergy there.

the hermitage of St Enodoc but we know nothing about him. Some parts of the church are Norman, and there is a Norman font; the tower with its crooked spire is thirteenth century. There was a painted wooden screen in the fifteenth century, but some time later the top of it was clumsily cut off. There are traces of a village which, like the church, was at some time suddenly overwhelmed by a sandstorm. By ecclesiastical law the Vicar had to be let down through a hole in the church roof once a year to conduct a service. In 1863–4 the church was dug out and restored, although parts of it are still below the level of the surrounding dunes. It is this that gives it its sense of mystery and holiness, together with its association with Betjeman, who wrote of his love for the place in his poem 'Sunday Afternoon Service in St Enodoc Church'.

Opening Times and Service Times
St Enodoc daily 07.30–dusk. Services Sunday 15.00, and July to August 08.00. Tel. 01208 862398

TINTAGEL
(Cornwall)

Off the A39 at Camelford, the B3266 and B3263 lead to the romantic cliff-top ruined castle of Tintagel. Take the small road beside The Cornishman Inn and you can drive to the church, then walk along the cliffs to the landward court of **Tintagel Castle**. Then there are steep steps down to the bridge and up to the island section of the castle. Alternatively you could walk, or take the official landrover, but not drive your own vehicle,

---

Sir John Betjeman (1906–84)

Sir John was an authority on English architecture, and his books on English churches are unsurpassed; he did much to popularize the then despised Victorian and Edwardian buildings and to protect them from destruction. His verse was light and humorous in style, but gave expression to a growing nostalgia in England for the vanishing countryside and the life of the middle classes; so popular was it that he was made Poet Laureate. His was a deep and conservative faith, and he gave eloquent expression to traditional Christianity in his verse. He died at Trebetherick, and refusing more splendid resting places was buried at his own request in the churchyard of St Enodoc.

King Arthur

There seems to have been a Romano-British Christian warlord called Arthur who resisted the advance of the Saxons in the fifth century. Cornish folklore was familiar with tales of Tristan and Iseult, and King Mark of Cornwall, and they seem to have blended with those of Arthur. It was Geoffrey of Monmouth, however, in his twelfth-century *History of the Kings of Britain*, who popularized the stories of King Arthur, born at Tintagel the son of Uther Pendragon, his knights, and the wizard Merlin, perhaps including, among the adventures of the knights of the round table, some of the stories of the missionary journeys of the Celtic monks who had originally lived there. By the time Sir Thomas Mallory had written his *Morte d'Arthur* the tales had become a glorification of the chivalry of the medieval knights, and Tennyson and T.H. White are among many who have continued to draw on the evocative mystery of the legends to stimulate contemporary resonance. Behind it all, however, lies the fact that the Christian faith has been for centuries a strong stimulus to acts of gallantry among the English.

down the half-mile (1 km) rough track from the village to the bridge. The walls you see are mostly from the chapel and great hall of the Norman stronghold built in 1145, and added to in the thirteenth century for the Earls of Cornwall, most of which had washed into the sea by the sixteenth century when they abandoned it. But on the headland there are important remains of the sixth-century Celtic settlement, which may have been a monastery, or the headquarters of a Cornish king, or even of King Arthur – recent excavations have found a sixth-century stone bearing the word ARTOGNU. An exhibition tells the story, and paths descend to 'Merlin's Cave'. The church on the cliffs is dedicated to **St Materiana**, a princess of Gwent who evangelized this area in about 500. There were probably Celtic and Saxon churches on this site, but the present building is almost exactly as the Normans left it, though with the addition of a thirteenth-century south porch, a fourteenth-century north porch, tower, and decorated north transept window; a reredos made from fifteenth-century bench ends, and a rood screen from about 1500; a pre-Reformation altar in the sacrament chapel, and a late Tudor bishop's chair. A Roman stone was found in the churchyard with the name of an emperor who was put to death by Constantine in 324.

Opening Times and Service Times

Tintagel Castle (English Heritage) daily April to September 10.00–18.00; October 10.00–17.00; November to March 10.00–16.00. Tel. 01840 770328
St Materiana's Services Sunday 10.00, 18.00 (1). Tel. 01840 770315

ISLE ABBOTS (Somerset)

The church at Isle Abbots stands at the end of a dream street of thatched cottages, on a side road between the A303 near Ilminster and the A378. One of the best of all the Somerset-style towers rises above the surrounding 'levels'; in the niches of the tower, there are fine pre-Reformation statues, and on the corners curious squatting figures known as 'Hunky-Punks'. There is a 'squint' (see Glossary) and a carved Norman font, as well as a rare example of a 'barrel organ', commonly used to accompany singing in church before live organists were commonly available.

Service Times
Isle Abbots church Sunday 08.00 (3), 09.30 (4), 11.15 (1). Tel. 01460 52610

BURRINGTON COMBE (Somerset)

On the northern side of the Mendip Hills, the B3134 runs in a valley down to the A368. Local tradition points out the cleft in a rock in this valley, Burrington Combe, where Augustus Toplady (1740–78), the curate at the parish church, while sheltering from a storm, wrote the hymn 'Rock of Ages, cleft for me' on a scrap of paper he happened to be carrying. This story may explain the appeal of the hymn to those who wish to pray for protection. The rock is opposite the carpark just uphill from the Burrington Inn.

BATH (Somerset)

The only hot springs in Britain surfaced in the west of England some 100,000 years ago. The Celtic tribe of Dobunni made the spring sacred to their god Sulis; the Romans later developed the whole area into a huge leisure complex, Aquae Sulis. You can visit the **Roman Baths** today and see the bronze head of Sulis-Minerva. When the Romans left, the drains became blocked and the whole area was covered in mud. On their arrival in 577, the Saxons built a town inside the Roman walls, and, in the reign of King Offa, between 757 and 796, a large monastery and abbey. Here the first English King, Edgar I, was crowned in 973 by St Dunstan. In 980 St Alfege became Abbot of Bath, before being made Archbishop of Canterbury. In the eleventh century the Bishop of Wells, who was a physician, bought Bath for £500 and began building a vast Benedictine priory and a Norman cathedral, new baths, a school and a palace. He intended it for Somerset's cathedral, but his successors, although called Bishops of Bath and Wells, preferred to make Wells their cathedral, because Bath had a troublesome monastic community. Bath was popularized when Queen Elizabeth I visited, and became fashionable in the eighteenth century under the direction of 'Beau' Nash; you can get an idea of social life at that time by visiting the **Pump Room** next to the Roman Baths. Jane Austen wrote several of her novels here, and *Northanger Abbey* is set largely in eighteenth-century Bath; there is a Jane Austen Centre in Gay Street with an exhibition about her life. Bath lies on the A4, the 'Great West Road' from London.

Bath Abbey is approached through the splendid west front; the Norman cathedral fell into decay, and in 1499 Bishop Oliver King pulled it down. He is supposed to have rebuilt the Abbey church because he saw a vision of angels ascending and descending at this spot (Genesis 28.10–17), and these are represented, along with his punning logo of a crown and an olive tree, in the carvings on the west front. The new abbey was in the Perpendicular style, but it was abandoned unfinished at the Dissolution of the Monasteries. Inside, the fan-vaulting was begun by the architects who had worked on Henry VII's chapel in Westminster Abbey, and finished by Sir George Gilbert Scott, who meticulously replicated the detail of the chancel in the vaulting of the nave so that they appear continuous. The fifteenth-century architects made the transepts and aisles small and the windows large, creating the impression of a roomful of light; but the eighteenth century crammed the building with memorials, including a tablet to Admiral Arthur Philip (1738–1814), the first Governor of New South Wales; and the Victorians added stained glass. Remains of the Norman cathedral are seen in the Gethsemane Chapel. Outside the southeast door are the Heritage Vaults, with sculpture, silver and reconstructions. The Abbey is south of the bridge over the River Avon and beside the Roman Baths: follow the signs for the Information Office.

Opening Times and Service Times

Roman Baths daily mid July to August 09.00–21.00; November to February 09.30–16.00; September to October, March to June 09.00–17.00. Tel. 01225 477785, Fax. 477743. http://www.romanbaths.co.uk
Bath Abbey Easter–October Monday to Saturday 09.00–18.00; November to Easter Monday to Saturday 09.00–16.30; all year Sunday 13.00–14.30, 16.30–17.30. Services Sunday 08.00, 09.15, 11.00, 12.15, 15.30, 18.30; Monday 08.30; Thursday 11.00; Friday 08.30. **Heritage Vaults** Monday to Saturday 10.00–16.00. Tel. 01225 422462, Fax. 429990. Email office@bathabbey.org; http://www.bathabbey.org
Jane Austen Centre daily 09.30–17.30. Tel. 01225 443000

BRISTOL (County Borough)

The City of Bristol is a former port city, associated with the great days of British shipping, but also with the shame of the slave trade (see p. 142). **Bristol Cathedral** is between Anchor Road and College Green. It was founded in 1140 as the Abbey Church of St Augustine. According to legend this was on the site where St Augustine of Canterbury met with leaders of the original Celtic church of Britain in the seventh century, and failed to win their support for his mission because he did not rise when they entered. That the meeting took place is attested by the Venerable Bede, but where it was we cannot be sure. The monks of Bristol were Augustinian Canons, who lived a life of poverty, chastity and obedience with regular prayer like Benedictine monks, but were more involved in work among the local community. Soon after the Dissolution of the Monasteries, the unfinished nave of the Abbey was demolished, and the remaining buildings were re-consecrated in 1542 as the city's Cathedral. The **choir** dates from the fourteenth century, and has notable capitals to the pillars and a unique design of vaulting. There are lively fifteenth-century misericords in the **choir stalls**. The **nave** was rebuilt in 1867–77 to designs by G.E. Street which effectively imitated the choir. The **Elder Lady Chapel** of 1210–20 – off the north transept – has joyful and curious carvings, including a monkey playing a bagpipes with a ram on a violin. The **Eastern Lady Chapel**, added in 1298–1330, has original glass dating from around 1340 in its window; the altar candlesticks were given in thanksgiving for the safe return of the ships that brought home the shipwrecked Alexander Selkirk, the model for Defoe's story of *Robinson Crusoe*. The **east end** of the church is described as a 'hall church' because the height of the aisles is the same as the chancel. In the **south transept** is a carved stone coffin-lid depicting the 'Harrowing of Hell', when Christ after his crucifixion brought the departed souls out of Hades. The elaborately ribbed **Chapter House**, off the south transept, was built between 1150 and 1170, and is one of the most elaborately carved Norman rooms in the country.

North of the Cathedral on the other side of College Green is the **Lord Mayor's Chapel**. This small church, with a late thirteenth-century nave, early fourteenth-century south aisle and Perpendicular chancel, was originally a part of St Mark's Hospital. In 1722 it was designated the official civic church of the city. The stained glass and the Spanish tiles are worth visiting.

Northeast of here, between the Horsefair and Broadmead, is **John Wesley's Chapel**. This is the oldest known Methodist Chapel in the world, built by John Wesley in 1739 and rebuilt by him in 1748. Both the chapel and the attached living quarters are preserved exactly as they were in Wesley's days, and outside the door is the stable for the itinerant preacher's horse. The double-decker pulpit is beneath a hidden upstairs window, from which John Wesley could watch the progress of his trainee preachers.

The other side of Broadmead is **Quaker's Friars**, so called because it was a building, dating from 1227, which had been used by Dominican Friars, and was used by the early Quakers from 1670 to 1956; George Fox, their founder, was married here, as was William Penn. The Quaker extension was built in 1747; now the whole building is used as Bristol Registry Office, where civil marriages take place.

South from here, between the Floating Harbour and the River Avon, is the great church of **St Mary Redcliffe**, showing the evolution of Gothic style from the thirteenth to the fifteenth centuries. Queen Elizabeth I called it 'the fairest parish church in England'. Here medieval pilgrims would say prayers for a safe journey before they set sail, and give thanks when they returned.

The spire, from 1872, replacing one that collapsed in 1446, soars to 89 metres (292 feet) high. The church is entered through an ornate hexagonal early fourteenth-century north porch, with decorations in a style brought back by Bristol traders from their journeys in the lands of Islam. The interior is full of intricately carved detail, including over 1000 carved roof bosses, picked out in gold leaf, in the lierne vaulting. The American or St John Chapel contains a wooden statue of Queen Elizabeth I in the style of a figurehead; the whale bone above the entrance is supposed to have been brought back from Newfoundland by John Cabot. There is a model of Cabot's boat over the north door. Admiral William Penn is buried in the south transept, and his armour is kept high on the wall at the west end. When he died, King Charles II owed him a large sum of money, so he gave to the admiral's son instead some lands in America, where William Penn the younger founded Pennsylvania (see p. 109). The Handel window, in the north choir aisle, is from 1859 and commemorates the composer, who played on the organ here. Above the north porch is the muniment room where in 1768 Thomas Chatterton claimed to have found the poems of a fifteenth-century monk called Thomas Rowley. When the brilliant forgeries were exposed, Chatterton committed suicide; there is a memorial to him in the south transept. In the north transept is the 'chaotic pendulum', a beautiful illustration of scientific 'chaos theory' and of the limitations on the scientist's ability to predict events (see http://www.clifton-scientific.org/stmary.htm).

Opening Times and Service Times

Bristol Cathedral daily 10.00–16.00. Services Sunday 07.40, 08.00, 10.00, 15.30; Monday to Saturday 08.30, 12.30, 17.15 (or Saturday 15.30). Tel. 0117 9264879, Fax. 0117 9253678. http://www.bristol-cathedral.co.uk

Wesley's Chapel Monday to Saturday 10.00–16.00. Prayers Friday 13.00. Tel. 0117 9264740. http://www.wesley.fen.bris.ac.uk

Lord Mayor's Chapel Tuesday to Saturday 10.00–16.00. Services Sunday 11.00. Tel. 0117 9294350

St Mary Redcliffe every Sunday 08.00–18.00; June to August Monday to Saturday 08.00–20.00; September to May 08.00–18.00. Services Sunday 08.00, 09.30, 11.15, 18.30; Monday to Saturday 09.15, 17.00; Tuesday 12.45; Wednesday 07.30, 10.00. Tel. and Fax. 0117 9291487. http://www.stmarys.ebusiness.co.uk

West of London

For the purposes of this book, I am going to return to London
to cover some attractive places that lie west of the capital.

WINDSOR; ETON
(Berkshire)

Windsor and Eton are just
south of Junction 6 of the
M4, 21 miles (34 km) west of
London. **Windsor Castle** has
been one of the favoured
residences of the British
Royal Family ever since, in
about 1080, William the
Conqueror built a simple
wooden 'motte and bailey' –
a tower with a moat round it
– where the **Round Tower**
now rises above all the
surrounding buildings. The
defensive walls and the
magnificent **State
apartments**, east of the
Round Tower, which are

open to the public, have been
rebuilt and extended many
times. At present all visitors
to the castle have to buy
tickets and pass through
security checks at the
entrance in St Alban's Street.
Opposite Henry VIII's
gateway is **St George's
Chapel.** King Henry III built
a chapel in the castle, which
Edward III enlarged in 1348,
and provided with a College
consisting of the Dean and
Canons and a choir; he
dedicated it to the Most
Noble Order of the Garter.
Edward IV replaced this with
a new chapel, which was
completed in 1528 and is a

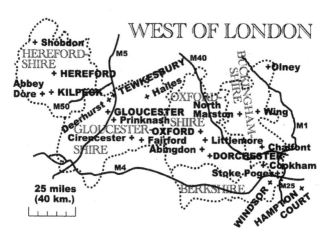

superb example of architecture in the Perpendicular style, where the ribs fan out from the piers to support the wide and almost flat tracery of a **lierne vault**. The huge **west window** shows 75 figures in mostly early sixteenth-century glass. Passing under the organ screen from the nave to the **chancel**, we find two sets of ornate **choir stalls**, with a wide space between them, arranged for antiphonal singing, and dating from 1478 to 1485, with elaborate misericords and other carvings. The back row is for the Knights of the Garter, and their colourful banners hang overhead; the middle row is for the Military Knights, minor canons and choir men; and the front rows for the choirboys. Those who arrive early for evensong on a weekday can usually be seated near the choir and listen to the magnificent singing. The nineteenth-century **east window** has 52 lights, representing the Resurrection of Jesus, the Visit by the Wise Men to Bethlehem, and in the lower tier incidents from the life of Prince Albert, consort to Queen Victoria. The **tomb of King Henry VI** (see p. 193), re-buried here in 1484, was associated with many miracles of healing, and pilgrims flocked to pray there until the Reformation. Other members of the Royal Family buried here include Edward IV, Henry VIII, Jane Seymour, Charles I (both body and head in the same place), George III, George IV, William IV, Edward VII and Queen Alexandra, George VI and Queen Elizabeth the Queen Mother.

Crossing a footbridge at the end of Thames Avenue in Windsor brings you to the small town of Eton. **Eton College,** one of the most famous of English public schools, was originally founded by King Henry VI in 1440 to provide a free education to 70 poor scholars and choristers. When it became fashionable, however, for the nobility to send their sons to Eton, pupil numbers increased and the fees of what was now a very exclusive private school became hugely expensive. The **College Chapel**, built between 1441 and 1480 in the Perpendicular style, is one of the best examples of this style in the country, although it was not until 1957 that the wooden ceiling was replaced with stone fan-vaulting, probably as Henry VI had intended. The **wall paintings,** dating from 1479 to 1488, are considered by some to be the finest in England. There are also a tapestry reredos and painted panelling by William Morris, to designs by Burne-Jones, and modern stained glass by

John Piper, Patrick
Reyntiens, Monica Forsyth
and Evie Holme. The organ
is from 1902 with over 4000
pipes up to 9.7 metres (32
feet) in length.

Opening Times
Eton College daily Easter and
summer school holidays
10.30–16.30; Easter term and
September 14.00–16.30. Chapel
closed weekdays 13.00–14.00;
Sunday 12.30–14.00. The
services are not usually open to
the public except on special
occasions. Tel. 01753 671177,
Fax. 671265. Email
webmaster@etoncollege.org.uk;
http://www.etoncollege.com
Windsor Castle Precincts, State
apartments, Queen Mary's Dolls'
House, the Gallery daily except
Good Friday, 14 June, 25–26
December, open 10.00–17.00
(last admission 16.00) subject to
change at short notice. **St
George's Chapel and Albert
Memorial Chapel** February to
December Monday to Saturday
10.00–16.00, Sunday
14.00–15.45. Evensong daily
17.15. Tel. 01753 868286 ext.
2235 or 01753 831118
(recorded message).
http://www.royal.gov.uk

OXFORD
(Oxfordshire)

Oxford developed in the
eighth century around the
nunnery of **St Frideswide**, a
Saxon princess of Mercia
who fled to Oxford to avoid
marriage with a
neighbouring prince. She
established a convent with

herself as abbess, which was
where Christ Church now
stands; when she died
around 735 it became a place
of pilgrimage. The original
street plan still shows, with a
main road (St Giles,
Magdalen Street,
Cornmarket Street, and St
Aldates) running from north
to south, intersecting at St
Mary Mag's with Broad
Street (The Broad) and at
Carfax with High Street (The
High) running from west to
east. A number of
monasteries were established,
and young people gathered
to hear the more well-
educated monks expounding
the Christian faith. Around
1200 this emerged as one of
Europe's earliest universities,
originally a federation of
monastic halls, and still
today made up of
autonomous colleges. During
the Reformation both
Catholics and Protestants
were martyred in Oxford:
Campion, Cranmer, Latimer
and Ridley; a small cross in
the road surface in the
middle of Broad Street marks
the spot where they died.
Orlando Gibbons, organist
and composer, was born in
Oxford in 1583.

There is plenty to see in
Oxford; it would best if
possible to take several days
over your visit, particularly
because some of the colleges
are open in the afternoons
only. We begin the tour in

the centre of Oxford at the crossroads known as **Carfax**, where the fourteenth-century tower is all that remains of the former St Martin's Church.

Walk south along St Aldate's, and you reach **Christ Church College**, founded by Cardinal Wolsey in 1525 as Cardinal's College. Visitors enter through the college gardens, and pay a fee, except those attending services in the Cathedral, who may enter through the main gate free. You pass the late Gothic **cloister**, and the early Gothic **Chapter House** with a Norman doorway, which is used as a shop, to enter 'Tom Quad'. The college chapel is also **Oxford Cathedral**, the smallest cathedral in England. This little gem is Late Norman, about 1150–1210, with a sixteenth-century roof in the nave and a stellar vaulted roof from the fifteenth century in the choir. The Noah window in the northwest corner is of painted glass, with a detailed depiction of the city of Nineveh. The windows in the northeast and southeast are by Burne-Jones. The glass in the Lucy Chapel dates from 1330 and shows the martyrdom of St Thomas à Becket. The Lady Chapel at the northeast contains the restored shrine of St Frideswide; since the

Reformation her remains have been buried beneath a slab. Wolsey planned to demolish this building and provide his college with a new chapel, and had taken down part of the cloister and most of the nave when he died in 1530, but Henry VIII preserved what was left, renamed it Christ Church, and made it Oxford's cathedral in 1542. One of the modern roof bosses is a portrait of Mahatma Gandhi. Notable former students of the college include Charles Dodgson (Lewis Carroll) and John Wesley.

If you then walk through the eighteenth-century Peckwater Quad to Oriel Square you will come to **Oriel College** (founded 1326, rebuilt 1619–42, with a second quadrangle from the eighteenth century and a library by James Wyatt), and, on the other side of Merton Street, **Corpus Christi College** (founded 1517, with an early Tudor Front Quad and gateway, a sixteenth-century hall with a hammerbeam roof and a sixteenth-century chapel with an altarpiece of *The Adoration of the Shepherds* from the studio of Rubens) and **Merton College**. Merton, founded in 1264, has the oldest college buildings in Oxford: Mob Quad and the library are fourteenth century, and the Chapel, built in 1294–97 in the Decorated style, has original glass.

Turning left into Logic Lane or back up Oriel Street brings you to High Street and **The Queen's College,** founded in 1340 to honour Queen Philippa and rebuilt in 1671–1760. Then turning right – east – along the High Street you find **Magdalen College** (pronounced 'maudlin'), by a famous bridge across the River Cherwell, where you can hire punts. Magdalen was founded in 1458 as the

Hospital of St John the Baptist; it has late Perpendicular style cloisters, chapel and bell tower; from the top of the tower the excellent choir sing a carol every year on the morning of the first of May.

Back along the High Street to Queen's College and up Queen's Lane and New College Lane brings you to **St Edmund Hall** (founded in about 1220 on a site given by St Edmund of Abingdon; the buildings are mid seventeenth-century), and the adjacent **Church of St Peter in the East,** now the college

---

Hugh Latimer (c. 1485–1555)

Hugh, the son of a yeoman farmer in Leicestershire, became a famous preacher, with a down-to-earth style and a ready wit. Although he preached against social abuses, and corruption in the Church, he was licensed to preach anywhere in England. He was rebuked for spreading Protestantism, but after the rift between Henry VIII and the Pope he became one of the King's advisors, and then Bishop of Worcester. He resigned rather than sign the Six Articles, which condemned Reformation doctrine. For a while he was kept a prisoner in the Tower of London, but was released when Edward VI came to the throne, and soon became a popular court preacher. Under Queen Mary's reign, however, he was again arrested and sent to the Tower. In 1554 together with Cranmer and Ridley he was taken to Oxford to debate Transubstantiation and the Sacrifice of the Mass. Refusing to accept the medieval doctrine he was excommunicated and burnt with Ridley. It shows remarkable faith and courage to be able to joke when one is being burnt at the stake: his last words were 'Be of good comfort, Master Ridley, and play the man. We shall this day light such a candle by God's grace in England, as (I trust) shall never be put out.'

library, with a crypt dating from about 1150; and **New College**. This was founded by William of Wykeham in 1379, shortly before he founded Winchester College in Winchester. The vast fifteenth-century chapel has fourteenth-century glass in the southwest, and a most unusual west window designed by Sir Joshua Reynolds in 1777, with his wife representing Faith and the actress Mrs Siddons as Hope. Beneath it is a moving modern sculpture by Sir Jacob Epstein of Lazarus rising from the dead. The college garden is surrounded on two sides by the twelfth-century wall of the city. **Hertford College**, founded in 1282 and re-established in the nineteenth century, has a bridge built in 1913 over New College Lane to link its two quadrangles.

Thomas Cranmer (1489–1556)

Cranmer was a fellow of Jesus College, Cambridge, when King Henry VIII was trying to have the divorce he wanted accepted by the Church. Cranmer suggested that as the Pope, who had waived the Church law to allow the marriage in the first place, was under the control of Henry's enemies, a debate in the universities of Europe might decide the matter. When the universities decided in Henry's favour, he appointed Cranmer Archbishop of Canterbury in gratitude. Cranmer accepted the office with great reluctance, but once appointed he used it to further his own plans for a theological Reformation in the Church. He had already secretly married; he compiled *The Litany*, the first service in the vernacular, in 1544, when Henry was at war with the Scots and the French. It was not, however, until the boy king Edward VI was on the throne that he could pursue his aim of introducing Protestant theology to the Church of England. *The Book of Common Prayer* of 1549 and its more Protestant revision of 1552 were largely his own compositions. Cranmer influenced and was influenced by the changes in the English language at this time to produce some of the finest expressions of Christian prayer in the history of the nation. When Mary became Queen he was accused of high treason, sentenced and pardoned, but then tried for heresy. He signed a recantation, accepting transubstantiation and papal supremacy, but then withdrew it and thrust first into the flames the hand which had signed it, when he was burnt at the stake in Oxford.

Opposite are the **Sheldonian Theatre**, designed by Sir Christopher Wren, and built in 1664–9 for formal University ceremonies; Hawksmoor's 1713 **Clarendon Building** in the Palladian style; and the **Bodleian Library**, one of the world's great book collections, established in the fourteenth century and rebuilt by Sir Thomas Bodley in the seventeenth century.

Then following Catte Street to the south, you pass the **Radcliffe Camera** (a Baroque rotunda designed by James Gibbs) and come to the entrance to **Brasenose College** on your right; the college takes its name from a brass doorknocker in the hall; it has a fourteenth-century kitchen; the

Gatehouse, Library and hall are from the early sixteenth century and the Library and Chapel mid-seventeenth. The **University Church of St Mary the Virgin** is on the south side of the square; a fifteenth-century church in the Perpendicular style, with a thirteenth-century tower in the Decorated style; a Baroque porch of 1637 by Nicholas Stone, and the fourteenth-century **Congregation House**, now used as a coffee shop, which was where the university started. It was in St Mary's Church that the trial of Thomas Cranmer was held, and notable preachers there include Ridley, Latimer, both the Wesley brothers, and John Henry Newman. **All Souls College**, with its entrance in the High Street, is

---

Nicholas Ridley (c. 1500–55)

After a short time as chaplain to Thomas Cranmer, Ridley became Master of Pembroke Hall, Cambridge. He then became Bishop of Rochester and finally Bishop of London. He was sympathetic to the Reformation, and under Edward VI he openly promoted Protestantism at Cambridge and helped to compile the first *Book of Common Prayer* in 1549. He preached on social injustice, and a sermon he preached to the King was partly instrumental in the foundation of Christ's Hospital (the Bluecoat School for orphans), St Thomas's Hospital, and the Bridewell as a home for vagrants, homeless children and petty criminals. He supported Lady Jane Grey's claim to the crown, and when Mary came to the throne he was removed from his bishopric. He was then excommunicated, and burned at the stake with Hugh Latimer in Oxford.

John Keble (1792–1866)

John Keble became a fellow at Oxford when he was only 19, but resigned 12 years later to become his father's curate in a country parish among the Cotswold Hills. There he wrote the series of poems called *The Christian Year*, which became immensely popular and influential during the Victorian period. In 1831 he was appointed Professor of Poetry at Oxford. Keble's University sermon in 1833 on 'National Apostasy' is regarded as the beginning of the Oxford Movement. He defended belief in the Real Presence of Jesus in the Holy Communion, and encouraged the clergy to take a high view of their duties, including praying for their parishioners by daily use of morning and evening prayer. Keble's hymns still in regular use include 'New every morning is the love' and 'Blest are the pure in heart'.

on your left; it was founded in 1438 to commemorate the souls of those who died in the Hundred Years War. The front Quadrangle dates from the mid-fifteenth century; the chapel is Perpendicular in style from 1442, with fifteenth-century glass and a medieval reredos; and Nicholas Hawksmoor's North Quad is from the eighteenth century. The colourful sundial was designed by Wren.

Turning into Turl Street, known as The Turl, **Lincoln College** is first on the right; it was founded in 1427 and in 1436 the Front Quad and Hall were built. The chapel dates from 1610–31, with original seventeenth-century Flemish glass; and between the two quads are the oak-panelled rooms where John Wesley used to meet with his student friends, and where their methodical pursuit of holiness led to the nickname 'Methodists'.

Behind Lincoln is **Exeter College,** founded 1314; Palmer's Tower dates from 1432; the chapel was designed by Gilbert Scott in 1857, and contains a tapestry by William Morris and Edward Burne-Jones, who were both undergraduates at this college. **Jesus College** is across Turl Street; founded in 1571, it has a late-Perpendicular east front.

On the far side of Broad Street is **Trinity College** – some of the buildings are designed by Sir Christopher Wren, with Grinling Gibbons

Edward Bouverie Pusey (1800–82)

Pusey spent his entire life from the age of 28 as Professor of Hebrew and Canon of Christ Church in Oxford. He contributed learned papers on the discipline of fasting, and on baptismal regeneration, to the series of *Tracts for the Times* which gave rise to the Tractarian Movement, and when Newman joined the Roman Catholic Church, Pusey became the leader of the Anglo-Catholics or Puseyites. He preached and wrote extensively on the Church of England as part of the worldwide Catholic Church, and on the Real Presence of Christ in the Holy Communion. He encouraged the translation of the Fathers of the Early Church, the revival of monasticism and sacramental confession.

carvings in the chapel – and **Balliol,** founded in 1282, with a fifteenth-century Front Quad and all the rest nineteenth century. A few yards to the south in Cornmarket Street, pedestrianized, is the church of **St Michael at the Northgate,** with a Saxon tower and a thirteenth-century interior. It is the oldest building in Oxford, and contains the oldest stained glass, from about 1290, in the east window, showing St Nicholas, St Edmund of Abingdon, St Michael the Archangel and the Virgin and Child.

Colleges' Opening Times and Service Times

Visiting times are usually displayed at the porter's lodge. Service times in college chapels, which may vary, normally only apply in 'full term', i.e. three periods of eight weeks beginning in January, after Easter, and in October. Christ Church, Magdalen, and New College have sung services during the choir school's term. All telephone numbers have the Oxford area code 01865. Each college has a website; consult http://www.ox.ac.uk/colleges, which also provides a map.

All Souls October to April Monday to Friday 14.00–16.00; April to October 14.00–16.30. Services open to Fellows only. Tel. 279379
Balliol daily 14.00–17.00. Services Sunday 17.45. Tel. 277777
Brasenose daily 10.00–11.30 (tour parties only), 14.00–16.30 or 17.00 during BST. Services Sunday 09.00, 18.00; Tuesday 18.00 except (3). Tel. 277830
Christ Church Monday to Saturday 09.00–17.30; Sunday 12.00–17.30. **Hall** as above daily except between 12.00 and 14.00. **Cathedral** Monday to Saturday 09.00–16.30; Sunday

The Oxford Movement

With slovenly standards in church life and the challenges to faith from scientific discoveries in the mid-nineteenth century, a need for Church reform was felt. Historical studies and the Romantic movement had made Christians aware of what they regarded as an ideal strength and purity of church life in the early centuries and the Middle Ages. There were too many Anglican bishops in Ireland claiming an income and a seat in the House of Lords when there were few Anglicans living in their dioceses, so the Government planned to suppress ten Irish bishoprics. This was seen as unjustified interference from the State by those who gave high importance to the independence of the Church as a society created by God – the High Churchmen. Centred mostly in Oxford they started what became known as the Oxford Movement. Keble, Newman and Pusey were regarded as leaders. Although Henry Manning, John Henry Newman and Frederick Faber were eventually received into the Roman Catholic Church, many Anglo-Catholics remained in the Church of England, and their emphasis on personal prayer and holiness influenced all wings of that Church and many Nonconformists also. At the beginning of the movement, the dignity of their simple worship, with candles on the altar and robed choirs, shocked many, and they were attacked and persecuted. In the next generation, this turned into the ritualist movement, with attempts to reconstruct what they regarded as medieval English traditions of worship. The rediscovery by the Oxford Movement of the importance of dignified ceremonial has changed church life all over the world.

13.00–16.30. Services Sunday 08.00, 10.00, 11.15, 18.00; Monday to Saturday 07.15, 07.35, 18.00; Wednesday 13.00. Cathedral time is five minutes later than standard time. Tel. 276492

Corpus Christi daily 13.30–16.30. For services Tel. 276700

Exeter daily 14.00–17.00. Services Sunday 09.00, 18.00; Monday to Friday 09.00, 18.55, except Tuesday and Friday 18.15. Tel. 279600

Hertford daily 10.00–12.00, 14.00–dusk. Services Sunday 17.45.Tel. 279400

Jesus daily 14.00–16.30. Services Sunday 17.45; Tuesday 08.15; Thursday 08.15, 09.00. Tel. 279700, Fax. 279700

Lincoln Monday to Saturday 14.00–17.00; Sunday, BH 11.00–17.00. Services Sunday 17.45. Tel. 279800

Clive Staples Lewis (1898–1963)

C.S. Lewis, lecturer at University College and Magdalene College, Oxford, and Professor of English at Cambridge, wrote the story of his own life in *Surprised by Joy*. He became widely known through his radio talks and popular books as one who could explain traditional Christian beliefs in a simple rational way. His Narnia books for children use the extended metaphor of Aslan the lion to represent Christ, and the space travel trilogy also use fiction to convey Christian truth. *The Screwtape Letters* are a witty series of messages purporting to be from a senior devil to a junior devil instructing him how to tempt a newly converted Christian. The play and film *Shadowlands* have made his thinking and the story of his marriage known to an even wider public. He died at his home on the Woodstock Road in Oxford.

Magdalen October to June 14.00–18.00 or dusk; late June to September 12.00–18.00. Tel. 276000

Merton Monday to Friday 14.00–16.00; Saturday to Sunday 10.00–16.00. Services Sunday 09.00, 18.00. Tel. 276310

New daily Easter to October 11.00–17.00; October to Easter 14.00–16.00. Services Sunday 18.00; Monday to Saturday 18.15. Tel. 279555

Oriel daily 14.00–17.00. Services Sunday 09.00, 18.00; for other times Tel. 276555

Queen's by prior appointment only, afternoons. Services Sunday 18.15; Friday 18.30. Tel. 279120

St Edmund Hall daily dawn–dusk (functions permitting). For services Tel. 279000

Trinity daily 10.00–12.00, 14.00–16.00. Services Sunday 18.00. Tel. 279900

St Mary's Church Services Sunday 10.00 (University Sermon), 11.00, 18.00; Monday to Thursday 12.15; Wednesday 18.15 sung evensong; from July to September Sunday 10.00 only. Tel. 279111. http://www.university-church.ox.ac.uk

St Michael at the Northgate daily April to October 10.00–17.00; November to March 10.00–16.00. Services Sunday 08.00, 10.30, 18.00. Tel. 240940

DORCHESTER-ON-THAMES (Oxfordshire)

Southeast of Oxford, off the A4074, is Dorchester-on-Thames in Oxfordshire, not to be confused with Dorchester in Dorset. It was first occupied in the Bronze Age; the Romans built a town here and called it

Dorocinum. It became the capital of Wessex, and in the seventh century St Birinus established a cathedral church. In 869 it became the cathedral for the great Diocese of Mercia, stretching from the Thames to the Humber. The Normans moved the centre of this diocese to Lincoln. In 1140 a new church was built, and the nave of the present **Abbey Church of St Peter and St Paul** is the west end of this church. New aisles and a new east end were added in the following centuries. It is still a huge building, which seems incongruous now in such a small village. Most of the church is in the Decorated style. The enormous east window contains some glass dating from 1340; scenes from the life of Christ are carved into the stone tracery. In the north wall is a fourteenth-century Jesse-Tree window, with the branches of the tree carved into the stone tracery, and the descendants of Jesse shown, sometimes in the stone and sometimes in the

glass panes. On the south side of the sanctuary are pinnacled sedilia, for the clergy to sit on, with thirteenth-century windows let into the back of them, and a piscina for washing the chalice after Mass. The rare lead font is from 1170, with images of the apostles, and is one of the finest in England. Behind it is a fourteenth-century corbel showing sleeping monks with the devil blowing a horn, as a warning against the sin of sloth. On a raised platform in the south aisle is an altar with wall paintings from the fourteenth century; there is another mural in the Lady Chapel, with scenes from the life of St Birinus; the oldest glass in the Abbey, dating from around 1225–50, is a roundel of the consecration of Birinus, situated in the northeast chapel. Recent excavations have revealed foundations of earlier churches, and the complete skeleton of a twelfth-century abbot. Work is well advanced to restore the shrine of St Birinus in the

---

St Birinus (d. 649/50)

Birinus was consecrated a bishop in Genoa, and landed in Wessex in 634. Birinus was successful in converting the West Saxons to the faith, and baptized King Cynegils of Wessex in the river at Dorchester-on-Thames. The Christian King Oswald of Northumbria joined with King Cynegils to give Dorchester to Birinus as the seat for his bishopric. In 647 or 648 he founded a church in Winchester, the predecessor of Winchester Cathedral.

southeast chapel, so that Dorchester may once again become a place of pilgrimage, and a centre for prayer for Christian unity and world peace. West of the Abbey is the Abbey guest house, now a well-displayed historical museum.

Opening Times and Service Times
St Peter and St Paul daily 09.00–19.00 or dusk. Services Sunday 08.00, 10.15. Tel. 01865 340007. http://www.dorchester-abbey.org.uk

TEWKESBURY
(Gloucestershire)

Tewkesbury is near to Junction 9 on the M5. **Tewkesbury Abbey** has a Norman tower which is 40 metres (132 feet) high, the largest Norman tower in the world. There was a Saxon Benedictine monastery here in the eighth century, but hardly anything of that survived a sacking by the Danes. The new abbey was founded in 1092 by a Norman nobleman, and the exterior recessed arch of the west front, at nearly 20 metres (65 feet) high, is the largest of its type in England. The nave has 14 solid Norman pillars, and a fourteenth-century stone vault which replaced an earlier timber roof. The choir has an impressive ceiling and stained-glass windows dating from 1335. There are beautiful memorials, and also the macabre Wakeman Cenotaph which shows the corpse of a bishop being consumed by enormous worms; the intention apparently was to warn the living to do good to others while they still had time. At the Dissolution of the Monasteries, the townspeople of Tewkesbury saved the Abbey from destruction by buying it for £453. Outside, the Abbey House and Gatehouse remain from the complex of monastic buildings.

Opening Times and Service Times
Tewkesbury Abbey all year Sunday 07.30–19.00; Monday to Saturday 07.30–18.00 (summer); 07.30–17.30 (winter). Services Sunday 08.00, 09.15, 11.00, 18.00. Evensong term time Monday to Thursday 17.00. Tel. 01684 850959, Fax. 273113. http://www.tewkesburyabbey.org.uk

GLOUCESTER
(Gloucestershire)

Gloucester is pronounced 'GLOSS-tuh', or by a real countryman even 'GLAS-trr'. Like most towns whose names end in '-cester', it was a Roman garrison, which became a colony for retired Roman soldiers, and an important trading post for ships coming up the River Severn. In Norman times it was of political importance

---

George Whitefield (1714–70)

Whitefield (WIT-field) was a Gloucester man who was influenced by the Wesleys and followed them to Georgia, USA, where he founded an orphanage. When he returned to England he began preaching in the open air and attracted large crowds; he also raised considerable sums for his orphanage. He was possibly a better preacher than the Wesleys, but his theology was narrow and Calvinist, and he disputed their offer of free salvation. The churches he founded through the patronage of Selina, Countess of Huntingdon, 'The Countess of Huntingdon's Connexion', did not survive, although the Calvinistic Methodists of Wales trace their origins to Whitefield, and his influence in America was enormous.

---

and in the Middle Ages a religious centre. It is approached from Junctions 11 or 11a of the M5. The **Cathedral** is west of the Roman roads called Southgate and Northgate. Here a Saxon abbey was founded in the seventh century, but replaced by Norman Benedictines beginning in 1069. King Edward II was murdered at the nearby Berkeley (BARK-lee) Castle in 1327; his body was welcomed into Gloucester Abbey and his shrine became a place of pilgrimage. The donations of the pilgrims paid for the refashioning of the Abbey in the new Perpendicular style; Henry VIII made it into a cathedral. The mid-fifteenth-century **tower** lifts its delicate pinnacles high above the **College Green** and the medieval **St Mary's Gate**. Inside the Cathedral, the sturdy pillars, reddened at the base by a fire in 1122, and the zigzag mouldings of the **nave** betray its Norman origins, but in the **choir**, the fine Perpendicular panels and tracery have been added on top and hide the Norman structure. Internal flying buttresses support the tower. The **east window**, from around 1350, commemorating the Battle of Crecy, 24 metres (almost 80 feet) high, is the tallest medieval window in Britain. The **Lady Chapel**, added in the fifteenth century, is full of light. **King Edward II's effigy**, north of the choir, has a delicate stone canopy from the fourteenth century. In the **presbytery** is the **tomb of Robert II**, the eldest son of William the Conqueror, who died in 1134, with a painted wooden effigy, made in 1290, of him in semi-warlike pose as a crusader. There is a

Whispering Gallery, entered from the north transept, where the echo enables even the softest sounds to travel across the vaulting. The **cloisters** of 1367 were the first example of fan-vaulting in England; they contain the **lavatorium** where the monks washed before meals. Leading off the cloister is the **Chapter House**. The **Three Choirs Festival** rotates each year between Gloucester, Hereford and Worcester cathedrals, and several great choral works received their first performance here.

Opening Times and Service Times
Gloucester Cathedral Monday to Friday 07.30–18.00; Saturday to Sunday, BH 07.00–18.00. Services Sunday 07.40, 08.00, 10.15, 12.15, 15.00; Monday to Friday 08.00, 08.35, 17.30; Wednesday 07.30, 12.45; Saturday 16.30. Tel. 01452 528095, Fax. 300469. http://www.gloucestercathedral. uk.com

HEREFORD
(Herefordshire)

The mostly agricultural county of Herefordshire (HERry-fud-shuh) contains some delightful scenery formed by the valley of the River Wye, and in the west the Black Mountains rise on the Welsh Borders, guarded since ancient times by the earthwork of Offa's Dyke. Hereford was a military garrison to defend the English border against the Welsh, strategically placed on the River Wye. The Saxons made it into a religious centre. In 794, King Offa of Mercia in central England offered his daughter in marriage to Ethelbert the King of East Anglia. But on the eve of the wedding, Ethelbert was beheaded by the unscrupulous Offa; legend has it that his ghost asked for the body to be buried in Hereford. There is a wonderful **memorial brass** in the **Cathedral** showing the decapitated monarch holding his head, literally, in his hands.

The Normans began building on the site of the Saxon Cathedral with a large **western tower**; not to be out-done, the builders in the fourteenth century added a larger **central tower**. Then in 1786 the Norman tower collapsed and destroyed most of the nave. Remaining Norman portions are the south transept and the impressive **Norman arches** at the east end of the nave. The rest of the building, depending on how you look at it, is either a hotch-potch of styles, or an example of how building from different periods can blend into a satisfying whole! The **choir** contains fourteenth-century choir stalls with misericords, and 'King Stephen's chair'

St Thomas de Cantelupe (c. 1218–82)

As Chancellor of Oxford he supported the Barons against King Henry III, and after the king's defeat at Lewes in 1265 he became Chancellor of England. In 1275 he was made Bishop of Hereford and adviser to King Edward I. He opposed simony and nepotism (the appointment to church office of those who bought their posts or had powerful relations), and defended his rights as a bishop against the barons and even the Archbishop of Canterbury. He was made a saint by popular demand in 1320.

from about 1200. The **north transept** is one of the finest examples of the Early English style, with high soaring windows. It holds the tomb of St Thomas of Hereford; it is one of the best-preserved medieval shrines in the country. In the Norman **south transept** is a sixteenth-century German painting of the **Adoration of the Magi,** and a rare early example of a **fireplace** in a church; our ancestors must have worn their outdoor clothes in church and stamped up and down during the service, if they went at all in winter. The cathedral's treasures are displayed in the modern **Mappa Mundi Centre,** entered from the cloisters. The Mappa Mundi is a map of the world, with Jerusalem at the centre, drawn in 1289 on parchment, measuring 165 cm by 135 cm (65 by 53 inches), the largest known example from such an early date. Donors including John Paul Getty, Jnr, gave £2.5 million to build an air-conditioned centre to preserve it in Hereford, with an interactive display explaining the map for visitors. Also on display are a **casket** that used to contain the alleged remains of St Thomas à Becket; a **Saxon Gospel** on vellum from the seventh century; and the world's largest **chained library,** some 1400 books and manuscripts attached to the shelves by chains to prevent theft.

Opening Times and Service Times

Hereford Cathedral Monday to Saturday 09.30–17.00. **Mappa Mundi Exhibition and Chained Library** Monday to Saturday 10.00–16.15 (summer); Sunday 11.00–15.15 (summer); Monday to Saturday 11.00–15.15 (winter); closed Sunday (winter). Services Sunday 08.00, 10.00, 11.30, 15.30; Monday to Saturday 07.30, 08.00, 17.30. Tel. 01432 374200, Fax. 374220. http://www. herefordcathedral.co.uk

KILPECK
(Herefordshire)

Eight miles (13 km) southwest of Hereford is the hamlet of **Kilpeck** with, beside the mound where a Norman castle used to stand, an amazing Norman church almost unchanged since it was built in 1135, replacing a Saxon church of 650. Around the south door in particular there are intricate carvings in sharp relief of the tree of life, dragons and angels. On the outside of the church there is a frieze with around 70 carvings of human and animal heads. The west wall carries dragon heads of Viking type, like the prows of their ships. Nowhere else in the country has such a wealth of Norman carving survived intact. Possibly one of the Norman knights from the castle returned from the crusades with some relics, and decided to build a worthy church so that pilgrims could visit the shrines. Kilpeck is signposted off the A49 or the A465, and is well worth the journey along the narrow country lanes.

Service Times
Kilpeck Church Sunday 10.00 every three weeks, check board for dates. Tel. 01981 240079

Corbels at Kilpeck, Herefordshire

COOKHAM
(Berkshire)

Between the River Thames and the A4158 is the attractive riverside village of Cookham, with red-brick cottages set round a green. It is notable for its parish church (**Holy Trinity**), and for the **Stanley Spencer Gallery**, in the former Wesleyan chapel that he attended as a boy, devoted to the highly original painter Stanley Spencer (1891–1959), who reinterpreted biblical stories, particularly the Resurrection of Christ, as though they had happened in contemporary Cookham. There is no doubt that he regarded Cookham as a holy place, though one of his greatest works is at Burghclere in Hampshire.

Opening Times and Service Times
Holy Trinity Church Services Sunday 08.00, 09.30, 18.30; Monday to Saturday 09.00; Monday 10.00; Wednesday 10.00, 18.30; Thursday 07.30. Tel. 01628 529661. http://www. holytrinitycookham.org
Stanley Spencer Gallery daily Easter to October 10.30–17.30; November to Easter Saturday to Sunday, BH 11.00–17.00. Tel. 01628 520890. http://www. stanleyspencer.org

OLNEY
(Buckinghamshire)

North of Milton Keynes on the A509 is the small town of Olney, where John Newton and William Cowper produced an influential book known as the *Olney Hymns*; you can visit the **Cowper and Newton Museum** in Orchard Side, Market Place. **St Peter and St Paul's Church** is on the edge of the town, on the banks of the River Ouse; most of it was built between 1330 and 1400. Olney is the birthplace of the architect George Gilbert Scott, who altered the east end of the church and designed the east window; the galleries were demolished at the same time. Cowper used to sit in the north gallery to hear Newton preach; Newton's pulpit is preserved at the west end of the south aisle. Windows show each of them, and also Dr Henry Gauntlett, who wrote over 1000 hymn tunes, including 'Once in Royal David's City'. Newton is buried to the south of the chancel. The church is the finishing line for the traditional Shrove Tuesday pancake race.

Opening Times and Service Times
Cowper and Newton Museum March to Christmas Tuesday to Saturday, BH 10.00–13.00, 14.00–17.00. Tel. 01234 711516, Fax. 0870 1640662. Email cnm@mkheritage.co.uk
St Peter and St Paul's Services Sunday 08.00 (2, 4), 08.30 (2, 4, 5), 09.00 (1, 3, 5), 10.00 (all); Tuesday, Friday 09.15, 17.00; Wednesday 09.30. Tel. 01234 713308

John Newton (1725–1807); William Cowper (1731–1800)

The young John Newton was captured by the press-gang and compelled to serve in the British Navy, where he had an adventurous career. In 1748 he was converted, and soon obtained the post of surveyor of tides at Liverpool. He was influenced at this time by George Whitefield, and studied Latin, Hebrew, Greek and Syriac. He was ordained in 1764 and made curate of Olney, where with William Cowper he wrote the *Olney Hymns*. Among his most popular hymns are 'Amazing Grace', 'Glorious things of thee are spoken' and 'How sweet the name of Jesus sounds'. For the last 27 years of his life he was rector of St Mary Woolnoth in London, and he supported William Wilberforce in his campaign against slavery.

The son of a Hertfordshire Rector, William Cowper became a barrister but began to suffer suicidal mental breakdowns. He was comforted in the home of a retired clergyman in Huntingdon, who died, and Cowper now moved to Olney with the widow, Mary Unwin. John Newton persuaded him to write hymns, and some of his best verse is among the 67 he contributed to the *Olney Hymns*: 'God moves in a mysterious way'; 'Hark, my soul, it is the Lord'; 'O for a closer walk with God'; and 'Jesus, where'er thy people meet'. His increasing insanity prevented him marrying Mrs Unwin, but she cared for him and persuaded him to write secular poetry also, including *The Ballad of John Gilpin*. It has been said that Cowper's hymns are written with 'the pen of misery dipped in the ink of despair', yet his flashes of insight into the love of God make them an encouragement for all who seek to pray out of the pit of depression.

WING; NORTH MARSTON (Buckinghamshire)

Wing is off the A418 west of Leighton Buzzard. **All Saints** seems to be an early Saxon church based on the pattern of a Roman basilica or law-court, with the altar replacing the magistrate's seat in the apse. Beneath the apse is a seventh-century crypt, which may be the 'shrine with relics' referred to in her will by Aelgifu, the founder of the church and sister-in-law of King Edgar. The round chancel arch, at 6.4 metres (21 feet) wide, is one of the widest Saxon arches in the country – there was some advanced technology during the 'Dark Ages'. Nothing was altered until the addition of a south aisle in the fourteenth century, and the insertion of a fifteenth-century clerestory and apse windows. The roof is in the Perpendicular style, and every surface is carved with saints, kings and musicians, which are hard to see without binoculars. Doorways high in the wall appear to have led in the tenth century to a gallery which may have been for dignitaries.

Off the A413 north of Aylesbury is **North Marston**. Now here's a curious story. The Rector of North Marston from 1290 to 1314 was Sir John Schorne. He was revered in his lifetime as a healer and a saint. Tradition has it that he had trapped the devil in a boot, which may be the origin of the 'Jack-in-a-box' toy. It is also said that during a drought he struck the ground with his staff and a spring appeared; perhaps an early example of dowsing? The spring is in Schorne Lane, off Church Street; it was said to have healing properties, but today it is covered with a wooden shutter, and the pump beside it no longer works. Instead the villagers have constructed an attractive village pond down the road. Sick people who

had asked for Sir John's prayers while he was alive continued to do so when his bones were buried in a niche beside the altar in the south aisle of the church, and so many pilgrims came that his relics were moved to Windsor in 1478, to become a centre for pilgrimage there until the focus shifted to the shrine of Henry VI. In compensation the Canons of Windsor gave North Marston a considerable sum to improve their church.

Service Times
All Saints, Wing Sunday 08.00, 10.00, 18.00 (2); Thursday 09.30. Tel. 01296 688496
St Mary's, North Marston Sunday 10.00. Tel. 01296 670298

CHALFONT ST GILES; STOKE POGES (Buckinghamshire)

In **Chalfont St Giles**, south of Amersham between the A355 and the A413, you can visit **Milton's Cottage**, where he stayed to escape the Great Plague in London, and where he completed *Paradise Lost* and began *Paradise Regained*. You can also visit the nearby group of houses called **Jordan's**, where the Quaker William Penn stayed before travelling to found Pennsylvania. The seventeenth-century meeting house is in almost original condition, and outside are buried William Penn, his first

William Penn (1644–1718)

The son of Admiral Sir William Penn (1621–70), he was sent down from Oxford for refusing to conform with the Anglican establishment after the Restoration of the Monarchy. In 1666 he heard a sermon that convinced him of the truth of Quakerism, then wrote books criticizing orthodox Christian doctrine, and was imprisoned for it in the Tower of London. While in prison he wrote the classic *No Cross, No Crown* (1669). From 1677 he and two other Friends became the Trustees of West New Jersey in north America, and gave it a constitution which would permit all forms of worship which were compatible with monotheism and religious liberty. He was one of 12 Quakers who in 1681 bought East New Jersey, and in the same year he was granted Pennsylvania. He visited America from 1681 to 1684 and 1699 to 1701 but in each case returned to England to protect the liberty of the colonies. In 1693 he wrote a book advocating a European Parliament.

and second wives and their children. The simplicity and peace are almost tangible. George Fox and William Penn worshipped in the kitchen of Jordans Farm, now Old Jordans Guest House; opposite is the Mayflower Barn, reputed to be constructed from the timbers of the Pilgrim Fathers' ship.

Stoke Poges, just north of Slough (rhymes with How), is a holy place because here Thomas Gray (1716–71) composed his poem 'Elegy in a Country Churchyard':

The curfew tolls the knell of passing day,
The lowing herd winds slowly o'er the lea . . .

It is still a peaceful spot, and the poet is buried in his mother's tomb outside the east wall. The church has two remarkable windows: the seventeenth-century 'naked cyclist' in the west window, and a sombre but vividly coloured piece of nineteenth-century sentimentality about a dying child and an angel, on the south side.

Opening Times and Service Times
Jordan's Quaker Meeting House Wednesday to Sunday, BH (summer); Saturday to Sunday (winter) 10.00–13.00, 14.15–18.00 or dusk. Tel. 01494 874146. http://www.oldjordans. co.uk
Milton's Cottage March to October Tuesday to Sunday

10.00–13.00, 14.00–18.00. Tel. 01494 872313. http://www. miltonscottage.org
Stoke Poges Church Services Sunday 08.00, 10.00 (1, 3), 11.15 (2, 4, 5), 18.30. Tel. 01753 642261

LITTLEMORE (Oxfordshire)

When John Henry Newman (see p. 131) was appointed Vicar of the University Church of St Mary in Oxford in 1828, one of his duties, which he took seriously and enjoyed, was to care for the village of **Littlemore**. There was no church, no school and no vicarage, so he took lodgings and obtained funds to build a school and a church. After the furore caused when he wrote Tract 90, he retreated to Littlemore and took a lease on an old barn, which had been turned into cottages and a stable, and converted them into a library and a **college**. It was here in 1845 that he completed his book *The Development of Doctrine*, and was received into the Roman Catholic Church. Today the College has been restored, including his room with its bare brick floor, and the chapel furnished as he knew it; there is a small community, and pilgrims come to honour Newman and pray for understanding and unity between Christians. Follow the signs to Littlemore from the

Oxford bypass at the Cowley roundabout, and turn left at the church; the college is on the corner of Cowley Road and College Lane.

Opening Times
Littlemore College Monday to Friday 10.30–12.00, 14.00–17.00; Saturday to Sunday (except last Sunday) 14.00–17.00. Tel. 01865 779743, Fax. 773397. http://www.thework-fso.org

ABINGDON (Oxfordshire)

South from Oxford on the A34 and A4183 lies the substantial market town of Abingdon. It began as a fortified settlement for the tribal Britons, and claims to be the oldest town in continuous occupation in England. An abbey was founded there in the seventh century, and sacked twice by Danish raiding parties. Under the Normans it became larger than Westminster Abbey is today, but Henry VIII dismantled it and used the stone for his own building projects, so all that remain are the fifteenth-century **Chequer Hall** and the **Long Gallery**, now used as the Unicorn Theatre, and the **Abbey Gate**. This stands beside **St Nicholas's Church**, which was built in about 1177 by the Abbey for their lay servants, tenants and possibly pilgrims. The west doorway has round Norman

St Edmund Rich (c. 1180–1240)

St Edmund was born at Abingdon in Oxfordshire. He taught logic at Oxford, and St Edmund Hall in that University is believed to have been built on the site of his Oxford home. As Archbishop of Canterbury he attempted, without success, to resist royal mismanagement of the Church's property, and the taxes imposed by the Pope, so he retired to Pontigny in self-imposed exile.

arches, but the blind arcades have the new pointed arches. **St Helen's** is probably on the site of the first church from the seventh century, but today it is mostly thirteenth-century work that we see. It was the church of the townspeople, and their rallying point when, furious at the Abbey's control of burial rights and local markets, they set fire to the Abbey in the fourteenth century. Because of the number of trades' guilds, each with their own chapel, the church has five aisles and is broader than it is long. Its glory is the painted ceiling, from 1391, in the Lady Chapel, the second aisle from the north. It is a unique treatment of the Jesse Tree, with King David and his father Jesse in the eastern panel on the south side, and their descendants in successive panels down one side and up the other, ending with St Joseph, and then Jesus on an unusual cross shaped like a lily. The organ case from 1727 has a huge wooden King David playing

passionately on the harp. Close to St Helen's are three sets of **almshouses,** founded in 1446 (with a long timber gallery), 1707 and 1718.

Service Times
St Helen's Sunday 08.00, 10.00, 18.30; Monday to Saturday 09.00, 17.30; Monday 07.15; Wednesday 10.30; Friday 12.15
St Nicholas's Sunday 08.00, 11.00. Tel. (both) 01235 520144

FAIRFORD (Gloucestershire)

The county of Gloucester straddles the Cotswold Hills, and so contains many towns and villages built of the glorious golden Cotswold stone. On the A417 east of Cirencester is the village of Fairford. Of all England's wonderful parish churches **St Mary's** is one you mustn't miss, because of its glorious stained glass, some of the best in the country, dating from about 1500. The windows truly act as 'the poor man's Bible', because they tell the whole story of salvation from beginning to end, in colours that could inspire even those who could not read. The 12 apostles face the 12 prophets, and in the clerestory the 12 martyrs are opposed to 12 persecutors of the Church. The life of Jesus is shown in the windows of the chancel. For many people their favourite is the window showing the Ascension, with the disciples gazing up into heaven and just the feet of Jesus appearing in the top of the window as he rises into the clouds. There are also some curious misericords.

Service Times
St Mary's Sunday 08.00, 09.30, 18.00; except on the last Sunday 08.00, 10.00, 11.00, 18.00. Tel. 01285 712611. Email st.mary-fairford@btconnect.com

CIRENCESTER
(Gloucestershire)

The A417 joins the A419 in Cirencester (SIGH-run-sess-tuh), a market town serving a large area and known as 'the capital of the Cotswolds'. The Romans founded a fort called Corinium at the junction of Ermin Street, Akeman Street and the Fosse Way; by the second century it had grown into the second largest city in Roman Britain. There was a Saxon abbey; its site is now occupied by the small park called the Abbey Grounds, where there is a fragment of the Roman wall. The **Church of St John the Baptist** is the largest in Gloucestershire, built at the expense of wool merchants who had grown rich from the flocks of Cotswold sheep. The nave was originally twelfth century, rebuilt in 1520. The lofty tower was built between 1400 and 1420; the three-storey porch which leads in from the market place served at one time as the town hall. The nave gives an impression of great space, light and height; angels on the tall piers bear the coats of arms of those who paid for the reconstruction of the church from 1516 to 1530. There is a stone wineglass-shaped pulpit carved in around 1450 – one of very few pulpits in Britain to have survived from pre-Reformation days – complete with sermon-timer; and a wealth of memorials and memorial brasses. North of the chancel is the Chapel of St Catherine, originally built in 1150, with superb fan-vaulting installed 350 years later, and the brightly coloured fragments of a fifteenth-century wall painting.

Service Times
Church of St John the Baptist Sunday 08.00, 10.00, 18.00; Monday to Saturday 16.45. Tel. 01285 659317

HAILES ABBEY
(Gloucestershire)

The next holy place we visit would be a little hard to find

except that brown signs with the English Heritage symbol point the way. From Stow-in-the-Wold, you turn west along the B4077 to Stanway. A short distance further on you turn left (south) onto the B4632, and **Hailes Abbey** is a mile (2 km) east of this road. Founded in 1246, this Cistercian Abbey was once a celebrated pilgrimage site, crammed with visitors wishing to see a phial which was supposed to be filled with the blood of Christ. Now all that you can see are the foundations, some arches from the cloister, the north wall of the refectory, and some finds which are kept in the museum on the site; the information panels show some helpful reconstructions.

Opening Times
Hailes Abbey (English Heritage, jointly with National Trust) daily April to September 10.00–18.00; October 10.00–17.00. Tel. 01242 602398

PRINKNASH
(Gloucestershire)

Turning off the A46 southeast of Gloucester, signs lead to Prinknash (pronounced PRINN-ush). The **Old Abbey** was founded in 1096 and rebuilt in 1520; it is now used as a retreat centre. The modern buildings of the **New Abbey** house a flourishing Roman Catholic community of Benedictine monks. The community was founded in the 1890s in the Church of England, and eventually settled on Caldey Island, in Wales, in 1906. In 1913 most of the brothers were received into the Roman Catholic Church; in 1928 they moved to Prinknash, and the new abbey was completed in 1972. There are about 25 monks. They have an important ministry of teaching and prayer, and support themselves by selling craft work, including the pottery for which they are famed.

Opening Times and Service Times
Prinknash Abbey all year Sunday 07.30–19.00; Monday to Saturday 07.30–18.00 (summer); 07.30–17.30 (winter). Services Sunday 06.30, 08.15, 12.20, 18.00, 20.10; Monday to Saturday 05.00, 06.30, 08.15, 12.20, 18.00, 20.10. To book retreats Tel. 01452 813592. http://www.prinknashabbey.org. uk

DEERHURST
(Gloucestershire)

Just west of the A38 south of Tewkesbury, the B4213 takes you to a turning leading to the tiny village of Deerhurst. This has two important Anglo-Saxon buildings: the first you come to is **St Mary's Church**, parts of which may date from an eighth-century monastery. Several features of the architecture are clear indications of its Saxon origin, and more clearly seen here than in many other churches of the period: a fine Saxon font; herring-bone patterns in the rough stones of the walls; a triangular-headed window leading from the tower into the nave; and carvings of beasts. The arch in the east wall originally led to an apse, which is now ruined, but high on the exterior surface is a carving of an angel. The font is acknowledged as the finest Saxon font in existence. Above the inner door into the church is a unique carving of the Virgin Mary with the Child Jesus represented as still within her womb; the features are blank because the detail was originally added with paint. St Alfege, the Archbishop of Canterbury who was martyred in 1012, had been a monk at Deerhurst Priory. Here a treaty was drawn up between King Edmund Ironside and King Canute the Dane in 1016. There is a fifteenth-century brass commemorating Sir John Cassey, his wife, and her pet dog, Terri, the only named animal on a medieval brass. Nearby is **Odda's Chapel**, which was built by Earl Odda in 1056 with a simple nave and chancel; absorbed later into the adjacent farmhouse, which it served as a kitchen; and only identified as a church in the nineteenth century.

Opening Times and Service Times
Odda's Chapel (English Heritage) daily April to September 10.00–18.00; October to March 10.00–16.00 **St Mary's** Services Sunday 10.30 (2), 18.00 (4). Tel. 01684 292562

ABBEY DORE (Herefordshire)

Abbey Dore is well signposted on the B4347, 12 miles (20 km) southwest of Hereford. It was originally the site of a Cistercian Abbey, founded in 1147; in 1632 the local landowner, Lord Scudamore, commissioned John Abel to restore the lofty chancel. He carved the magnificent screen out of Hereford Oak, and used 204 tons of timber to rebuild the roof. Only fragments of the nave and the other monastic buildings remain, but the chancel and transepts form an enormous building to find in the depths of the Hereford countryside. It is now one of very few out of the many former Cistercian churches in England still in use for regular worship.

Service Times
Abbey Dore Sunday 09.00 every three weeks; first Wednesday 16.00. Tel. 01981 240079. http://www.doreabbey.org.uk

SHOBDON
(Herefordshire)

West of Leominster is the hamlet of Shobdon, where **St John's Church** was apparently a richly decorated Norman building like Kilpeck, until in 1752–6 Sir Richard Bateman demolished it, using some arches in a much weathered folly nearby, and built in its place a flight of rococo fancy, the only such church in England. It was probably influenced by Horace Walpole's Gothic villa at Strawberry Hill in Old Windsor. The arches, the pews, the window frames, and the triple-decker pulpit are all distinguished by elaborate S-shaped curves, known as 'ogee' curves, picked out in pastel blue-grey against the white walls and ceiling. The Bateman family pew in the south transept is complete with fireplace; their servants in the north transept had to do without. The church is approached down a fine avenue of lime-trees from a turning off the B4362.

Opening Times and Service Times

St John's Church closes May to October 19.30; November to April 16.00. For service times Tel. 01544 230525

The Western Midlands

In the heart of England, but west of the spine of hills that runs down the centre of the country, are a group of ancient counties, and one new county which has been carved out of them and given the name of the West Midlands. They contain some cities and towns that used to be industrial and grimy – 'The Black Country' – but have now been much improved, and from them you can reach some of England's most attractive countryside.

WORCESTER
(Worcestershire)

Worcester (pronounced WOO-stuh, with a short 'oo' as in 'wood') is famous for its porcelain. The cricket-pitch beside the River Severn has as its background the great sandstone **Cathedral**, standing photogenically in a bend of the river. You enter the cathedral precincts through the fortified **Edgar Tower**, built to defend the entrance to the medieval monastery. St Oswald established a Saxon monastery here in 983. The **crypt** was built for the Cathedral begun in 1084 by St Wulstan, and is the largest Norman crypt in the country; much of the rest of the Cathedral was reconstructed in the fourteenth century. The **nave** shows the transition between the Norman style and pointed Gothic arches; the carvings of fruit on the pillars were started by stonemasons from Lincoln, most of whom died

in the Black Death, and they were finished off by less skilled workmen. The **choir** is of Early English architecture, and a very fine example of the style; with slender pillars and intricately worked choir stalls. Among the many monuments are the **Tomb of King John** (d. 1216) in front of the high altar in the choir, between the tombs of St Wulstan and St Oswald, as he requested; and the fourteenth-century **Beauchamp** (BEE-chum) tomb in the nave. The design of **Prince Arthur's Chantry** is late Perpendicular, with delicate tracery; it was built in 1504 by King Henry VII for his son, who died during his honeymoon with Catherine of Aragon, who was later to be married to Arthur's brother Henry VIII. In the **southeast transept** is a fine alabaster statue of the **Virgin and Child** dating from around 1470. The **cloisters** date from the 1374 reconstruction; from there

THE WESTERN MIDLANDS

0   25 miles (40 km.)

DERBYSHIRE

STAFFORDSHIRE

SHROPSHIRE

WEST MIDLANDS

WORCESTERSHIRE

WARWICKSHIRE

+Eyam
M1
+Cheadle + Tissington
+ Ashbourne
+ Oswestry M6
Melbourne
A5
+ Shrewsbury
+ Hoar Cross
M54
+ LICHFIELD
A5 +Polesworth
M42
+ Birmingham
M6
+ Ludlow + Kidderminster COVENTRY
+Gt Witley
+ Warwick
+ WORCESTER + Stratford-upon-Avon
Malvern + M40
+ Pershore
M5 + Evesham
M50

St Wulfstan (c.1009–95)

Wulfstan (or Wulstan) was for 25 years a member of a monastery at Worcester, where he was so admired for his humility that he was elected Bishop to popular acclaim; but he was so humble that it was hard to persuade him to accept the post. Once enthroned, however, he administered the diocese with great efficiency, and helped Archbishop Lanfranc to suppress the slave trade between England and Ireland. He was the only Saxon bishop whom William the Conqueror allowed to remain in place when he appointed Norman bishops to the other sees.

you can enter the circular Norman **Chapter House** of about 1150, one of the first attempts to build vaulting without the support of a central shaft.

Opening Times and Service Times
Worcester Cathedral daily 07.30–18.00. Services Sunday 07.30, 08.00, 10.30, 16.00, 18.30; Monday to Tuesday, Thursday to Saturday 08.00, 17.30; Tuesday 13.05; Wednesday 08.00, 08.30, 13.05, 17.30; Friday 11.30. Tel. 01905 28854, Fax. 611139. Email info@worcestercathedral.org.uk; http://www.cofe-worcester.org.uk

COVENTRY
(West Midlands)

In Saxon times Coventry vied with Lichfield over which was to be regarded as the capital of the Kingdom of Mercia, and a Benedictine Priory was founded there in 1043 by Leofric, Earl of Mercia. The legendary story of Leofric's wife, Lady Godiva, riding naked through the streets on horseback – the citizens, with the exception of Peeping Tom, all averted their gaze – to persuade him to lessen the burden of taxes on the people, may also have some reminiscence of pre-Christian sacrifices on this holy spot to a horse god. The pious Godiva, real name Godgifu, survived her husband by ten years and gave money and land to the church. Recently, the archaeologists from the television programme *Time Team* discovered the foundations of the Saxon Cathedral.

Coventry prospered through the wool and cloth trade, and a new church was built in around 1200; it was made a cathedral in 1918, when the motor industry had given the city a new lease of life, and set ablaze when the city of Coventry was devastated in a bombing raid on 14 November 1940. The ruins of the **Old Cathedral** are joined to the new one, and are the site of the open-air re-enactment of the medieval Coventry Mystery Plays every three years. The soaring spire is the third highest in England. After the firestorm a fireman put two charred beams together in the shape of a cross; a replica forms the centrepiece of the east end of the ruined cathedral, with the simple words 'Father, forgive' chiselled beneath; not 'forgive them' or 'forgive us', just 'forgive'. The Coventry Litany of Reconciliation, with this response, is said here every Friday, and the Cross of Nails, formed of medieval nails picked up from the ashes of the roof, has been sent to many churches around the world which are willing to pray for reconciliation.

Mystery Plays

The re-enactment of the Last Supper in the Eucharist or Mass is a form of drama; in the Middle Ages the Church supported re-enactments of other Bible stories, either in church or on carts around the streets of the town. These evolved into the Passion Plays of Oberammergau and many other places, processions such as that at Bruges, and the Mystery Plays in England. The text of parts of the Cycles from York, Chester, Wakefield and Coventry has survived. Different scenes would be performed by the members of appropriate trade guilds. In this way, and through the stained-glass windows, the ordinary illiterate people of the Middle Ages probably knew more of the Bible than many educated people today. The well-known 'Coventry carol' was written to be sung by the women of Bethlehem, at the massacre of the innocents by King Herod, in the Coventry Mystery Plays: 'Lully, lullay, thou little tiny child'. It is a moving experience to attend a performance of the Coventry Cycle in the ruins of the old cathedral, with different scenes taking place in different areas.

The superb **New Cathedral of St Michael,** built alongside the old and consecrated in 1962, was designed by Sir Basil Spence; it uses modern materials yet retains the long, thin design of medieval cathedrals. The entrance to the porch linking the two cathedrals – from death to resurrection – is marked by Jacob Epstein's striking **bronze of St Michael Defeating the Devil** (Revelation 12.7). A glass screen forms the west wall of the new cathedral, with figures of saints and angels etched into the glass by John Hutton; we see Christ through the lives of the saints, for dominating the east wall is the great 23 metres (75 feet) high **tapestry of Christ in Glory** by Graham Sutherland. The figure of Christ is surrounded by the symbols of the four Gospels: angel for Matthew, lion for Mark, ox for Luke and eagle for John. Beneath are a tiny figure of Adam, a chalice, and a stark crucifix. There is also a modern gold cross on the **high altar** in front of the tapestry. The **choir stalls** are designed to remind us of Christ's crown of thorns. The **stained-glass windows,** representing the stages of life – birth, youth, maturity, old age and the afterlife – are only visible as you return from the altar.

The **font** is formed from a boulder brought from the hillside at Bethlehem; behind it is a window designed by John Piper representing Jesus the Light of God bursting into the world. On the walls are **texts** from the Bible carved in stone by Ralph Beyer, with bold irregular lettering inspired by the catacombs in Rome. The **Lady Chapel** houses a statue of the Virgin Mary, and on the left of it is a new **Millennium Chapel**; there is a mosaic of the Angel with the Shining Chalice in the **Chapel of Christ in Gethsemane**, and the **Chapel of Christ the Servant** has a hanging cross and a Crown of Thorns. The **Chapel of Unity**, a separate building though linked to the Cathedral and shaped like a crusader's tent, is controlled by a Joint Council formed from different denominations, and prayer for reunion is held there regularly. Below the cathedral are exhibition rooms and resource centres, a bookshop and the headquarters of the **International Centre of Reconciliation**. The consecration of the new cathedral was marked by the first performance of Benjamin Britten's specially written *War Requiem*, the greatest choral work of the twentieth century.

Opening Times and Service Times

Coventry Cathedral daily 09.00–18.00. Services Sunday 07.40, 08.00, 10.30, 17.00; Monday to Saturday 08.30, 12.00 (except Thursday), 12.40, 17.00. Tel. 02476 227597, Fax. 631448. Email information@coventrycathedral.org; http://www.coventrycathedral.org **International Centre for Reconciliation** Tel. 552654, Fax. 267004. Email reconciliation@globalnet.co.uk. Belgrade Theatre Mystery Plays 2003 and every three years Tel. 553055. http://www.belgrade.co.uk

LICHFIELD (Staffordshire)

The pretty cathedral city of Lichfield, 18 miles (29 km) north of Birmingham, originally a Roman town at the crossroads of the Riknild Street, the present A38, and Watling Street (now the A5), was for most of the Saxon period the capital of the enormous Kingdom of Mercia. For that reason St Chad made it his centre when he came down from Northumbria to evangelize the Midlands, though he spent most of his time on the move. He died here in 672, and a shrine was built for his relics; the Normans began a **cathedral** on the site in 1085, but the present red sandstone building originates mostly from 1195, and was largely rebuilt in the thirteenth and fourteenth centuries. The three **spires** of the cathedral – more than any other English cathedral, and known as 'the three sisters of the vale' – are visible from far outside the city. This is one of the smallest and most perfectly proportioned, and therefore probably the prettiest, of all the cathedrals of England. It was bombarded during the Civil War and the central spire collapsed in 1646. It was repaired in the 1660s, and the interior remodelled by Wyatt in the eighteenth century. But Sir Giles Gilbert Scott restored it to its medieval splendour between 1857 and 1901.

Its chief glory is the magnificent **west front**, with over 100 figures carved in the mellow red sandstone, representing biblical personalities, the ancestors of Christ, and English kings. Some of them are from the thirteenth century but the rest were replaced by Scott. The interior of the **nave** is quite narrow, with decorated **capitals** on the pillars, which lean out slightly, and coloured **roof bosses**; from the west of the nave you can see the full length of the Cathedral past the Transitional-style **crossing** and the **choir,** the first three bays of which were completed in the Early English style in the twelfth century, to the **Lady Chapel** and the fine sixteenth-

Doorway, Lichfield Cathedral

St Chad (d. 672)

The story of St Chad is told by the Venerable Bede. He was born in Northumbria and trained by St Aidan in the monastery of Lindisfarne. He studied in Ireland, and settled at the Abbey of Lastingham in Yorkshire which his brother St Cedd had founded; when Cedd died, Chad succeeded him as Abbot. St Wilfrid had been appointed Archbishop of York, and gone to France to seek consecration, but he was away a long time and King Oswy, fearing he would never return, appointed Chad as archbishop in his place, which he was not authorized to do. Chad went to Canterbury to be consecrated, but found there was no bishop there at the time, so he went on to be consecrated by the Bishop of the West Saxons and the other English bishops, and served faithfully in York for three years. Eventually Wilfrid did come back, and Archbishop Theodore of Canterbury declared that Chad's appointment was invalid. With glad humility Chad stepped down, saying that he had never desired the office but only accepted it out of obedience, and returned to Lastingham. But in the same year, 669, he was appointed Bishop of the Kingdom of Mercia, which stretched the full width of England from east to west, and spent his time travelling around his enormous diocese on foot, because he was too humble to ride. He chose Lichfield as his see city. Theodore, riding a horse, met Chad walking along the road one day, and the Archbishop dismounted and himself lifted Chad onto his own horse. Chad converted many of the pagan Mercians to Christianity by his example, and his popularity is shown by the number of churches dedicated to him.

century **Flemish glass** at the east end. These windows were in fact bought from the Cistercian Abbey of Herckenrode in Belgium in 1802. On the south side of the choir is the thirteenth-century Saint Chad's Head Chapel, where the head, covered in gold leaf, was displayed to pilgrims from the gallery. The **monuments** include Samuel Johnson, David Garrick and Erasmus Darwin. *The Sleeping Children* is a beautiful and tender alabaster carving by Sir Francis Chantrey. In the **Chapter House,** the Lichfield Gospels, an incomplete illustrated Anglo-Saxon manuscript the equal of the Lindisfarne Gospels and the Book of Kells, is displayed

Dr Samuel Johnson (1709–84)

Samuel Johnson was born above his father's bookshop in the market square in Lichfield. He went to Oxford, but never took his degree and returned to Staffordshire as a teacher. Moving to Birmingham he published his first articles in the *Birmingham Journal*, and married Elizabeth Porter, the widow of a friend and 20 years older than him. He had another go at teaching before moving with his wife to London, accompanied by young David Garrick – his star pupil, and later to become a famous actor. Eventually he was asked to compile a dictionary of the English language – a task that had never been attempted before – and which took him eight years until 1755 and nearly broke him financially and in health before it was finished. It was written with wit and humour, made his name, and the new king George III gave him a pension. In 1763 he met the Scot, James Boswell, who accompanied him on a tour of the Western Isles and wrote an account of their journey, and after Johnson's death, a *Life of Johnson*, which became the most famous biography in the English language. Johnson showed in his personal religion a deep sense of unworthiness, a strong faith, and a fear of enthusiasm.

from Easter to Christmas. Its decorations blend Coptic, Celtic and oriental influences. The **Cathedral Close** contains canons' houses, the **Deanery** of 1704 and a **Bishop's Palace** from 1687 which is now a school. In Breadmarket Street, near the Cathedral, is the **Samuel Johnson Museum**, in the house, built by his father in 1708, where he was born.

Opening Times and Service Times

Lichfield Cathedral daily 07.40–18.30. Services Sunday 08.00,10.30, 15.30; Monday to Friday 07.40, 09.30, 17.30; Saturday 09.30, 17.30. Tel. 01543 306100, Fax. 306109. Email enquiries@lichfield-cathedral.org; http://www.lichfield-cathedral.org **Samuel Johnson Museum** daily March to September, October to February Monday to Saturday 10.30–16.15. Tel. 01543 264972, Fax. 414779. Email sjmuseum@lichfield.gov.uk; http://www.lichfield.gov.uk/sjmuseum

KIDDERMINSTER; GREAT WITLEY (Worcestershire)

We can tell from its name that there was a minster at **Kidderminster**, possibly founded by St Chad in the seventh century. No trace of this remains, but the chancel and tower of the parish church of **St Mary's and All Saints** are fourteenth century, and were apparently not attached to each other, as the nave was built later to join them. A brass, which was originally in the chancel, celebrates with a Latin verse Sir John Phelp, who died after the siege of Harfleur in 1415. Outside the church (which stands on a hill by the A456 bypass) there is a statue of its most famous incumbent, Richard Baxter; his chair stands in the sanctuary, but his table is in the URC 'Baxter Church' and his pulpit in the Unitarian Church. Over where the pulpit used to stand in the parish church is written on the pillar:

> We preach not ourselves but Jesus Christ our Lord. We are not as the most part are which chop and change with the word of God.

Witley Court in **Great Witley** was built in the seventeenth century, and in the 1730s a new church was built, the village people being forced to move a mile (2 km) away to make room for it. For this church many of the pictures and windows, and the organ, were bought from the auction of the contents of the Duke of Chandos's 'Canons Estate' in Edgware. Witley Court burnt down in 1937 and is still a ruin, but the

---

Richard Baxter (1615–91)

Richard Baxter was pastor of the parish church in Kidderminster in Cromwell's time, but then when the Act of Uniformity in 1662 insisted that he should use nothing but *The Book of Common Prayer* he found the demand too restrictive. Reluctantly he left the established Church and became the leader of the moderate or 'Presbyterian' Nonconformists. He attempted to reconcile those who disagreed on religious matters in his day, and is one of the most attractive members of the Puritan faction, the very opposite of the usual picture of a narrow killjoy. In *The Saints' Everlasting Rest* he wrote that Christians should enjoy the beauty of nature, music and poetry, and so begin to long for the even greater delights of heavenly bliss:

> Lord, it belongs not to my care
> Whether I die or live;
> To love and serve thee is my share,
> And this thy grace must give.

church remains the parish church of Great Witley, and may be England's only example of a church decorated throughout in the Baroque style, with all the figures caught in extravagant gestures. The ceiling paintings group around a representation of Jesus ascending into heaven, in shortened perspective as though seen from below. All the Duke of Chandos's children were sickly and died except one, who became bankrupt and sold the estate. It is thought that some of the cherubs in the ceiling paintings may be portraits of these dead children. The windows are the best collection of eighteenth-century glass in the country, and were painted in enamel on the glass and signed by a Yorkshireman, Joshua Price; only the robes of the principal characters are in stained, as opposed to painted, glass. The organ from Canons is one on which Handel accompanied his *Chandos Anthems*. Great Witley Church is approached by a long rough lane, turning off the A443 well to the west of the entrance to Witley Court.

Opening Times and Service Times
St Mary's and All Saints
Monday, Wednesday to Saturday 10.30–12.30; Monday to Tuesday 14.00–16.00. Services Sunday 08.00, 10.30;

Thursday 12.30; Friday 08.00. Tel. 01562 751923
Great Witley Church For opening and service times Tel. 01229 896210 or 01905 620489. http://www. greatwitleychurch.org.uk

GREAT MALVERN; PERSHORE; EVESHAM (Worcestershire)

Southwest from Worcester on the A449 brings you to Great Malvern at the foot of the **Malvern Hills**. They have been associated with a surprising amount of artistic activity: on or near their slopes William Langland (c. 1330–c.1400) wrote his great Christian poem *Piers Plowman*, probably in Colwall, where much of the scenery remains as he described it; Elizabeth Barrett Browning (1806–61) and John Masefield (1878–1967) spent their childhoods here; and the Roman Catholic Sir Edward Elgar (1857–1934) composed much of his music, including the great oratorios on Christian themes, in the area. **Great Malvern Priory** was founded in 1085; Langland may have been educated there. The Priory church has sturdy Norman pillars, and there are traces of all subsequent periods of architecture also, until with the Dissolution of the Monasteries the Lady Chapel, south transept and most of the monastic buildings were destroyed and the local people bought the church for £20. Its medieval glass is among the best in England, and the great east window from the fifteenth century is one of the largest in any English parish church. The window of the north transept commemorates Prince Arthur, whose chantry we have seen in Worcester. There are also hundreds of detailed fifteenth-century wall-tiles, and misericords from 1350 to 1380 showing mythological and domestic scenes, and, from 1450 to 1480, the labours of the months of the year.

On the A44 southeast from Worcester you can find the small town of **Pershore**. **Pershore Abbey** was begun in the eleventh century on the site of a Saxon church, and there are many Norman features in the Abbey church. After a fire in 1223, the chancel and tower were rebuilt in the Early English style; about 50 years later the lierne roof was added in the Early Decorated style. At the Dissolution the nave and one transept were demolished, and the chancel with the other transept became the parish church. It was sympathetically restored in 1864 by George Gilbert Scott, who built a new east wall, and let light from the tower windows into the crossing by suspending the

bell-ringers' chamber from the roof like a hovering spacecraft. The history of Pershore is told in excellent nineteenth-century glass by John Hardman in the south aisle.

Further east on the A44 is the agricultural town of Evesham. **Evesham Abbey** was founded early in the eighth century by St Egwin, Bishop of Worcester, on the spot where a swineherd named Eoves had a vision of the Virgin Mary. Many pilgrims came to pray to Mary, and others came to visit the place where Simon de Montfort was defeated in the Battle of Evesham in 1265. He was not a saint, but a popular leader of those who resented the power of the king. Only a gateway and a superb bell-tower containing 14 bells survive from the Abbey church built in the 1530s; they are now incorporated, together with St Lawrence's, which has been declared redundant, in the complex of buildings around Evesham Parish Church, **All Saints,** which was begun in Norman times but largely rebuilt in the 1870s. In the south aisle is a ceiling boss of a Green Man (see Glossary) with the original colouring restored.

Opening Times and Service Times
Great Malvern Priory Church
daily March to October

09.00–18.30; November to February 09.00–16.30. Services Sunday 08.00, 10.30, 12.00 (2, 4), 18.30; Monday to Saturday 09.15; Thursday 11.30. Tel. and Fax. 01684 561020. Email gmpriory@hotmail.com; http:// www.greatmalvernpriory.org.uk
Pershore Abbey Services Sunday 08.00, 10.00, 11.45, 18.30; Wednesday 07.30; Thursday 08.00; Friday 11.00. Tel. 01386 552071. Email vicar@ pershoreabbey.fsnet.co.uk
All Saints, Evesham Services Sunday 08.00, 10.00, 18.00; Monday to Saturday 12.00; Thursday 10.00. Tel. 01386 442213, Fax. 761214. http://www.allsaintsevesham. swinternet.co.uk

STRATFORD-UPON-AVON
(Warwickshire)

Shakespeare was England's greatest poet and playwright, so it is natural that his birthplace should receive more visitors than it can really cope with in summer, but it is a charming place behind all the crowds, and it is well worth booking in advance to see a performance in one of the theatres. **Holy Trinity Church** is worth a visit, not only because it holds Shakespeare's tomb, but also because it is an excellent example of medieval English church architecture. The tower and north transept were built in 1210, and the rest of the church between 1280 and 1480. There are 26 fifteenth-century misericords. As in many other churches there have been changes, and the wooden spire was replaced in 1763 with the present one built in stone. Many of the stained-glass windows date

---

William Shakespeare (1564–1616)

Passages of Shakespeare that seem puzzling on the page can leap to life in a good stage production as brilliant dramatic effects. As a good playwright Shakespeare never reveals his own beliefs, only those of his characters, but he probably shared the faith of his time, and in particular that 'there's a divinity that shapes our ends, rough-hew them how we will' (*Hamlet*), and it is the outworking of this Providence that is portrayed in the dramas. Shakespeare makes King Henry V say, after the Battle of Agincourt:

O God, thy arm was here;
And not to us, but to thy arm alone,
Ascribe we all.

It is related that after the battle the English army sang on their knees the first verse of Psalm 115: 'Not unto us, O Lord, not unto us, but unto thy name give the praise'.

from the fourteenth century, especially in the south aisle. The monument on Shakespeare's tomb in the chancel was placed there only seven years after his death; there is a charge to enter the chancel, which is not unreasonable when you consider the cost of maintaining a building that receives so many visitors. On the church door is a thirteenth-century sanctuary knocker; by using this a fugitive could claim protection in the church from their pursuers for 37 days, long enough to work out a compromise.

Opening Times and Service Times

Holy Trinity Church March to October Monday to Saturday 08.30–18.00, November to February 09.00–16.00; Sunday all year 14.00–17.00. Services Sunday 08.00, 10.30, 18.00; Monday to Saturday 08.00 (09.30 Monday, Saturday), 17.30 (15.30 November to February). Tel. 01789 266316. Email office@stratford-upon-avon.org; http://www.stratford-upon-avon.org Theatres Booking Office Tel. 01789 403403

WARWICK (Warwickshire)

North of Junction 15 on the M40, by the A46, is the county town of Warwickshire (WORR-ik-shuh). On the site of a Saxon church, the first Earl of Warwick (1088–1119) built a church in 1123, of which the crypt is the only part remaining, and established a college consisting of a dean and seven canons. The **Collegiate Church of St Mary**, in Church Street opposite Castle Street, was burnt down in 1694 and rebuilt in a strange mixture of Gothic and Renaissance styles, but has a wonderfully wide nave, full of light from its large windows. On the south wall of the nave are shelves for loaves of bread to be distributed to the poor. The fourteenth-century **chancel** survived the fire, and is in Perpendicular style, with amazing flying ribs in the roof. On the right of the chancel is the **Beauchamp Chapel** (BEE-chum) from 1439, said to be the most beautiful chantry chapel in England. It contains many wonderful tombs, starting with the gilded bronze effigy, in full Italian armour, of Richard de Beauchamp, Earl of Warwick, and including the alabaster tomb of Robert Dudley, Earl of Leicester, one of Queen Elizabeth I's favourite advisers, and the founder of the almshouses known as the **Lord Leycester Hospital** in Warwick's High Street.

Opening Times and Service Times

Collegiate Church of St Mary April to October Monday to Saturday 10.00–18.00, Sunday 12.00–18.00; November to

March Monday to Saturday 09.00–15.40, Sunday 12.00–16.30. Services Sunday (1) 08.00, 10.00, 11.00, 18.00; Sunday (2–5) 08.00, 10.30, 18.30; Wednesday 10.00; Wednesday, Friday in term time 17.30. Tel. 01926 403940, Fax. 402118. http://www. saintmaryswarwick.org.uk

POLESWORTH
(Warwickshire)

The county of Warwickshire curves round the east side of the West Midlands conurbation, so **Polesworth** is most conveniently reached from the M42; it lies northeast of Junction 10. **Polesworth Abbey** was founded in 827 by King Egbert of Wessex for his daughter Editha, who was still a child; the first Abbess was St Modwinna. There is no clear record of what Editha did or when she died, but before the end of the century St Editha of Polesworth was commemorated locally in the central prayer of the Mass, and pilgrims came to Polesworth to pray for healing. She is not the same person as St Editha of Tamworth, who lived in the next century. Today you turn north off the A5, the old Roman Watling Street, and on the far edge of the village of Polesworth turn right until you come to a medieval archway. Going through this you pass the church to arrive

at the vicarage, preferably by appointment. You walk through the vicarage to the church, where the Norman nave retains its round arches. The vicarage garden contains part of the nuns' cloister, and has a healing atmosphere of calm.

Service Times
Polesworth Abbey Sunday 10.00; Monday to Saturday 08.30, 18.00. Tel. 01827 892340. Email Polesworthabbey@aol.com; http://www.Polesworthabbey.co. uk

BIRMINGHAM
(West Midlands)

Birmingham is Britain's second largest city, and at the hub of its road, rail and air networks. Rising from humble trades such as nail-making in family workshops, its pool of skilled workers made it a centre for the Industrial Revolution. It has now cast off its grimy image with an imaginative rebuild of the city centre. **St Martin's in the Bull Ring** is a large fourteenth-century church, which was almost completely rebuilt at the end of the nineteenth century. In 2002 there was a major programme of cleaning and development. When Birmingham was first made a Diocese of the Church of England in 1905 its first bishop was the Anglo-Catholic Charles Gore

(1853–1932). St Martin's would have been the obvious choice for his cathedral, but the appointment of the Rector of St Martin's was in the hands of an Evangelical Trust, so to avoid having to work with a Provost with whom he was not in sympathy, Gore chose instead to make **St Philip's, Colmore Row**, into **Birmingham Cathedral**. A church designed by Thomas Archer in the English classical Baroque manner, it had been built between 1711 and 1715 as an overspill for St Martin's. It was enlarged in the 1880s, when Edward Burne-Jones was commissioned to design four beautiful and colourful stained-glass windows, prime examples of his work in the Pre-Raphaelite artistic style. They represent the Nativity, the Crucifixion, the Ascension and the Last Judgement.

St Chad's Cathedral, by St Chad's Circus behind Snow Hill Station, was the first Roman Catholic Cathedral to be built in England, between 1839 and 1841, since the Reformation. It was designed by Pugin in brick, and the exterior is now soot-blackened. But step inside and you find a glorious sanctuary in which every possible surface seems to have been gilded, and a shrine lifted high above the

---

Sir Edward Burne-Jones (1833–98)

Born in Birmingham and christened in St Philip's, Colmore Row, Burne-Jones went to study Divinity at Exeter College in Oxford. Also studying on the same course in the same college was the artist and poet William Morris. When they met the artist Dante Gabriel Rossetti in 1856, Burne-Jones left Oxford without graduating, and settled with Morris in London as an artist, under the guidance of Rossetti. Eschewing the fleshy models of Raphael and other later romantic artists, they returned to the more ascetic style of Filippo and Filippino Lippi and Sandro Botticelli, and established a school of English art called the Pre-Raphaelites, marked by subjects of medieval chivalry, detailed painting of foliage, and a romantic, melancholy and mystical expression on the faces of their models, who were often the women of their own circle. They also designed tapestries and stained glass, and pioneered a concept of the artist-craftsman which influenced nineteenth-century industrial design and the decoration of many English churches.

John Henry Newman (1801–90)

Newman was a Fellow of Oriel College and Vicar of St Mary's Church in Oxford, and was preparing a study of the Church in the fourth century when he made a tour of Southern Europe and met vigorous Roman Catholicism. On his return he became the leader of the Oxford Movement, seeking to restore to the Church of England an awareness that it is part of a worldwide church which is continuous with that of the first few centuries. His *Parochial and Plain Sermons* made a deep impression with their simple but profound spirituality. He wrote many of the *Tracts for the Times*, arguing for a middle way between 'Popery and Dissent'. They encountered so much opposition that he began to doubt his position in the Church of England and gradually withdrew to the village of Littlemore where in 1845 he was received into the Roman Catholic Church. His *Essay on the Development of Christian Doctrine*, published at this time, together with *The Grammar of Assent* in 1870, showed how theology can change while remaining true to its origins, and developed his psychology of faith. The *Apologia pro Vita Sua* was a frank autobiography written as a response to a controversy with Charles Kingsley. He established the Birmingham Oratory, a community of secular priests living together without vows, modelled on the Oratory of St Philip Neri in Rome, and was for a while Rector of Dublin University, writing the seminal *Idea of a University*. But although he was made Cardinal, his relationship with Rome was almost as strained as had been his place in the Church of England, perhaps because he was at heart a romantic poet. His hymn 'Lead, kindly light', and the visionary poem *The Dream of Gerontius*, written in 1865 when he thought he was dying, have moved generations of Christians of all denominations.

altar to contain the relics of St Chad, 'rescued' from Lichfield at the Reformation; his story is told in the stained glass. At the southern end of Broad Street, past the International Convention Centre and the Birmingham Repertory Theatre, is Five Ways junction, Edgbaston and just beyond that on the right hand side – north – of the Hagley Road A456 is the **Birmingham Oratory**, founded by Cardinal Newman. There is a fine church in classical style, and the education provided by the Oratory School is in great demand; the original buildings are occupied by the religious community of the Oratorians.

Opening Times and Service Times
St Chad's Cathedral Services Sunday 09.00, 11.00, 17.00; Monday to Friday 12.15, 17.40, 18.00; Friday 17.00; Saturday 10.00, 10.30, 12.00, 16.30. Tel. 0121 2362251, Fax. 2306279. Email cathedral.dean@ rc_birmingham.org
St Martin's Monday 11.00–16.00; Tuesday to Saturday 10.00–16.00. Services Sunday 09.30, 11.00, 18.00, 19.30; Tuesday, Thursday 12.30; Saturday 14.30. Tel. 0121 6435428 or 6006024, Fax. 6337808
St Philip's Cathedral Open between Morning Prayer and the end of Evensong. Services Sunday 09.00, 11.00, 16.00; Monday to Friday 07.15, 18.00; Saturday 09.00, 16.00. Tel. 0121 2364333, Fax. 2120868
The Oratory Services Sunday 08.30, 10.30 (Latin), 12.00, 19.30; Monday to Friday 07.30, 12.15, 17.45, 19.45; Saturday 08.00, 11.00, 17.45. Tel. 0121 4540496, Fax. 4558160. Email oratory@globalnet.co.uk; http://www.birmingham-oratory.org.uk

SHREWSBURY (Shropshire)

The county of Shropshire, abbreviated to Salop, lies on the Welsh Borders, and has gained its wealth from its connections with Wales, as well as its own hilly countryside. The county town of **Shrewsbury** is situated in a natural defensive position in a loop of the River Severn, and so was settled in the fifth century, after the Roman legions had left the nearby garrison of Wroxeter. The two main bridges over the Severn are known as Welsh Bridge and English Bridge; just across English Bridge outside the town, stands **St Mary's Abbey**. The Benedictine monastery was founded in 1083 by Roger de Montgomery, who also built the first stone castle in Shrewsbury. The relics of St Winefride were brought from Wales by Abbot Herbert in the twelfth century, and Shrewsbury became a great centre for pilgrimage; a fragment of her shrine remains. The Abbey became immensely powerful, and, in 1283, one of the first democratic parliaments in England was held in the now demolished Chapter House. But at the Dissolution the pilgrimages reverted to Holywell in Flintshire. Instead of being demolished as so many were, the Abbey church became the parish church and was continuously cared for, though road-making in 1830 led to the demolition of most of the

'Brother Cadfael'

When Ellis Peters created the character of Brother Cadfael for her novel, *A Morbid Taste for Bones*, she can have had no idea that the medieval detective would be the hero of 19 novels and a series of made-for-television dramas. It was an amusing twist on the genre to make the detective a medieval monk in Shrewsbury, but the number of visitors who now come to Shrewsbury specially to see the places described in the stories, show how effectively she created the series. She lived in Shrewsbury until her death, and had researched carefully into the history of the period, and in particular into the way of life of the Benedictine monks of the Abbey. Brother Cadfael emerges as an unassuming but acute member of the community, but above all as a sincere Christian believer. His compassion for the victims, and even the villains, of the crimes he investigates springs directly from his belief in divine mercy. Though he does not conform to the conventional expectations of the community, the books portray as good a picture of the life of contemplative prayer and intercession as you will find anywhere in fiction.

monastery buildings. The tower was built in the fourteenth century during the reign of King Edward II, whose statue is contained in a niche. The font is made from the inverted base of a Roman column from Wroxeter. The window to St Benedict is in memory of Edith Pargeter, who wrote under the name of Ellis Peters.

Opening Times and Service Times

St Mary's Abbey daily Easter to November 09.30–17.30; December to Easter 10.30–15.00. Services Sunday 09.45, 16.00; Tuesday 08.00; Thursday 12.00. Tel. 01743 232723, Fax. 240172. Email shrewsburyabbey@rm1083. fsnet.co.uk; http://www.virtual-shropshire.co.uk/shrewsbury-abbey

LUDLOW (Shropshire)

Ludlow stands picturesquely on top of a hill, with its black-and-white timber buildings gathered round the rugged, ruined **castle**. The Saxons built a defensive settlement here near the Welsh border, but the Normans under Roger de Lacey started work in stone in 1085, and the castle continued to grow in succeeding centuries. The rich and powerful Roger Mortimer came here in 1326 and built the Solar and the Great Hall, where the first performance of Milton's masque of *Comus* was given in 1634. Arthur, Prince of Wales, brought his bride Catherine of Aragon here for their honeymoon in 1501 and died here a few months later. Some of the castle was destroyed in the Civil War, but you can still see the tall Norman keep, and a round chapel with an ornamented west door, built in 1120. The Ludlow festival features an open-air performance of a Shakespeare play inside the castle walls in June and July. At the opposite end of Broad Street from the castle, the **Church of St Laurence** has huge stained-glass windows. Originally built in Saxon times and enlarged in 1199, parts of it show a Transitional style between Norman and Early English architecture. The north transept is Decorated. 1440 saw the construction of the nave and chancel roofs, and the decoration of the latter in the nineteenth century was modelled on surviving fragments of the original design. The 28 misericords are from 1447, and among the finest in England; some of them are allegorical, but others mix Lancastrian and Yorkist designs because at the time of the Wars of the Roses the King, Henry IV, was of the red rose party, and the local landlord was

Richard, Duke of York, and the townsfolk wanted to hedge their bets. There is a 'Palmers' Chapel: palmers were pilgrims who returned from the Holy Land with a branch from a palmtree. Ludlow was in effect ruled by the Palmers' Guild, though the legend of their foundation by King Edward the Confessor, illustrated in the beautiful window, is largely mythical.

Opening Times and Service Times

Ludlow Castle daily May to July, September 10.00–17.00; August 10.00–19.00; October to April 10.00–16.00, but only open weekends in January. Tel. 01584 873355

St Laurence's April to October Monday to Friday 10.00–17.30, Sunday 14.30–17.30; November to May Monday to Friday 11.00–15.00. Services Sunday 08.00, 09.30, 11.15, 17.30; Monday to Friday 17.30; Wednesday 11.00; Thursday 08.00. Tel. 01584 872073

OSWESTRY (Shropshire)

It is possible that **Oswestry**, close to the Welsh border and the Offa's Dyke path, takes its name from Oswald's Tree where St Oswald was martyred. The tower of **St Oswald's Church** dates from 1085, but the spire, the springers of which can still be seen, was removed in

1640. The rest of the church is from the thirteenth century, but there was a major reconstruction of the church following the Civil War, and in 1872–4 the architect G.E. Street reordered and extended it.

Service Times
St Oswald's Sunday 07.30, 08.00, 10.30, 18.30; Monday to Saturday 08.15. Tel. 01691 653467, Fax. 655235

HOAR CROSS
(Staffordshire)

North of Lichfield and to the west of the A515 lies a tiny village that has a most amazing church. The **Church of the Holy Angels** was built in advanced Anglo-Catholic ritualistic fashion by Emily, the widow of Hugo Francis Meynell Ingram, in his memory, and to hold his remains, between 1872 and

---

St Oswald (c. 605–42)

Northern England was pagan. Ethelfrith the Ravager usurped the throne of Northumbria from his brother-in-law Edwin. When Edwin came back from exile and regained his kingdom, he killed the Ravager and banished his children to Scotland. Among them was an 11-year-old called Oswald. He listened eagerly as the monks of Iona told him of their master Columba, not many years dead, and he became a Christian. When the Welsh King Caedwalla killed Edwin in 633, he allowed Oswald's two brothers to divide Northumbria between them and rule it under him, provided they renounced their Christianity. Within a year, however, he had killed them both, so Oswald returned and defeated King Caedwalla in 634 at the Battle of Heaven's Field, near Hadrian's Wall, after setting up a large wooden cross on the battlefield and instructing his soldiers to pray to Jesus. Oswald was now King of Northumbria; he sent for St Aidan to come from Iona to Lindisfarne, and travelled round with him acting as his interpreter while they set about evangelizing the people of his kingdom. In the seventh year of his reign, the pagan King Penda of Mercia defeated him at a place called Maserfield and decapitated him, hanging his mutilated body on Oswald's Tree on the battlefield, though it is not certain where this was. His head, which had been guarded by a wolf, was placed in St Cuthbert's coffin in Durham and found there in 1827. He was honoured as a Christian martyr not only in England but also all over Europe during the Middle Ages.

1876. She was wealthy and childless, and the sister of Lord Halifax who was the lay leader of the Anglo-Catholics. She employed G.F. Bodley as architect, and John Betjeman said that it was his masterpiece. It is quite dark inside, with windows and statues portraying the saints. The chantry chapel contains the memorial tombs of Emily and Hugo; they were married for seven years and she survived him by 33 years. It is a curiously ornate building to find in a small village; visitors come to see full Anglo-Catholic worship and the culmination of Victorian Gothic architecture.

Service Times
Church of the Holy Angels
Sunday 10.00. Tel. 01283 575738

CHEADLE
(Staffordshire)

St Giles' is a Roman Catholic Church designed by Augustus Pugin in 1841, and must be considered *his* masterpiece. The Gothic-Revival movement reacted against the plainness of Protestant churches, and working for the wealthy Roman Catholic sixteenth Earl of Shrewsbury, who lived in nearby Alton Towers, Pugin could be quite unrestrained in putting his principles into practice with the most costly materials. He has recreated a dream of what a medieval church might have looked like if they had had the resources of the nineteenth century to hand. Cheadle is on the A522 east of Stoke on Trent; this is not the Cheadle in Greater Manchester.

Opening Times and Service Times
St Giles' daily dawn to dusk. Mass Saturday 17.30; Sunday 10.00. For weekday services Tel. 01538 753130.
http://www.puginsgem.co.uk

EYAM; TISSINGTON
(Derbyshire)

Eyam (pronounced Eem) is the village which laid down its life that others might live. It is situated in the hilly area known as the **Peak District**, on the B6521 southwest of Sheffield. When a parcel of cloth arrived in the village from London in 1665, it was infested with the fleas that spread the bubonic plague. In the summer of 1666 there were 130 deaths in two months. The Puritan Rector, Thomas Stanley, had been ejected at the Restoration of the Monarchy, but still lived in the parish; he was replaced by the young William Mompesson; working together in a surprisingly early example of ecumenical cooperation, they persuaded the villagers to isolate themselves so that the plague would not spread beyond the village. By collecting food left on the village boundaries and paying for it with coins soaked in vinegar, they did so until the plague died out. A modern window in the parish church tells the story; they have over 120,000 visitors each year, so moving is the recollection of the villagers' sacrifice. In the churchyard is one of the country's best Celtic crosses, from the eighth century.

Tissington is a small village on the southern edge of the Peak District, off the A515. It has six wells and is where the custom of '**well-dressing**' on Ascension Day began. In many villages of the Derbyshire Peak District, the village well is adorned with a carpet of flowers forming a picture, usually of a scene from the Bible. Tissington is worth visiting at other times, with buildings gathered round a village green, the parish church and Tissington Hall forming the twin foci.

Service Times
Eyam Church Sunday 08.00, 10.30, 18.15. Tel. 01433 630930 or 630821
Tissington Church Sunday 11.00 (1), 18.30 (2, 4). Tel. 01335 390226

ASHBOURNE (Derbyshire)

St Oswald's Church is delightfully situated beside a row of ancient almshouses and a field where horses graze, at the west end of the small town of Ashbourne, south of Tissington and northeast of Derby, where the A52 crosses the A515. The novelist George Eliot described it as 'the finest . . . parish church in the kingdom'. It has a 65-metre-tall (212 feet) slender spire. The interior is full of curious carvings, and a chapel in the north transept is filled with memorials to the Cockayne and Boothby families. Two poignant memorials to children are enough to draw the pilgrims. Thomas Banks has carved Penelope Boothby, who died aged five in 1791, as if she is lying asleep. Queen Charlotte is said to have burst into tears on seeing the tender image. Then in the south aisle is a 1904 window by Christopher Whall in Arts and Crafts style, full of most unusual shades of violet and pink. It commemorates a wife and daughter who died as the result of a fire. Girls and children in medieval costumes have lifelike faces which must be portraits; the heavenly city glows behind a thicket of thorns as though it were the Sleeping Beauty's castle.

Opening Times and Service Times
St Oswald's daily 09.00–17.00. Services Sunday 08.00, 10.30, 18.30. Tel. 01335 343052 or 343129. Email office@ saintoswald.freeserve.co.uk

MELBOURNE
(Derbyshire)

South of Derby you can turn onto the A515 and side roads to reach a small town called Melbourne. There are thatched and whitewashed cottages, and remains of a fourteenth-century castle. **St Michael with St Mary** is the dedication of one of the finest Norman churches in Britain. It is said that when Scottish raiders threatened Carlisle in 1120, the bishop decided to build himself an alternative cathedral to fall back to, and chose the village of Melbourne, at a very safe distance. Whether or not that is true, the church has always been too big for the village, and there was no need to modify it according to changing fashion. There is a large narthex, curious animal carvings on the capitals at the crossing, and a 'squint'. The east end was squared off in the fifteenth century, and another storey added to the tower, which contains a peal of 12 bells. Melbourne gave its name to Lord Melbourne the Victorian Prime Minister, who gave his name to the city in Australia, so there are Australian flags to show the connection.

Opening Times and Service Times

St Michael with St Mary daily 08.45–17.15. Services Sunday 08.00, 10.00, 18.30. Tel. 01332 862153 or 862347. http://www. melbourneparishchurch.co.uk

The North-West

The 'dark Satanic mills' which belched smoke across the North-West and ground the faces of the poor have long since gone; now we can enjoy the wonderful hill scenery – the northerners are keen walkers – and the associations with Christian folk of centuries past. The two cathedrals of Liverpool are chosen to begin this section.

LIVERPOOL
(Merseyside)

As the River Dee silted up, the Roman port of Chester became unusable, and the small port of Liverpool on the River Mersey, founded by a charter from King John in 1207, emerged into prominence until it became England's second port after London. Liverpool expanded with the growth of trade to the Caribbean, including slaves. After the end of the slave trade it became the embarkation point for millions of emigrants to the Americas and Australia. Now what is left of the docks is mechanized; and the Albert Dock area has been restored with shops and restaurants and the northern branch of the Tate Museum of Modern Art. Today many visitors come to Liverpool, at the western end of the M62, to relive the era of the Beatles, and listen out for the scouse accent.

Liverpool is remarkable for having two modern cathedrals, Roman Catholic and Anglican, linked by **Hope Street,** a perhaps unconscious symbol of the dream of eventual reunion between the churches. Already much has been achieved; the two bishops work together for social justice, and the cathedrals publish a joint leaflet. **Liverpool Anglican Cathedral,** in red sandstone, was begun in 1904 under the inspiration of Bishop Chavasse; one of a family of bishops, he is buried in the **south choir aisle.** The architect was Sir Giles Gilbert Scott (1880–1960), a Roman Catholic, who is buried outside what we must call the **'west door';** although the cathedral is not orientated east–west it is traditional to speak of the end where the high altar is as the east end. From the **nave bridge** you can see the **two great windows:** that at the 'west end' is based on the *Benedicite*, 'O all ye works of the Lord, bless ye the Lord...' and the 'east

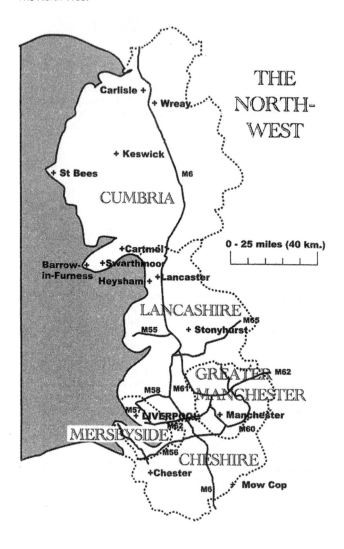

window' illustrates the *Te Deum*, 'We praise thee, O God...' The **tower** is 100 metres (331 feet) high and extends the full width of the building; it contains the heaviest **peal of bells** in the world that can all be rung, 31 tonnes in all. The **organ** is also notable for its size and fine tone; it is the largest church organ in the world. There is fine wood carving in the font cover in the **southwest transept**; the **choir** has the mythical Liver (pronounced LIE-vuh) birds, from which the city is alleged to have taken its name, carved on the steps; and the **Lady Chapel,** the first part of the cathedral to be completed, contains a fifteenth-century plaque of the Madonna by Giovanni della Robbia. In this cathedral the vast size of the building produces a feeling of religious awe.

The Metropolitan Cathedral of Christ the King, the Roman Catholic Cathedral, is in a totally different style of architecture. It was built on the site of the workhouse or Poor Law Institute, which the Diocesan authorities thought was appropriate for a church dedicated to caring for the needy. The first designs by Pugin in the mid-nineteenth century were abandoned because of lack of funds. Ambitious plans for one of the largest cathedrals in the world were then drawn up in a traditional style by Sir Edward Lutyens, but the crypt alone, begun in 1933, had been almost completed when building stopped during the Second World War. In the austerity years after the war it was impossible to complete the original design, as inflation had spiralled the cost to £27 million. A competition was held for a new design, incorporating the existing crypt, which would be finished in five years and cost no more than £1 million. The

---

Bishop John Charles Ryle (1816–1900)

Although educated at Eton and Christ Church Oxford, John Ryle, a Macclesfield boy, was too poor to become a Member of Parliament, his first ambition, and decided to be ordained instead. In 1880 he was made the first bishop of the newly formed Anglican Diocese of Liverpool, and saw it through its first 20 years. He expressed his strong Evangelical convictions in simple language in a number of popular publications. He was once asked whether answers to prayer were merely coincidence. 'All I know,' he replied, 'is that when I pray, coincidences happen, and when I don't, they don't.'

winning design was by Sir Frederick Gibberd, and was the first major church in the country that took into account the newly emerging liturgical thinking, which sees the congregation at Mass, with the priest, gathered around the altar celebrating a common meal. It was therefore built, between 1962 and 1967, in a circular design with the altar at the centre of a saucer shape, and a crown of pinnacles above it. Because so many Roman Catholics in Liverpool originated from Ireland, it was affectionately christened 'Paddy's Wigwam'. It will seat a congregation of 2300 worshippers, each one of whom can clearly see the celebrant standing at the altar. It was here that the Council of Churches for Britain and Ireland was launched in 1990. Unfortunately as with so

---

The Slave Trade

Although slavery was the basis of Greek and Roman, Egyptian and Mesopotamian, Arab and African, and even Celtic and Saxon societies, it had almost died out in Europe when the European nations began to expand their empires in the sixteenth and subsequent centuries. Arab slave dealers either bought Africans from their tribal chiefs or captured them at the point of a gun, then took them to the markets such as Zanzibar to sell to the Europeans. They were then shipped to ports such as Bristol and Liverpool, and onwards across the Atlantic, in appallingly crowded conditions, to provide labour for the plantations in the New World. It became a triangular trade, with firearms, alcohol and cloth traded with Africa in exchange for the slaves, who were shipped to the Caribbean and America, where their place in the holds was taken by tobacco, raw cotton and sugar for Europe. At first few voices were raised against this, and John Newton before his conversion had no conscience about acting as the captain of a slaving vessel. But gradually Christians began to see that scriptures such as Paul's letter to Philemon, in which he asks the slave owner to welcome back his escaped slave as a Christian brother, had made slavery incompatible with Christian compassion. The speeches of Evangelicals such as William Wilberforce in Parliament led to the ending of the British end of the slave trade; after that the British Navy patrolled the coast of Africa intercepting the Arab dhows and setting the slaves free.

many buildings of the same period there have been problems with the roof leaking. Ask one of the cathedral guides to show you the Lutyens Crypt; the **Chapel of the Tombs**, where the Archbishops are buried, has a rolling six-tonne marble stone door, like that which sealed the tomb of Christ in Jerusalem.

Opening Times and Service Times

Anglican Cathedral Services Sunday 08.00, 10.30, 15.00, 16.00; Monday to Friday 08.00, 12.05, 17.30; Saturday 08.00, 15.00. Tel. 0151 7096271, Fax. 7027292. http://www. liverpoolcathedral.org.uk
Metropolitan Cathedral daily 07.30–18.00; Sunday 07.30–17.00 (winter). Services Sunday 08.30, 10.00, 11.00, 15.00, 19.00; Monday to Friday 07.45, 08.00, 12.15, 17.15 (or Thursday, Friday 17.45); Saturday 08.45, 09.00, 18.30. Tel. 0151 7099222, Fax. 7087274. http://www.liverpool-rc-cathedral.org.uk

MOW COP (Cheshire)

Mow Cop (rhymes with How) is where Primitive Methodism began. By a tower on a prominent hilltop, in 1807 Hugh Bourne and William Clowes gathered several thousand Methodists, who thought that Wesleyan Methodists were not evangelical enough, and founded the Primitive Methodists, popularly known as the Ranters, who were particularly successful in arranging American-style 'camp-meetings'. They were expelled from the Wesleyans, and it was not until 1932 that the two branches of Methodism in England were reunited. Still every year pilgrims gather in the **Methodist Memorial Church**, next to the field where the first meeting was held, to sing:

> Sing glory hallelujah, the Lord is with us still; The little clouds increasing that arose on Mow Hill.

The former Wesleyan Methodist Chapel has been made into a **Museum of Methodism and Local History**; the tower on the hilltop is in the care of the National Trust. Signposts to Mow Cop lead from the A34 south of Congleton.

Opening Times and Service Times

Museum of Methodism and Local History May to September Saturday to Sunday 14.00–18.00; Wednesday to Friday 14.00–17.00; BH 11.00–18.00. Tel. 01782 522004
Methodist Memorial Church Services Sunday 09.30, 14.30. Tel. 01782 513218 or 810109
National Trust carpark closes at dusk

CHESTER
(Cheshire)

The county town of Cheshire is Chester, originally Deva Castra, the largest known Roman camp in Britain. It lies at the southern end of the M53, 40 miles (65 km) southwest of Manchester, and is surrounded by an almost continuous circuit of 2 miles (3 km) of **medieval walls**, some stones in which are recognizable as Roman or Saxon in origin. You can walk along the top of the walls, and the view is magnificent. From **King Charles Tower**, in the northeast corner, Charles I is supposed to have watched the royalist forces being defeated at the Battle of Rowton Moor in 1645 at the end of a two-year siege; it now holds a Civil War museum. **The Rows** are unique two-storey shops, partly dating from medieval times; a Roman hypocaust can be seen in the cellar of one, and a thirteenth-century crypt below another.

Chester Cathedral was first built in the tenth century to house the **Shrine of St Werburgh**, a seventh-century Saxon princess, daughter of Wulfhere, King of Mercia, which attracted many pilgrims. A new shrine was made in the fourteenth century and has been restored in the **Lady Chapel**. In 1092 the church was made into a Benedictine abbey, and a Norman arch and arcade from the eleventh-century building can still be seen in the **north transept**. In 1541 the Abbey was made the cathedral of the Diocese. The present building was mostly erected between 1250 and 1540; the tower is held up by intersecting flying arches on the interior, called the Crown of Stone, a feature that is unique to this cathedral. But the original red sandstone crumbled and the cathedral was restored by Gilbert Scott in the nineteenth century. The excellent carved **misericords**, dating from 1380, are to be found in the choir stalls, with elaborately carved medieval canopies above them. In the north clerestory of the nave is the stone carving known as the **Chester Imp**. Through the doors in the north wall of the nave, you can visit the cool sixteenth-century **cloisters**, surrounded by several of the old Abbey buildings. The thirteenth-century **Chapter House** is still used for meetings of the Dean and Chapter; at the Dissolution, Henry VIII made the last Abbot the first Dean of the new cathedral. The **refectory** has a beautifully restored hammerbeam roof. The Chester cycle of **Mystery Plays** remains one of the most famous dramatizations of the Bible story (see p.

119). Chester horse races have been held since 1540 on a piece of land by the river called **The Roodee**, an Anglo-Saxon word for the Island of the Cross.

Opening Times and Service Times

Chester Cathedral daily 07.30–18.30. Services Sunday 07.45, 08.00, 10.00, 11.30, 15.30, 18.30; Monday to Friday 07.30, 17.30; Saturday 07.30, 08.00, 16.15; Monday, Friday 13.10; Tuesday 12.30; Wednesday 08.00; Thursday 11.30. Tel. and Fax. 01244 324756. http://www.chestercathedral.com

MANCHESTER (Greater Manchester)

Manchester is a fine big city, rapidly being cleaned, opened up and modernized. **Manchester Cathedral** is the third church on the site since the ninth century, but the Perpendicular style has been almost lost in the many enlargements. The supports for the roof beams in the nave are in the form of angels holding fifteenth-century musical instruments. There is a unique carved and gilded wooden choir screen, and to the left of it, the 'Angel Stone', possibly dating back as far as the eighth century, with a figure of an angel and the Saxon words 'Into thy hands, O Lord, I commend my spirit'. There are fine misericords in the choir. It

was made a cathedral in 1847.

Opening Times and Service Times

Manchester Cathedral daily 07.30–18.00. Services Sunday 08.45, 09.00, 10.30, 18.30; Monday to Saturday 07.45, 08.00; Wednesday to Friday 13.10; Monday to Friday 17.30; Saturday 15.30. Tel. 0161 8332220, Fax. 8396226. http://www.manchestercathedral.co.uk

STONYHURST COLLEGE (Lancashire)

Turning east at Junction 31 of the M6 along the valley of the River Ribble and the A59, you turn left – north – near Whalley Abbey onto the B6246 following signs to Hurst Green, and then left again on the B6243, to reach Stonyhurst College, at the end of the village of Hurst Green. Stonyhurst is the largest Roman Catholic School in England, tracing its origin to the school for English boys founded in 1592 in St-Omer in France and moved subsequently to Bruges in 1762 and Liège in 1773. Moving to Stonyhurst Hall in Lancashire in 1794, its teachers are Jesuits and among the most famous was the poet Gerard Manley Hopkins. During a tour of the Grade I listed buildings, which stand at the end of an impressive drive in beautiful

---

Gerard Manley Hopkins (1844–89)

Hopkins was born at Stratford in London, and studied at Balliol College in Oxford, where he was influenced by the Tractarians. He followed Newman into the Roman Catholic Church in 1866, and became a Jesuit. He taught at Stonyhurst College, then became Professor of Greek at University College, Dublin. An exceptionally sensitive and compassionate poet, he invented what he called 'sprung rhythm', in which the pattern of stresses is more important than the number of syllables. None of his verse was published in his lifetime, but his friend Robert Bridges, whom he had met in Oxford, brought out a full edition in 1918, ranging from major works such as 'The Wreck of the Deutschland', about the death of a group of nuns, to beautiful miniatures such as 'Glory be to God for dappled things'.

Grade II* listed gardens, Stonyhurst visitors will see the chapels and the Great Hall, and how present-day pupils live.

Opening Times and Service Times
Stonyhurst College House 15 July to 26 August; Gardens 1 July to 26 August; Saturday to Thursday 13.00–17.00; otherwise by appointment. Sunday Mass at Stonyhurst St Peter's Church, 10.00 in term time, is open to the public. Tel. 01254 826345, Fax. 826732. http://www.stonyhurst.ac.uk

LANCASTER; HEYSHAM (Lancashire)

The county town of Lancashire is dominated by **Lancaster Castle**, rebuilt in 1407 on the site of the Roman Fort guarding the crossing of the River Lune,

and later used for many years as a prison. Beside it on the same hill stands **Lancaster Priory Church of St Mary**. It is believed that there was a church there in Roman times, and in a church built in 630 a religious order was founded in 1094. There is a south porch doorway dating from about 1180, but the church we see now is mostly in the Perpendicular style, and is reputed to be one of the finest medieval church buildings in Lancashire. The glorious fourteenth-century **chancel stalls** are elaborately carved with foliage.

In the nearby seaside village of **Heysham** (pronounced HEE-shum) are two Saxon churches, **St Patrick's Chapel** and **St Peter's Church**, both probably dating from the eighth century. Only two ruined walls of St Patrick's survive, but it has a fine Saxon doorway; west of the chapel are a number of graves cut into the rock, unique in England. St Peter's is still in use as the parish church, and Saxon portions can be seen amid the later alterations. There is a **Norman 'hogsback' tombstone** carved with symbols of both Norse mythology and traditional Christianity. Follow signs to Heysham village.

Opening Times and Service Times
Lancaster Castle part-tour daily Easter to September 10.30–16.00; full tour August Saturday to Sunday 10.30–16.00. Tel. 01524 64998. http://www.lancastercastle.com
Priory Church of St Mary, Lancaster daily 10.00–16.30. Services Sunday 08.00, 10.00, 11.30 (1), 18.30; Monday, Thursday 12.30; Tuesday 10.15; Wednesday 15.30; Friday 10.30. Tel. 01524 65338. Email lancasterpriory@yahoo.co.uk; http://www.priory.lancaster.ac.uk
St Peter's, Heysham visiting by appointment only. Services Sunday 11.00, 16.00 (winter; 18.30 summer). Tel. and Fax. 01524 851422.
St Patrick's Chapel For further information Tel. Lancaster Museums 01524 64637

CARTMEL (Cumbria)

The county of Cumbria has rugged scenery stretching from the Lake District north to the Scottish border. On the A590 travelling west, before reaching romantic Lake Windermere you should turn off on the minor road south signposted to Cartmel.

The **Priory Church of Cartmel** is astonishingly large for such a small village, but it was originally built for a Priory of Augustinian Canons who served all the villages on this part of Morecambe Bay. In 675 King Ecgfrith of Northumbria gave the land of Cartmel to St Cuthbert. There was probably an earlier church on the promontory called Kirkhead when William Marshall, who had been granted the land following the Norman Conquest, gained permission to establish a priory at Cartmel. At first the church consisted of a choir, a crossing with a low tower, transepts, two chapels and a short nave. The carved **Norman south door** is from this period. In the fourteenth century the monastic buildings, which had been on the south side, were rebuilt on the north side, possibly for protection against Scots raiders under Robert the Bruce, and the **Priory Gatehouse** was built. This subsequently became the courthouse, then a school, and is now cared for by the National Trust. In the

147

fifteenth century the great **east window** was constructed; much of the original stained glass has been taken to other churches and replaced with plain glass. An upper level was added at this time to the **tower,** diagonally to the lower section. Brilliantly carved **misericords** were added to the choir stalls. At the Dissolution the townsfolk petitioned to keep the church as their parish church, and it is one of the very few monastic churches to survive the Reformation intact. One of the monks was appointed as the first parish priest. In 1618 the roofs were repaired and given a plaster ceiling, and the beautifully carved **screen** and **choir stalls,** symbolizing Christ the True Vine, were added, together with two curiously carved **chairs.** Parliamentary troops stabled their horses in the church during the Civil War, which so infuriated the parishioners that they fired at the soldiers through what is known as the '**Cromwell Door**'. Modern additions include a beautiful **reredos** painted in 1932 by the Wareham Guild, and an unusual **statue of the Holy Family** resting on the flight to Egypt.

Opening Times and Service Times
Priory Church of Cartmel
09.00–17.30 (summer);
09.00–15.30 (winter). Services Sunday 08.00, 10.45, 18.30; Monday to Saturday 08.00, 18.00; Wednesday 12.00; Thursday 10.15. Tel. and Fax. 01539 536261
Cartmel Priory Gatehouse
(National Trust) Easter to October Wednesday to Sunday 10.00–16.00; November to Easter Saturday to Sunday 10.00–16.00. Tel. 01539 536874, Fax. 536636. Email cartmelpriory@ntrust.org.uk

SWARTHMOOR HALL (Cumbria)

Swarthmoor Hall was built in 1586 by the father of Judge Thomas Fell. Judge Fell was away on business, leaving his young wife Margaret to care for the house, when **George Fox,** founder of the Quaker movement, paid a visit in 1652. When she heard him speak the following day she was convinced and became a follower. The Judge never became a Quaker, but allowed the hall to be used for Meetings for Worship and as the headquarters of the new movement. Eleven years after Thomas died, Margaret Fell married George Fox. The house has been much altered, but has now been equipped with period furniture and a number of items associated with George Fox, to become a place of pilgrimage for members of the Society of Friends from all over the

George Fox (1624–91)

How the Society of Friends came to be known as Quakers is a matter of dispute: some say it was because ecstatic trembling broke out at the early meetings, some that it was a name taken over from an earlier group, while some say that it was given to George Fox by Justice Bennett when Fox told him to 'tremble at the word of the Lord'. To this day they bear witness to silence in worship, pacifism, and simplicity of life. George Fox was born in Leicestershire and apprenticed to a Nottingham shoemaker. At the age of 19 he rebelled against family and friends, social convention and the State-controlled Church. He interrupted church services all over the country, acknowledging no authority except the Bible and the 'Inner Light' which he said was in everyone. Priests, lawyers and soldiers were all abhorrent to him. He called his followers the 'Friends of the Truth', and travelled around Britain, to the Caribbean, North America and Holland spreading his message, for which he and his numerous followers were often imprisoned.

world, a place of peace and a conference centre. Swarthmoor Hall is signposted 1 mile (2 km) south of Ulverston Station.

Opening Times
Swarthmoor Hall Gardens 10.00–17.00. Guided tours of the Hall mid-March to mid-October Thursday, Friday, Sunday 14.30. Groups, holiday and conference facilities by arrangement, Tel. 01229 583204. Email swarthmrhall@ gn.apc.org; http://www. swarthmoorhall.co.uk

FURNESS ABBEY (Cumbria)

At the western end of the A590 is Barrow-in-Furness, a mile and a half (2½ km) on the northwest side of which lie the ruins of **Furness Abbey**; follow signs from the A590. In 1123 a branch of the religious community of Savigny in Normandy was founded on a site near Preston, given by the Count of Boulogne who later became King Stephen of England. In 1147 the Savignacs were placed in the care of the equally austere Cistercian order. Only four years later they moved to a more secluded site in Furness. It was once the most powerful abbey in the North-West, the landlord of much of Cumbria, and the Abbot was the equivalent of a feudal baron. It survived two raids by the Scots in the fourteenth century, but the roof was destroyed following the Dissolution of the Monasteries. The ruins, situated in the secluded 'Valley of Deadly Nightshade', are nonetheless among Cumbria's finest, in warm red sandstone, with the **tower**, the **transepts** and **choir walls** standing to almost their original height. In the south wall of the presbytery are **sedilia** – seats for the clergy – and a **piscina** – a bowl for washing the chalice – with the carvings of their canopies almost undamaged. The **Chapter House** and its **vestibule** are characteristic of the simple style of thirteenth-century Cistercian buildings. Some of the best carvings are kept in a small **museum** on the site.

Opening Times
Furness Abbey (English Heritage) daily April to September 10.00–18.00; daily October 10.00–17.00; November to March Wednesday to Sunday 10.00–13.00, 14.00–16.00. Tel. 01229 823420

ST BEES
(Cumbria)

The A595 runs north from Furness up the coast. Just before reaching Egremont and Whitehaven you should turn west onto the B5345 which leads to the coastal village of St Bees. It is alleged to be on the site of the hermitage of an Irish nun

Bega, who gave her name to the place. There was a convent here in the seventh century; the present **St Bees Priory** was built in the twelfth century. Although it was damaged at the Dissolution, it was restored by Butterfield in 1867–9. There are magnificent Norman arches above the west door, and a collection of ancient gravestones in the nave. The organ is one of the finest built by 'Father' Henry Willis, in 1899. A legend recounts that St Bega was still a child when she fled from Ireland in around 900 and was shipwrecked at this spot, where she had a vision of the Virgin and Child; a pair of beautiful modern statues represent this story in the north transept. The chancel contains only one bay of the monks' choir; the remainder, beyond the east wall, was re-roofed as the St Bees' School music room, but the walls remain largely Early English, unchanged by the Victorians. St Bees' School was opened in 1587, endowed with lands removed from the Priory, one of the happier consequences of the Dissolution of the Monasteries. From 1817 to 1894 the church was home to a theological college founded by the Bishop of Chester.

Service Times
St Bees Priory Sunday 08.00,

10.30, 18.00 (4); Monday to Saturday 18.00 (winter 15.00). Tel. 01946 822279. http://www.stbees.org.uk

KESWICK
(Cumbria)

At the 'crossroads of the Lake District', where the east–west A66 meets the north–south A591, stands Keswick, the site of the world's first pencil factory, and an ideal centre for exploring Borrowdale and the lovely Derwent Water. Here also each year for three weeks in July is held the Keswick Convention, an influential gathering of Evangelical Christians. There are now similar family conferences held all over England, including the enormously successful 'Spring Harvest' Festivals.

General Information
Keswick Convention Trust PO Box 105, Uckfield, East Sussex TN22 5GY. Tel. 01435 8660343. Email office@keswickconv.com; http://www.keswickconv.com
Spring Harvest 14 Horsted Square, Uckfield, East Sussex TN22 1QG. Tel. 01825 769000, Fax. 769141. Email info@springharvest.org; http://www.springharvest.org

CARLISLE; WREAY
(Cumbria)

Carlisle (car-LILE) is the county town of Cumbria. **Carlisle Cathedral** is on a site where a church may have been established in the sixth century by St Kentigern, often known as St Mungo and the first Bishop of Glasgow. St Patrick and St Ninian of Whithorn in Galloway are also claimed as men of Cumbria. St Cuthbert came to Carlisle in 685 and found a well-established monastery here. In about 1100 Walter the Priest established a priory, and King Henry I in 1122 made the Augustinian friars responsible for it. In 1133 Carlisle was made a diocese. The **south transept** and two bays of the **nave** are all of the Norman building that survived the battles with the Scots. Under Hugh of Beaulieu (BEW-lee) work was begun in 1225 on a new **choir** three metres (12 feet) wider than the nave. There are ornate **canons' stalls** from 1425, and a unique series of 14 **capitals** on the pillars, 12 of which are carved with the activities of the country people during each month of the year. The **east window**, a fine example from about 1350 of tracery in the Decorated style, contains in the upper part some of the best fourteenth-century stained glass in the country. In the north transept, the **Brougham triptych** (Broom) is a masterpiece of Flemish art from Antwerp in about 1515, carved in wood in deep relief. At the Dissolution, Prior Lancelot

Salkeld, the last superior of the Priory, became the first Dean of the Cathedral; he gave the **Salkeld Screen**. The **ceiling** was restored in 1856 and decorated with gold stars on a bright blue sky. Underground at the west end, the newly built **treasury** displays the cathedral silver, and an excellent series of wall panels tell clearly the story of Christianity in Cumbria.

Wreay (pronounced REE-ah) is unique among English Churches in being entirely designed and paid for by one woman, Sarah Losh (1785–1853). Its layout was based on the early Roman basilica style of church, in the form that she had seen in Italy on her Grand Tour in 1817, with an apse surrounded by an arcade of pillars. The church was built in memory of her sister and parents, and also of a local hero Major William Thain, who sent her a pine cone, the classical symbol of eternal life, shortly before he was killed in Afghanistan in 1842. The decoration is full of this and many other symbols, but seems to have been entirely her own inspiration. She had met the poet William Wordsworth, and maybe under his influence she represents the whole world of nature worshipping God, with birds, insects and flowers

everywhere, even fossils and a tortoise. She employed her gardener as woodcarver, and sent her mason to Italy to improve his technique. The altar is a slab of green Italian marble supported by two brass eagles. The font, carved by Miss Losh herself, resembles a lily-pond; there is a frieze of carved wooden angels and palm trees above the chancel arch, and two life-size wooden angels on either side of it. The lectern is a naturalistic wooden eagle, standing on a pillar of bog-oak, and is matched on the other side of the arch by a reading desk in the shape of a pelican with its bill lifted high. The whole church is quite fantastic, and if it isn't a place of pilgrimage yet, it ought to be. It is on a side road between Carlisle and the M6.

Opening Times and Service Times

Carlisle Cathedral Monday to Saturday 07.45–18.15; Sunday 07.45–17.00. Services Sunday 07.45, 08.00, 10.30, 15.00; Monday to Saturday 07.45, 08.00, 17.30; Wednesday, Friday 12.30. Tel. 01228 548151, Fax. 548151. http://www.carlislecathedral.org. uk

St Mary's, Wreay Services Sunday 11.15 (1, 2, 3), 18.00 (4); Wednesday 09.45. Tel. 01228 710215

The North-East

In an attempt to keep out the warlike Picts, the Romans, following a visit by Emperor Hadrian in 122, built the magnificent Hadrian's Wall, which strides across the hills of northern England between Carlisle in Cumbria and Newcastle-upon-Tyne in the new county of Tyne and Wear. A good idea of the life of the Roman army on the northern border of the Roman Empire can be gained by walking along the wall, or visiting the remains and displays at Birdoswald, Housesteads, Vindolanda, Chesters, Corbridge, or the Roman Army Museum at Carvoran. At Carrowburgh Temple of Mithras you get an impression of one of the rival faiths to Christianity. Northeast of the wall lies the county of Northumbria, on the border with Scotland; we can travel south from there down the east coast of England, a region of people of sturdy independence, partly derived from the Norse and Danish people who invaded and occupied this part of the island. Durham, Fountains Abbey, York and Lincoln are among the most holy places.

DURHAM
(County Durham)

Dramatically situated atop the high cliffs of a wooded gorge in a bend of the River Wear, an ideal situation for defending the Christian community against attacks by the Danes, **Durham Cathedral**, in golden sandstone, is one of the purest examples of Norman architecture. The monks of Lindisfarne, carrying with them the bones of St Cuthbert, after a long journey to escape the invaders, eventually settled here in the tenth century. From about 1070 onwards the Normans improved the defences, building the castle on the narrow neck of the peninsula. The bishops of Durham acquired the unique status of Prince Bishops, the spiritual and secular leader of the community and entrusted to take military action to defend it.

Durham Cathedral was mostly built between 1095 and 1133, so that although there have been later additions, the style of the interior is quintessentially Norman. You enter through the **northwest portal**, where the lion's head **sanctuary knocker** is a reproduction of one dating from the twelfth century. The **nave** is dominated by the round arches, carved with deep

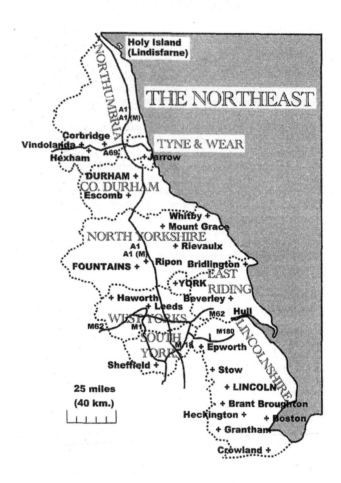

zigzags, supported by massive pillars deeply etched with chevrons, spirals, diamonds and vertical fluting, said to be influenced by Moorish architecture. The **roof vault** was the largest ribbed stone vault in the world when it was built in the early thirteenth century; it is supported, for the first time in England, by semicircular ribs, which form a pointed arch over every two bays, a step in the direction of Gothic architecture. When you reach the **crossing,** you can look up into the high vault underneath the central tower. The **south transept** contains the painted **Prior Castell's Clock** of about 1519. From here you can climb the 325 steps to the top of the **central tower,** built between 1465 and 1490, and admire the view. In the **choir** there are good carved **choir stalls** from 1662, and the vainglorious Bishop Hatfield's fourteenth-century **tomb,** and his **throne,** reputedly the highest in Christendom at the time it was erected. The fine stone-carving of the **Neville screen** separates the east end of the choir from the simple space where **St Cuthbert** is buried. His plain slab tombstone in the floor looks up to a hanging representation of Christ in glory. There is a sense of holiness here as pilgrims come to pray at one

Nave, Durham Cathedral

of the oldest shrines in England. The **Chapel of the Nine Altars,** with its rose window, occupies the east end and was added between 1242 and 1280; it is in the Early English style. To give a sense of light and height the floor has been lowered, and the windows made extremely tall; the bosses and capitals are very richly carved. At the far west end of the cathedral is the **Galilee chapel,** added in 1175, where the **Venerable Bede,** England's first historian, is buried, the roof above his tomb supported by 12 slender columns with zigzag carvings on the arches, supposedly in imitation of the great mosque of Cordoba in Spain. The Benedictine monks used to hold a procession round the Cathedral on Sundays which passed through the stages of Jesus' life and ended here with a commemoration of his resurrection appearances in Galilee; hence the name. The **cloisters** are entered through a door opposite the Cathedral's main entrance; around them are gathered the Abbey buildings, including the **monks' dormitory**, with a fourteenth-century wooden roof, and the **Cathedral Treasury** where you can see Anglo-Saxon embroidery, silver and gold, and manuscripts. The **relics of St Cuthbert** – his pectoral cross, his tiny portable altar, and his carved oak coffin – enable the imagination to leap the centuries and see him as if he were a contemporary.

Opening Times and Service Times

Durham Cathedral daily June to September 09.30–20.00; October to May Monday to Saturday 09.30–18.15, Sunday 09.30–17.00. Services Sunday 08.00, 10.00, 11.15, 15.30; Monday to Saturday 07.30, 08.45, 17.15; Wednesday to Friday 12.30. **Treasury** Monday to Saturday 10.00–16.30; February to November Sunday 14.00–16.30; December to January Sunday 14.00–16.15. **Monks' dormitory** April to September Monday to Saturday 10.00–15.30, Sunday 12.30–15.15. To enquire about exhibitions, the tower and guided tours Tel. 0191 3864266,

---

John Cosin (1594–1672)

Cosin was a rector in County Durham, and was asked by King Charles I to compile a book of prayers for Queen Henrietta Maria's maids of honour. *A Collection of Private Devotions 1627* was the result, but it did nothing to ingratiate him with the Puritans, who already opposed him because he was a personal friend of William Laud. He was elected Master of Peterhouse in Cambridge, and then Dean of Peterborough, but the Long Parliament deprived him of these positions because of his 'popish innovations'. He fled to Paris, where he ministered to members of the exiled Queen's household, and became a friend of the Huguenots. After the Restoration of the Monarchy he was made Bishop of Durham, and tried in vain to bring about a reconciliation between the Church of England and the Puritans at the Savoy Conference of 1661. He liked dignified ceremonial, and contributed to *The Book of Common Prayer* of 1662.

Fax. 3864267. Email visits@
durhamcathedral.co.uk; http:
//www.durhamcathedral.co.uk

FOUNTAINS ABBEY;
STUDLEY ROYAL
(North Yorkshire)

So much remains of the
complex of buildings that
made up Fountains Abbey, in
a delightful wooded valley,
that of all England's
ecclesiastical ruins it is surely
the most evocative. It is
signposted off the B6265
from Ripon. In 1132, 13
Benedictine monks, who felt
that the discipline was too
slack in their abbey in York,
appealed to St Bernard to be
allowed to join the austere
Cistercian order and build a
new house in a 'place remote
from all the world'.
Encouraged by the success of
Rievaulx, which had just
been founded, they started
building at Fountains, and at
the same time transforming
the barren landscape with
their agriculture. A century
later they controlled
agricultural land, forestry
and sheep-farming, iron-
workings and fish-farms over
a wide area, and the receipts
from this paid for an
ambitious building
programme. The lay-
brothers' buildings are larger
than those for the professed
monks, indicating the
proportions in the
community. The amount of
wealth in the hands of the
monks in the sixteenth

century led King Henry VIII
to dissolve the monasteries,
the communities were
dispersed and the buildings
fell into decay. Some of the
stone from Fountains Abbey
was used between 1598 and
1611 to build the five-storey
Jacobean mansion of
Fountains Hall nearby. Then
from 1720 to 1742 John
Aisabie, who had retired in
disgrace from the post of
Chancellor of the Exchequer
(the top government financial
position) because of the
collapse of an investment
scheme known as 'The South
Sea Bubble', made the
romantic ruins the centre
feature of his remodelling of
the valley landscape into a

**Fountains Abbey,
N. Yorkshire**

157

complex of lakes, cascades, woods and walks which is called **Studley Royal**. The whole area is now in the hands of the National Trust and English Heritage, to be enjoyed by everyone as it never could be before.

You enter the site at a **visitor centre**, which gives information on the history of the site and what to see; from there you can walk or take a mini-bus to Fountains Hall, then walk to the **watermill**, one of the finest examples of its kind in Britain, opened to the public in 2001 for the first time in 800 years, containing a **museum**, with a large model of the Abbey. As you walk towards the Abbey, the **guest house** and **lay brothers' infirmary** are on your right, and in front of you the **cellarium** or **undercroft**, a huge vaulted area underneath the monks' dormitory for storing the annual harvest of 13 tonnes of fleeces, and many other agricultural products, until they were bought up by merchants from Venice and Florence on their regular visits to the monasteries. You enter the roofless **nave** of the **Abbey church** under the imposing **west facade**. The area known as the **choir**, where all the singing monks worshipped, was under the crossing, and the tall **tower**, built in about 1500, is to your left over the north

transept. Beyond the choir is the presbytery, which was for those monks who were ordained priests. This leads to the high altar, behind which is the beautiful **Chapel of the Nine Altars**, with soaring arches and a large window in the Perpendicular style, an imaginative innovation that was copied at Durham. From the south transept you can enter the **cloister**, with the **kitchen**, a **warming room** and the **great refectory** – with a magnificently carved doorway – where the monks ate their meals, on the south side of the quadrangle. On the east side is the **Chapter House** with a triple-arched Norman entrance, and the complex of buildings leading to the **Abbot's house** and the **monks' infirmary**, both of which only survive as low walls and foundations. All the dormitories have a **latrine** or **reredorter** at one end over the river, and both the infirmaries are built over the river, so that sewage could be flushed away by the River Skell after drinking water had been taken from it upstream. If you continue a walk through Studley Royal park, don't miss **St Mary's Church**, a gem of high Victorian Gothic designed in 1871 by William Burges, with prolific decoration and brightly coloured glass.

Opening Times
Fountains Abbey; Fountains
Hall; Studley Royal Water
Garden (National Trust and
English Heritage) daily April to
September 10.00–18.00; daily
October 10.00–17.00;
November to January Saturday
to Thursday 10.00–16.00 or
dusk; **St Mary's Church**
(National Trust) daily April to
September 13.00–17.00; organ
recitals 14.30–15.30 most
Saturdays and Sundays. For
information on free guided tours
and on the **Mill** Tel. 01765
608888, Fax. 601002. http://
www.fountainsabbey.org.uk

YORK
(North Yorkshire)

A fortress called Eboracum
was built by the Romans in
71, and in 306 Constantine
the Great, whose father was
the Governor of Northern
Britain, was proclaimed
Emperor here, the only
Roman Emperor to be
proclaimed in Britain; later
he became the first Christian
Emperor. Eborius, Bishop of
York, together with bishops
from London and Lincoln,
attended the Council of Arles
as early as 314. The Anglo-
Saxons made York the
capital of their Kingdom of
Northumbria, and in 627
King Edwin was baptized by
Bishop Paulinus. After the
acceptance of Roman
traditions at the Synod of
Whitby in 664, the church in
York was dedicated to St
Peter. For 100 years in the
ninth and tenth centuries the
city was ruled by the Vikings,
who called it Jorvic. In the
Middle Ages York was rich
from the wool trade, and had
40 churches. The York cycle
of **Mystery Plays** became
famous (see p. 119), and
they are revived every
three years.

York Minster, at 160 metres
(534 feet) long by 76 metres
(249 feet) wide at the
transepts, is one of the
largest Gothic churches in
Europe. The result of this
enormous size is that the
walls could not possibly
support the weight of the
vault that would be required
to span them if it were made
of stone, so York Minster
has always had roofs made
of wood, painted to look like
stone, which of course
brought an additional fire
risk. The **western towers** are
60 metres (198 feet) high,
and the **central tower**, rebuilt
in 1480 after it collapsed in
1407, is 71 metres (234 feet)
high. Entering under the **west
front**, completed in 1470,
you find that the **nave** is in
Decorated style, built
between 1291 and 1350.
Turning round you will
see the great .west **window**,
known as 'The Heart of
Yorkshire' because of its
heart-shaped tracery, and
with glass painted in 1339
for Archbishop William
de Melton by Master
Robert Ketelbarn. York
Minster contains the

St Paulinus (d. 644)

Paulinus was one of the monks who was sent by Pope Gregory from Rome in the second wave of evangelism, after Augustine had laid the foundations of the mission to England in Canterbury. Edwin, King of Northumbria, wanted to marry Ethelburga the Christian sister of the king of Kent, and a condition was made that he should allow her to bring a bishop with her to conduct services. Paulinus was consecrated and went with her, and a few years later baptized Edwin in a wooden church in York. This was followed by the baptism of many of the nobles and people of the kingdom, in the river. Six years later York was made a Minster and Paulinus the first Archbishop. He extended his mission to the south and built a stone church at Lincoln. But when King Edwin was killed in battle, Paulinus returned with Ethelburga to Kent and spent the rest of his life as Bishop of Rochester. His story is told by the Venerable Bede, who described him as 'a tall man with a slight stoop, who had black hair, a thin face and a narrow, aquiline nose, his presence being venerable and awe-inspiring'.

largest collection of medieval stained glass in England. On the south side of the nave, the **Jesse Window** showing Jesus' ancestors starting with Jesse the father of King David, was made in 1310. On the north side of the nave, the **Pilgrimage Window** is from about 1312, with hunting scenes, a monkey's funeral and other grotesques, and the **Bellfounders' Window**, from 1330, shows the process of casting and tuning a bell. The **transepts**, in the Early English style, date from the mid-thirteenth century and are the oldest part of the building. In the **north transept** is the famous **Five Sisters Window**, with five 15-metre-high (50 feet) lancets of *grisaille*, a frosted, silvery-grey type of glass. High on the wall are two 400-year-old oak figures of knights which strike the hours and quarters, although the clock's movement was renewed in 1749. From here you can visit the octagonal **Chapter House**, from around 1300, and admire its wooden vaulted ceiling, obviating the need for a central pillar. The magnificent **choir screen** was made late in the fifteenth century by William Hyndeley, with statues of 15 English kings from William the Conqueror to Henry VI. The **choir** is from between 1361 and 1472, in the

St Wilfrid (c. 633–709)

Wilfrid was born in Northumbria, the son of a nobleman, and educated at Lindisfarne. He travelled to Canterbury and then to Rome. When he returned to Britain he was appointed Abbot of Ripon. He became the leader of those who argued for the adoption of Roman customs at the Synod of Whitby. He was chosen to be Archbishop of York, but as there were too few bishops to consecrate him in England he went to France to be consecrated. He stayed too long, and on his return he found that his royal patron was dead and his place as Archbishop of York had been taken by St Chad. Wilfrid gave way and retired to Ripon, but Archbishop Theodore ruled in his favour and Chad stepped down. Wilfrid built many churches, including one at Hexham which was then reckoned to be the finest north of the Alps. But his lavish lifestyle invited criticism, and eventually Archbishop Theodore divided Wilfrid's diocese without his consent. He appealed to Rome, but this was followed by a long and confused period of exile and imprisonment. Eventually he agreed to serve as Bishop of Hexham, and in 709 he died at the age of 76, giving away his fortune to good causes.

Perpendicular style. East of the Choir is the **Lady Chapel**, with the **East Window**, painted between 1405 and 1408 by John Thornton of Coventry. This has been claimed as the largest expanse of medieval glass in the world; it portrays scenes from the beginning of Genesis to the end of Revelation. The roof of the **south transept** was damaged by a fire started by lightning in 1984, together with the remarkable **Rose Window** of 1486, made from 17,000 pieces of glass, so we are told, to mark the marriage of King Henry VII with Elizabeth of York and the

end of the Wars of the Roses; they were restored in 1987. Here you find the **Tomb of Archbishop Walter de Grey**, archbishop for 40 years up until his death in 1255, who started the process of building the medieval cathedral.

Also in the south transept are the stairs down into the **Foundation Museum**, well worth the charge for admission. As a result of repairs to the foundations begun in 1967, you can now see the foundations of the Roman headquarters building, and of the early Norman cathedral built between about 1080 and 1110. You can also see the Saxon graveyard with the stone coffin of St William of York, and the modern strengthening of the medieval foundations. From the Foundation Museum you can visit the **Treasury**, and then return to the transept to exit through the **Cathedral Shop**.

At number 35 The Shambles, in a quaint street of leaning medieval butchers' shops, is a shrine to **Margaret Clitherow**, the Roman Catholic wife of one of the butchers, who was accused of sheltering priests and crushed to death in 1586 by rocks piled on top of a board, on the Ouse Bridge.

Opening Times and Service Times
Margaret Clitherow Shrine
Mass Saturday 09.45
York Minster daily 07.00–20.30 (summer); 07.00–18.00 (winter). Services Sunday 08.00, 10.00, 11.30, 16.00; Monday to Friday 07.30, 07.50, 12.30, 17.00; Saturday 07.30, 07.45, 16.00. Tel. 01904 557216, Fax. 557218. Email visitors@yorkminster.org; http://www.yorkminster.org
York Mystery Plays Every three years; York Early Music Festival Tel. 01904 632220

LINCOLN (Lincolnshire)

South of the River Humber and on the East coast is the county of Lincolnshire, with popular seaside resorts, and the great historic cathedral of Lincoln. Before visiting in Lincolnshire ask for a leaflet listing many more Lincolnshire churches than there is room for here, from the Church Tourism Network (Church House, The Old Palace, Lincoln LN2 1PB. Tel. 01522 529241. Email church.tourism@ lincoln.anglican.org; http://www.churchtourism.org).

Lincoln lies on the dead-straight A15, the old Roman Ermine Street; a Roman colony, it became the capital of the Anglo-Saxon kingdom of Lindsey and was converted to Christianity in about 630. In the Middle Ages it became rich with the wool trade. The great church music composer and 'Parent of English Music' **William Byrd** (1542/3–1623) is believed to have been born in Lincoln. Although by sympathy a Roman Catholic, and the composer of three great Latin Masses, he was admired throughout the Church of England for the music he wrote for the Chapel Royal.

The three great fourteenth-century towers of **Lincoln Cathedral** rise up above the

St Hugh of Lincoln (c.1140–1200)

Hugh was born in France; his father was Lord of Avalon in Burgundy. When Hugh's mother died, the father took his eight-year-old son with him to an Augustinian monastery, where he grew up. When he was 19 he was taken on a visit to the Grande Chartreuse, the mother house of the Carthusian order, who emphasized physical hardship and long periods of silence. So impressed was he that he begged to remain, and became a Carthusian monk. Meanwhile King Henry II of England, in penitence for the murder of Thomas à Becket, had founded a Carthusian monastery – or Charterhouse as they were called – at Witham Friary, between Bruton and Frome in Somerset. The first two priors, however, were ineffective, and the King, hearing of the reputation of Hugh, sent for him to come from France and take charge. He came unwillingly, but at once won the support of the monks, the peasants – who, he insisted, must be fairly compensated for the lands they had lost when they were given to the monastery – and the King himself.

Part of the chapel of the Carthusians remains incorporated in the parish church of Witham Friary. After only a few years, the King sent for Hugh again, and made him Bishop of Lincoln, with a huge diocese stretching as far as Oxford. But Hugh insisted that every year he must be allowed to return for one month to the austerities and prayerful atmosphere of Witham. He cared personally for the lepers of Lincoln. But he was not gloomy or solemn, and entertained all and sundry at his table. He was roused to anger by injustice, and stood up for the common people against the King's foresters, who had power to inflict vicious punishments on any Lincolnshire poacher. He stood up against riotous mobs who were attacking Jews in Lincoln and Northampton. And he stood up to three kings in succession: Henry, Richard I and John. He refused to pay taxes to finance Richard's wars in France, setting a precedent in relations between Church and State. St Hugh is frequently drawn with the emblem of solitude, a white swan, probably because a large and fierce swan was so tamed by the Bishop that it followed him tamely about his home. Hugh began to rebuild Lincoln Cathedral, the first in England in the new Gothic style. Before it was complete, he went to France on the King's business. On his return he fell ill in London. 'Now my doctors and my diseases may fight it out as they will,' he said, 'for I have little care for either. I have given myself to God, I will hold him and rest fast in him.' He died in Lincoln's Inn, and was buried in his new cathedral, which became a place of pilgrimage second only to Canterbury.

magnificent west front and are visible from several miles away. The first early Norman cathedral was built between 1072 and 1092 by the first bishop, Remigius (who had transferred the bishopric from Dorchester-on-Thames), and re-roofed in 1141 by Alexander, the third bishop, following a fire. This was destroyed by an earthquake in 1185, and St Hugh started to build the present cathedral in the Early English style. It gives a sense of balanced proportion, because the choir is as long as the nave and the two west towers almost as high as the great central tower. The central sections of the **West Front** are Norman, and either side is what is often described as a cliff-face of superb Early English blind arcades. A band of twelfth-century carved panels, based on a similar one in Modena, Italy, shows biblical scenes, full of vitality. On the south are the famous carvings of

Robert Grosseteste (c.1175–1253)

Robert came from a poor Suffolk family, whose surname means 'a large tile'. He studied at Oxford and probably also at Paris, and returned to Oxford as a teacher at the Franciscan house that he helped to establish there. He became famous as a scholar, and translated many books of philosophy from Latin into English. His experiments in natural science influenced Roger Bacon. In 1235 he was elected Bishop of Lincoln, and immediately began to tour his huge diocese on a journey of inspection. He deposed many abbots and priors who failed to appoint clergy to care for the parish churches for which they were responsible. In 1250 he visited Rome, and made a famous speech criticizing the number of Italians, not English-speakers, who were appointed to receive the income of rich parishes in England but had no interest in leaving Italy. He refused to recognize the appointment of the Pope's nephew as a Canon of Lincoln, and for this reason, probably, he was never made a saint.

Edward King (1829–1910)

Edward King was Principal of Cuddesdon Theological College, near Oxford, then Bishop of Lincoln, and was widely recognized as a saint in his own lifetime. His *Spiritual Letters* convey a sense of holiness without narrowness. An attempt was made to prosecute him for high church practices, but when Archbishop Benson decided in his favour it put an end to the practice of taking matters of church ritual before the courts.

---

the **Galilee Porch** and the **Judgement Porch**; the **east end** is Decorated in style with fine buttresses. Inside is a perfect example of Early English architecture, with pointed arches made from Lincoln oolitic limestone, and Purbeck marble shafts decorating the pillars. There is a **font** of Tournai marble from 1135 in the second of the seven bays of the nave, on the south side. The **north transept** is lit by the thirteenth-century glass of the window known as the **Dean's Eye**, and the south transept has the **Bishop's Eye**, with fourteenth-century leaf-pattern tracery filled with fragments of medieval stained glass. The stone **choir screen** is from the fourteenth century; above a doorway to the left is another example of a **Green Man** carving, watched by a dragon. **St Hugh's choir**, as it is called, is filled with fourteenth-century carved oak choir stalls, with interesting **misericords** – carvings of Alexander the Great and King Arthur are all mixed up with biblical characters and creatures from folklore. Over this soars the '**crazy vault of Lincoln**', the first rib vault in Europe to be built purely for decorative purposes, and fascinating for its lack of symmetry. To the east of St Hugh's choir, the **Angel Choir**, named from the 28 carved angels in the spandrels below the upper windows, is late Early English, completed in 1280 in order to create more space for the crowds of pilgrims coming to visit the shrine of St Hugh. The **East Window**, from 1275, was the first Gothic window to be built with eight lights in it; like the windows in the nave it is filled with good Victorian glass. On the first pier from the east end on the north side, the famous stone carving of the '**Lincoln Imp**' looks down from on high on the **shrine of St Hugh**. From the north aisle of the choir you can go through a door to the **cloister**, from the thirteenth century, which has wooden vaulting with amusing carved bosses. The north range of the cloister is formed by Sir Christopher Wren's **Library,** over a loggia in the Classical style. The early thirteenth-century ten-sided **Chapter House** rises to the east of the cloister, with a central shaft and external flying buttresses supporting the vaulting; here some of the first English Parliaments met under Edward I and Edward II.

Opening Times and Service Times

Lincoln Cathedral daily until 18.00 (winter); until 20.00 (summer). Services Sunday 07.45, 08.00, 09.30, 11.15, 12.30, 15.45; Monday to Saturday 07.40, 08.00, 17.15; Tuesday, Thursday 10.30; Friday 07.15. Tel. 01522 544544. http://www.lincolncathedral.com

VINDOLANDA; CORBRIDGE; HEXHAM (Northumbria)

There are many Roman remains along **Hadrian's Wall. Vindolanda** or Chesterholm is 1¼ miles (2 km) east of the National Park Information Centre at Once Brewed, on a minor road off the B6318. There in 1997 the foundations of a fifth-century Christian church, with a semicircular apse, were discovered above the remains of the Roman Governor's House, showing that after the legions withdrew, some of the people who remained were Christian. A Christian gravestone from the sixth century has also been found.

The **Church of St Andrew** in **Corbridge,** on the A69, has a Saxon doorway and tower; the round arch supporting the tower may have been brought from some demolished Roman building.

Turning south onto the A695 brings you into Hexham (HEX-um). The impressive **Hexham Abbey** was begun in 674 by St Wilfrid, using stones from the Roman town of Corbridge, on land granted to him by Queen Etheldreda. The large **Saxon crypt** remains from this building. Wilfrid's building was destroyed by Vikings and rebuilt; it was re-founded as an Augustinian priory in 1113 but the nave was destroyed by Scots troops led by William Wallace in the thirteenth century and never rebuilt. The **choir and transepts** in the Early English style are from the period from 1180 to 1250. In the south transept, near the entrance, is a unique broad staircase, which used to serve as the **night stair** down which the monks, called canons, came straight into church from their dorter or dormitory. At the foot is a first-century tombstone honouring

Josephine Butler (1828–1906)

Josephine Butler was born at Milfield but spent her childhood at Corbridge, where her father, John Grey, an energetic social reformer himself, built Dilston Hall and where both her parents are buried to the north of the chancel. In Corbridge Church Josephine married George Butler, who was subsequently ordained and supported her throughout his life. It was when they moved to Liverpool that she became aware of the terrible life of women who were driven into prostitution. She campaigned successfully against the Contagious Diseases Acts. These laid down that prostitutes had to undergo regular health inspection by the police; these examinations were often brutal and unjust. She also tried to suppress the 'white slave traffic' which procured young girls in Britain and from abroad to work as prostitutes. She supported higher education and the social and political rights of women. George Butler died in 1890 in Winchester, where there is a memorial to Josephine. At the end of her life she returned to Northumberland and is buried at Kirknewton.

Flavinus, a standard-bearer in the Roman army, which had been used in the Saxon foundations. Between the nave and the choir is a sixteenth-century **rood screen**, with portraits of local bishops between the complex tracery. In the chancel is the so-called **frith stool**, probably a bishop's throne dating from the eighth century not long after the time of St Wilfrid. Near the high altar is a gloomy painting entitled *Dance of Death*, from the fifteenth century. The **Leschman Chantry** dates from 1491 and shows a sense of humour in the stone carving, and an eye for beauty in the delicate woodwork above it. The

tower has a heavy peal of bells.

Opening Times and Service Times

Hadrian's Wall National Park Visitors' Centre, Military Road, Bardon Mill, NE47 7AN. Tel. 01434 322002. Email info@hadrians-wall.org; http://www.hadrians-wall.org

St Andrew's, Corbridge Services Sunday 08.00 (except 5), 09.00 (except 5), 10.00 (5); Thursday 10.00. Tel. 01289 306136

Hexham Abbey daily May to September 09.00–19.00; October to April 09.00–17.00. Services Sunday 08.00, 08.30, 10.00, 11.30 (1), 18.30; Monday to Saturday 09.00–17.00; Tuesday 12.00; Wednesday, Friday 08.30; Thursday 10.30.

St Aidan (d. 651)

In 634 King Oswald of Northumbria sent messengers to the island-monastery of Iona in Scotland, established by St Columba, asking them to send one of their monks to evangelize his kingdom. St Aidan was sent, and after being appointed Bishop he promptly established his base on the island of Lindisfarne. He decided that he must train native English priests to share and continue his mission, and established a monastery in the Celtic tradition to train boys for this task. With the help of the king, who often translated for him, he and the monks from his monastery quickly won many converts, cared for the needy, and also gained a reputation in scholarship and the arts; the superbly illustrated Lindisfarne Gospels are now in the British Museum in London. Aidan followed a lifestyle of simplicity and poverty. He died at Bamburgh in 651.

Tel. 01434 602031, Fax. 606116. Email hexhamabbey@ukonline.co.uk; http://www.hexhamabbey.org.uk **Vindolanda** (10% discount for English Heritage members) daily April to October 10.00–17.30; February, March, November 10.00–16.00. Tel. 01434 344277. Email info@vindolanda.com; http://www.vindolanda.com

LINDISFARNE (Northumbria)

Off the northeast coast of England, just south of the border with Scotland, is Holy Island, originally called **Lindisfarne**, the cradle of Christianity in the north of England. For about five hours twice a day the causeway that joins it to the mainland is covered by the sea; it could be dangerous to be on it when the tide comes in, and frustrating to be trapped on the island, so visitors are advised to consult the signs or telephone the Berwick Tourist Information Centre.

In 635 St Aidan chose Lindisfarne as the headquarters of his mission to northern England, and built a church there. Probably this eventually became the parish church, dedicated to St Mary. In the seventh century Bishop Finan built a church dedicated to St Peter. St Cuthbert was made Prior in 673 and Bishop in 684; he died on the Farne Islands in 687 and was buried on Lindisfarne. In 698 his body was dug up and found to be undecayed; in the same year the Lindisfarne Gospels were completed. Vikings invaded in 793 and

St Cuthbert (c. 634–87)

Of the 16 bishops of Lindisfarne the most famous is St Cuthbert, who had to be persuaded by King Ecgfrith to accept the post. Following the Synod of Whitby in 664, this Celtic monastery had agreed to follow the Rule of St Benedict, and he ruled it with fairness and compassion. He also followed the example of St Aidan in walking all over his diocese on missionary journeys. After only two years, however, he returned to his cell on the isolated Farne Islands, to the south, to resume a life of solitary contemplation and fellowship with God. Many stories were told of how the otters and seals played with him when he spent a night of prayer standing in the sea, and how they and the seabirds enjoyed his company and cared for him. When he died on the Farne Islands, his body was brought back to Lindisfarne, which became a place of pilgrimage from then until 875, when, from fear of Viking invasions, the island was abandoned and his body was taken on its long journey. Eventually it was re-interred in Durham Cathedral, which became the centre of a growing movement of pilgrimage to visit the shrines of people whose holiness shines as an example to all.

875, and in the latter year the monks left, taking with them St Cuthbert's body and the Lindisfarne Gospels. They were brought back in 1069 by monks from Durham, who were afraid of what William the Conqueror might do to them, but they returned to Durham in 1170, and in the next two centuries Benedictine monks from Durham built **Lindisfarne Priory** on the site of St Peter's Church, and extended the parish church. In the thirteenth and fourteenth centuries the Early English sections were added to both churches. The **Priory** is now a romantic ruin, but the lively **Parish Church of St Mary the Virgin** is a centre for the study of Celtic spirituality; they have over 140,000 visitors each year. There are traces of a **Saxon arch** and a Saxon high doorway in the wall that separates the chancel from the nave. It reached its present form in the thirteenth century. There is a reproduction of the Lindisfarne Gospels; the highly decorated page at the beginning of each Gospel has always been known as the 'carpet page', and the women of the island have had the imaginative idea of weaving colourful carpets for the

---

Benedict Biscop (628–89)

Benedict Biscop was born to a family of the Northumbrian nobility and served at the court of King Oswy. He accompanied St Wilfrid on his pilgrimage to Rome to visit the tombs of the apostles, and then made a second journey to accompany the King's son. On his way home he became a monk at the Abbey of Lérins. On his third journey to Rome he met Theodore of Tarsus, and returned with him to England when Theodore was appointed Archbishop of Canterbury. Theodore made him Abbot of St Augustine's Abbey in Canterbury in 669, and five years later he established his own monastery in the north at Wearmouth, which he endowed with a huge library. He encouraged scholarship, and the writing of manuscripts in the new uncial script, and he introduced the customs, music and learning of the Roman church to the Celtic Christians of Britain.

---

church copying the design of two of these pages.

Opening Times and Service Times

Berwick Tourist Information 106 Marygate, TD15 1BN. Tel. 01289 330733, Fax. 330448. http://www.berwick-on-tweed.gov.uk

Lindisfarne Heritage Centre http://www.lindisfarne-heritage-centre.org

Farne Islands can only be visited by boat when the birds in the sanctuary are not breeding

Lindisfarne Castle (National Trust) April to October Saturday to Thursday 12.00–14.30 plus 1¼ hours before or after depending on tides. Tel. 01289 389244, Fax. 389349

Lindisfarne Priory (English Heritage) daily April to September 10.00–18.00; October 10.00–17.00; November to March 10.00–16.00. Tel. 01289 389200

St Mary's, Lindisfarne Services Sunday 08.00, 10.45, 18.00 (Easter to September) or 15.00 (October to Palm Sunday); Monday to Saturday 07.30, 08.00, 17.30

JARROW (Tyne and Wear)

Jarrow is now part of the Newcastle-upon-Tyne conurbation; it is on the south bank of the river near the Tyne Tunnel. At Church Bank, a 15-minute walk from Bede Metro Station, is **Bede's World**, a museum near the junction between the A185 and A19. It is a newly opened display that provides a vivid experience of what life was like at the time of the Venerable Bede, who was a monk at the monastery founded by Benedict Biscop in Jarrow from 681 to 735. It

The Venerable Bede (672/3–735)

Bede became a monk of Wearmouth when still a child. In 681 when the Wearmouth monks built a new church and community at Jarrow, he transferred to the new monastery. There he wrote the history of his abbey, and expositions of the Bible, which gave him a great reputation among his contemporaries. He also wrote *The History of the English Church and People*, the major source for the events and personalities of the period when the Anglo-Saxon invaders were being converted. The width of his learning is astonishing.

also gives, through wall panels, archaeological discoveries and reconstructions, with models and audiovisuals, a stunning insight into the story of our ancestors' conversion to Christianity and its importance. There is also a working farm demonstrating farming methods at the time. Nearby are the foundations of the seventh-century monastery where Bede lived, beneath the ground but traced by stone slabs, and some walls from the eleventh-century monastery which replaced it, next to **St Paul's Church**. In the church are traces of the monastery church where Bede worshipped, and a slightly later Saxon chancel, possibly built as a separate chapel within the monastery; there is a medieval bishop's chair, and a fragment of Saxon glass in one of the southern windows alleged to be the oldest stained glass in Western Europe.

Opening Times and Service Times
Bede's World (English Heritage members half price) April to October Monday to Saturday 10.00–17.30, Sunday 12.00–17.30; November to March Monday to Saturday 10.00–16.30, Sunday 12.00–16.30. Tel. 0191 4892106, Fax. 4282361. Email visitor.info@bedesworld.co.uk; http://www.bedesworld.co.uk
St Paul's Monday to Saturday 10.00–16.00; Sunday 14.30–16.00. Services Sunday 10.30, 16.30; Monday to Saturday 16.30; Wednesday 19.00; Saturday 09.30. Tel. 0191 4897052

ESCOMB
(County Durham)

Escomb Saxon Church, on a country road north of Bishop Auckland, is a strikingly simple building, probably dating from between 670 and 690, in the purest Saxon style, using Roman stones from the nearby fort of Binchester. The arch between the nave and the chancel was probably a complete Roman arch, and there are Roman inscriptions on stones used on their sides or upside down in the north wall. There is an unusual Saxon sundial on the south wall. Apart from a short while when it was abandoned in the nineteenth century, Christian worship has been offered here continuously for 1300 years. The churchyard is oval in plan, which often indicates that it was the site of a pagan shrine before being converted into a Christian burial-ground.

Opening Times and Service Times
Escomb Saxon Church
09.00–20.00 (summer); 09.00–16.00 (winter); key from 22 Saxon Green, behind the church. Tel. 01388 602861 or 662265. Services Sunday 11.00.

WHITBY
(North Yorkshire)

Formerly the enormous county of Yorkshire was divided into Ridings; the word comes from 'thirdings'. Now it is divided for administrative purposes into four sections. On the east coast, and at the edge of the North Yorkshire Moors, stands one of the most popular towns for visitors in the North-East, Whitby, with its famous Abbey. The small fishing village was transformed in the eighteenth century into a centre for whaling and ship-building. **Church Street** retains an eighteenth-century atmosphere, and at the end of it is **Church Stairs**, a flight of 199 stone steps built originally in wood for carrying coffins up to St Mary's Church. In Bram Stoker's novel *Dracula*, the notorious count bounds up the stairs in the form of a black dog. **St Mary's Church** has a Norman chancel, with some evidence of Saxon windows. The wide chancel arch has a 'Green Man' on one pillar, and what may be the pole star blowing helpful winds to the formalized representations of ships on the opposite pillar. After the Reformation, the wooden galleries that were put in appear to have been constructed by ship-builders. It contains the best set of box pews (with high panelled sides and a door, to keep out the draught) in the country. There is also a triple-decker pulpit, with different levels for the preacher and the parish clerk, and built-in ear-trumpets for the benefit of a deaf rector's wife.

In a striking situation on top of the cliff are the ruins of **Whitby Abbey**. A community of monks and nuns was founded in 657 by King Oswy of Northumbria, and he put his daughter, St Hilda of Hartlepool, in charge of

The Synod of Whitby (664)

When St Augustine came to bring Christianity to the Anglo-Saxons he discovered that there was already a Christian church among the previous Celtic inhabitants. As his mission moved out into the areas in the west and north of England to which the Celtic Christians had retreated, the two groups discovered that, although they shared the same faith, there were important differences in their practice, principally over the date of Easter, the shape of the tonsure into which monks cut their hair, and the role of the bishop. The Celts had inherited a largely Eastern tradition, based on the first hermits of the Egyptian desert, though mixed with local customs. Augustine's mission was based on a much more hierarchical Western tradition practised at Rome. Not only was it inconvenient to have two sets of customs in one country, but it could also lead to rivalry and strife, so in 664 a council was called at Whitby to resolve the issue. St Colman of Lindisfarne argued for the Celtic side, and St Wilfrid led the Romanizing faction. The president was King Oswiu of Northumbria, who favoured the Celts, but largely due to the reconciling work of St Hilda it was agreed that the whole of England should follow the practices of the church in Rome. The story is reported by the Venerable Bede, who thought it was a good decision.

both. Archaeologists have recently discovered that although the site may have begun as a collection of individual cells, by the eighth century it was an urban settlement, and by 750 the whole landscape was full of structures. There were links with the settlements at Hartlepool, Jarrow and Lindisfarne. The communities were destroyed by Viking invaders in the ninth century, and under King William the Conqueror, Reinfrid, a monk from Evesham, built the soaring abbey buildings we now see, but for monks only this time. They were completed by 1320, and became ruins after King Henry VIII dissolved the monasteries. A new **visitor centre** was completed in 2002, suspended within the shell of an abandoned seventeenth-century mansion.

Opening Times and Service Times
Whitby Abbey (English Heritage) daily April to September 10.00–18.00; October 10.00–17.00; November to

---

St Hilda (614–80)

Hilda was a great-niece of King Edwin of Northumbria, where she was born in 614. St Aidan, who was beginning his great mission to northern England based in Lindisfarne, appointed her Abbess of Hartlepool in 649. Later she established a mixed monastery at Whitby, for both women and men, which seems to have been not uncommon in the Celtic tradition of monasticism and to have worked well without scandal. The Abbey developed a reputation for learning, and kings and archbishops came to her for advice. Such was her reputation as a reconciler that Whitby was chosen for the great conference called to unite the Celtic and Anglo-Saxon churches in England. Abbess Hilda seems to have been a powerful woman well able to issue orders to bishops, but she used her influence to persuade her fellow Celts to adopt the Roman customs. She also encouraged the poetic gifts of Caedmon, a herdsman, who composed many poems on biblical subjects; he was the first poet to write in the newly emerging English language.

March 10.00–16.00. Tel. 01947 603568
St Mary's Church daily June to September 10.00–17.00; October to March 10.00–12.00; March to May 10.00–15.00. Services Sunday 11.00. Tel. 01947 603421

MOUNT GRACE
(North Yorkshire)

South of Stockton-on-Tees on the busy A19 is **Mount Grace Priory**. It was a house of Carthusian monks, who took a vow of silence, each living alone in a two-storey cell, each with its own garden, their meals served through a hatch beside the door, and meeting only for worship in the church. The priory is the most important of the nine English Carthusian ruins, and one of the cells has been reconstructed to give an idea of how the monks lived.

Opening Times
Mount Grace Priory (National Trust and English Heritage) daily April to September 10.00–18.00; daily October 10.00–17.00; November to March Wednesday to Sunday 10.00–13.00, 14.00–16.00. Tel. 01609 883494

RIEVAULX
(North Yorkshire)

The A170 climbs the very steep incline known as Sutton Bank, at the southern edge of the North Yorkshire Moors, and to the east of this the B1257 turns off to the north.

It brings you to one of the beautiful ruined Cistercian Abbeys, in a romantic valley setting, for which Yorkshire is famous. The Cistercian order of monks, from Clairvaux in France, was founded by St Bernard; when they first came to England, **Rievaulx** was one of the first monasteries they built, starting in about 1132. They chose a remote setting to help them to meditate, but with the new agricultural methods they introduced, they soon became very wealthy and could afford to erect large buildings. The **nave** of the Abbey church, from about 1135–40, still stands to a good height, and is austere and simple. The walls of the thirteenth-century **presbytery**, still standing three storeys high, are by contrast of an ornate Early English design. The first Abbot was called William, and the remains of his shrine, which was visited by many pilgrims, is in the west wall of the Chapter House. Later the tomb of Abbot Aelred was also honoured. Enough survives of the domestic buildings, kitchens, infirmary and warming-house to give a good idea of how the monks lived their life. The Abbey is at the bottom of the hill and administered by English Heritage; the National Trust have the terrace and temples above.

Opening Times
Rievaulx Abbey (English Heritage) daily April to mid July, mid August to September 10.00–18.00; mid July to mid August 09.30–18.00; October 10.00–17.00; November to March 10.00–16.00. Tel. 01439 798228

RIPON CATHEDRAL (North Yorkshire)

When St Wilfrid returned from Rome in 672, he built at Ripon one of the first churches in Britain to be made of stone; you can still visit the **crypt** of this church beneath the present cathedral. The crypt was intended by Wilfrid to house some of the relics of the saints that he had brought back from Rome; the vaulting, with stone ribs, is of a technique unique in England, and possibly brought by masons who accompanied him from France and Italy. You can squeeze into the tiny crypt down the steps to the south of the nave altar. In around 1080 the first Norman Archbishop of York began to rebuild the church that was above the crypt, but in 1180 this was again rebuilt in the Norman Transitional style. The **Chapter House, north transept** and part of the **nave** are Norman. Many people believe that the Early English **west front,** with twin towers added in 1220, is the finest in England. In about 1300 the east end was enlarged in the Decorated style. Half the **central tower**, which was in the Transitional style, collapsed in 1450, and the south and east walls of the tower were rebuilt in the new Perpendicular fashion, the same style as most of the **nave**. In the **south aisle** is a **medieval font**, and above are a few roundels of **fourteenth-century glass**, all that remains of the great east window which was shot at and destroyed by Parliamentary soldiers in 1643. They also destroyed the images on the **choir screen**, which the Puritans thought were idolatrous; during the Second World War a single craftsman carved a complete set of replacements. In a similarly short time William Bromflete and his companions carved the **choir stalls** and **misericords** at the end of the fifteenth century. They became known as the Ripon school of craftsmen, and their work can also be seen at Beverley. One of the misericords depicts an 'Elephant and Castle', thought by some to be the punning badge of the 'Infanta of Castile', the wife of King Edward I, and used as a pub sign throughout the land. The fantastic and comical creatures are said to have inspired Lewis Carroll (Revd Charles Dodgson) when he wrote *Alice in Wonderland*. The church was not made a cathedral until 1836. The pulpit is in the *art nouveau* style from 1913, and the reredos is by Sir Ninian Comper. There is a modern metal screen in the **Chapel of the Holy Spirit**, which symbolizes the tongues of flame which the Bible says were seen on the heads of the 12 disciples at Pentecost (Acts 2.3). The **treasury** has an exhibition of silverware given to the Cathedral, and the '**Ripon Jewel**', which is a Saxon gold brooch, with semi-precious stones of amber and garnet, thought to have been made on the orders of St Wilfrid, which was found nearby in 1976. Ripon is on the A61 west of Junction 49 of the A1(M).

Opening Times and Service Times
Ripon Cathedral daily 07.30–18.30. Services Sunday 08.00, 09.30, 11.30, 12.30, 17.30; Monday to Saturday 08.30; Monday to Tuesday, Thursday to Saturday 17.30. Tel. 01765 602609. http://www.riponcathedral.org.uk

BRIDLINGTON (East Riding of Yorkshire)

Where the A165 runs north–south close to the East Yorkshire coast, the A166 from York meets it at the seaside resort of Bridlington. The parish church contains

Prior John of Bridlington (c. 1320–79)

Prior John was born in the village of Thwing in the Yorkshire Wolds. He became a friar, when he was only 14 years old, at the Priory of St Mary, Bridlington, and was the Prior there from 1362 until he died in 1379. During his life he gained a reputation for holiness, and for miraculous healings. After he died, Bridlington became a place for pilgrims wishing to pray at his tomb. He was the last English person to be canonized as a saint before the Reformation. King Henry V went to pray there before the Battle of Agincourt, and returned to give thanks for his victory.

all that remains of the twelfth-century **Priory of St Mary**, which was once second only to York among the Yorkshire monasteries. The last Prior joined the 'Pilgrimage of Grace' to protest at the Dissolution and was executed, so all except the nave and one gateway of the Priory was demolished; yet the nave forms an enormous building. Many carved bosses and capitals and a marble slab are exhibited beneath the west window.

Opening Times and Service Times
Priory of St Mary Monday to Friday 10.00–16.00; Saturday 10.00–12.00; Sunday 14.00–16.00. Services Sunday 08.00, 10.30, 18.30; Tuesday to Saturday 08.30; Wednesday 10.00. Tel. 01262 672221. http://www.bridlingtonpriory.co.uk

BEVERLEY
(East Riding of Yorkshire)

Beverley is where the A1035 crosses the A164; it is dominated by the twin towers of **Beverley Minster**. John of Beverley, Bishop of Hexham and later Bishop of York, retired to join a religious community in Beverley; he was buried here in 721 and made a saint in 1037. Pilgrims came from far and wide to pray at his tomb, which is now in the centre of the nave, and made substantial donations for the beautifying of the Minster church. The **central tower** collapsed in a fire in 1213, and several centuries of rebuilding transformed the Minster into one of the finest Gothic churches in the country. The **west front**, completed in 1420, is superlative, and was restored by the architect Nicholas Hawksmoor in the eighteenth century. The sumptuously carved fourteenth-century **Percy Tomb** is considered one of the masterpieces of medieval art. The **choir** from 1520–24 has 68 magnificently carved **misericords**. Beverley had a famous band of itinerant minstrels, who provided the money for the sixteenth-century carvings in the **north aisle**, with amusing caricatures of players on different types of musical instruments.

The small town of Beverley has two fine medieval churches: at the other end of the town from the Minster is **St Mary's**, founded in the twelfth century for the townsfolk and merchants. Facing the preacher in the pulpit is a colourful capital carved with five members of a music group, donated by the minstrels' guild. The misericords include an 'elephant and castle'. The chancel ceiling is painted with kings of England from the mythical Brutus of Troy to Henry VI; it originated in the fifteenth century and was repainted in 1863.

Opening Times and Service Times

Beverley Minster Monday to Saturday 09.00–18.00 (summer); 09.00–16.00 (winter). Services Sunday 08.00, 10.30, 18.30; Monday to Saturday 08.30, 17.00; Wednesday 07.15; Thursday 10.00, 19.30 (except August). Tel. 01482 868540.

http://www. beverleyminster.co.uk

St Mary's April to September Monday to Friday 09.15–12.00, 13.30–17.00 (18.30 on Friday in June, July and August), Saturday 10.30–18.00, Sunday 14.00–17.00. October to March Monday to Friday 09.15–12.00, 13.00–16.15. Services Sunday 08:00, 10.00, 18.30; Monday to Friday 09.00; Thursday 11.00; Saturday 11.30. Tel. 01482 865709 or Tel. and Fax. 881437. http://www.stmarysbeverley. org.uk

KINGSTON-UPON-HULL (East Riding of Yorkshire)

Kingston, commonly known as Hull, lies on the north bank of the estuary of the River Humber, near the famous suspension bridge; it can be reached on the A63 from Junction 38 of the M62. Hull was an important sea port since it was laid out in 1299 by Edward I. The closure of its gates against Charles I in 1642 was the first act of rebellion in the Civil War. **Holy Trinity Church** is the largest parish church in England at 87 metres (285 feet) long. The lowest part of the **tower** and the **transepts** were built in about 1330, with bricks from the municipal brickyard established in 1303. In South Church Side is the **Old Grammar School** dating from 1583; it continues the work of education by housing the 'Hands-On History' Museum, and

---

William Wilberforce (1759–1833)

The Member of Parliament for Kingston-upon-Hull, where he was born, Wilberforce read the New Testament assiduously and was converted to Evangelicalism. John Newton persuaded him that it would be a waste of his talents to be ordained, and he promoted Christian causes in Parliament instead. He was appalled at the injustice of slavery, and after many set-backs he pushed through Parliament two bills, to abolish the slave trade in 1807, and to emancipate all slaves in the British Dominions in 1833. He settled in Clapham, where he became the acknowledged leader of The Clapham Sect (see p. 22). Together they helped found the Church Missionary Society in 1798 and the British and Foreign Bible Society in 1803. Wilberforce's most influential book was *A Practical View of the Prevailing Religious System of Professed Christians*, published in 1797, which was largely responsible for the earnest transformation of English society from the dissipations of the previous century to what we call Victorian morality.

---

counted among its pupils William Wilberforce. His birthplace in the High Street houses the **Wilberforce House Museum** with a revealing exhibition about slavery.

Opening Times and Service Times
Grammar School 'Hands-On History' school holidays Monday to Friday 10.00–17.00; all year Saturday 10.00–17.00, Sunday 13.30–16.30
Holy Trinity Church April to September Monday to Friday 11.00–15.00; October to March Tuesday to Friday 11.00–14.00; all year Saturday 09.30–12.00. Services Sunday 08.00, 09.30, 11.00, 18.30. Tel. 01482 324835 or 446757. http://www.holy-trinity.org.uk

Wilberforce House Museum
Monday to Saturday 10.00–17.00; Sunday 13.30–16.30. Tel. 01482 613902. http://www.hullcc.gov.uk/wilberforce

LEEDS
(West Yorkshire)

Leeds, and its near neighbour Bradford, is at the junction of the M1, M62 and M67 motorways. **Leeds Parish Church of St Peter** is in the southeast of the city, tucked away in Kirkgate by the canal and the new Royal Armaments Museum. A wooden church on this site was burnt down in 633; a stone church followed this, then a Norman church, with an extension around 1500.

In 1837 Dr Walter Hook became Vicar of Leeds; he started to repair the church but found it to be unsafe, so he built a completely new church to seat 2000 worshippers, and it was opened in 1841. There is a 'Penny Window' bought with the contributions of the poorer members of the congregation. He brought in Samuel Wesley as organist, and established a tradition of dignified worship, with daily sung services, which was influential far beyond Leeds, and continues to this day. During the rebuilding a Saxon cross was found built into the foundations; it now stands to the right of the altar, and may have been the preaching cross where an early missionary gathered the people before there was a church. It seems to include figures from Norse mythology; perhaps this was a way of weaning the converts gently into their new faith.

Kirkstall Abbey lies 2 miles (3 km) northwest of the centre of Leeds, on Abbey Road (A65). It was built by Cistercian monks from nearby Fountains Abbey between 1152 and 1182. The **crossing tower** was raised in height between 1509 and 1528. The sign at the gate describes it as 'the finest early monastic site in Britain'; it must be one of the largest,

with the walls of the roofless nave rising to full height, the chancel still with its stone vault, and half the tower still standing, with walls of many other monastic buildings.

Opening Times and Service Times
St Peter's, Leeds Services Sunday 09.15, 10.30, 18.30; Monday to Friday 15.00; Thursday 13.05; Friday 12.00. Tel. 0113 2454012. http://www.leedsparishchurch. org.uk
Kirkstall Abbey daily all year dawn–dusk. **Museum** For opening times Tel. 0113 2755821

HAWORTH (West Yorkshire)

Turning off the A629 south of Keighley, the A6033 brings you to the town of Haworth. A quarter of a million visitors come each year to this village as a literary pilgrimage to the home of the Brontë sisters. Up a pedestrian cobbled street at the top of the hill in Haworth is the parish church of **St Michael's**, of which only the tower remains from the Brontës' day; it is where Charlotte was married in 1854, and contains the family vault. The **Brontë Parsonage Museum** is situated behind the church. Patrick Brontë bought this Georgian house in 1820 to bring up his family. His wife and two oldest daughters

The Brontë Sisters

Patrick Prunty or Bronty changed his name to honour Admiral Lord Nelson, who was made the Duke of Brontë. He was ordained and became vicar of the parish of Thornton from 1816 to 1820, where his four youngest children were born. After the death of their mother they were educated at home and amused themselves by writing stories. Later Charlotte and Emily spent a year in Brussels learning French, and they and Anne taught at local schools. Bramwell, however, sank deeper into debt, due to alcohol and drugs. In 1846 the sisters printed some of their poems privately under male pseudonyms, but it was Charlotte's *Jane Eyre* that first received celebrity in 1847. This was followed by Emily's *Wuthering Heights*, with Anne's *Agnes Grey* and *The Tenant of Wildfell Hall*, still under the names of Currer, Ellis and Acton Bell. But soon after, Emily, Anne and Bramwell died of consumption. Charlotte lived for another six years, revealed her true identity, and married her father's curate, Revd Arthur Bell Nicholls, who moved into the Parsonage; she died only nine months after that in the early stages of pregnancy. Those who enjoy the novels of the Brontë sisters may not realize that their personal questioning faith comes out most strongly in their poetry.

died there soon afterwards, and the surviving children, Anne, Emily, Charlotte and Bramwell, spent the rest of their short lives there. The Parsonage is furnished as it was in their day, and contains manuscripts, pictures, books and personal belongings.

Opening Times and Service Times
Brontë Parsonage Museum daily April to September 10.00–17.00; October to March 11.00–16.30. Tel. 01535 642323, Fax. 647131. Email bronte@bronte.prestel.co.uk;

http://www.bronte.info
St Michael's Services Sunday 08.30, 09.30, 10.45, 18.00. Tel. 01535 669534. http://www. haworthchurch.dial.pipex.com

SHEFFIELD (South Yorkshire)

The M1 leads to the important city of Sheffield, famed for its steel cutlery. The **Cathedral of St Peter and St Paul** is a beautiful but confusing building. A church was founded on this site in the twelfth century, though the older part of the present building is mostly

> ### *James Montgomery (1771–1854)*
>
> James was the son of a Moravian pastor in Irvine, and after various occupations started the *Sheffield Iris* newspaper, writing against injustice and slavery. He edited a hymn book for the Church of England parish he had joined in Sheffield, and was taken to court under a law forbidding hymns 'of human composition'. He was fined and spent three months in prison for printing a 'seditious ballad'. The Archbishop of York had the law repealed in 1821 – thanks to Montgomery it is now legal to sing hymns in the Church of England. Many of his deeply religious poems have passed into the hymn books, including the carol 'Angels from the realms of glory'.

Perpendicular from the fifteenth century. It was made a cathedral in 1914, and ambitious plans were made to enlarge it by building a new chancel and sanctuary on the north side of the old church, with a new nave on the south. The northern sections were beautifully completed by the outbreak of war in 1939, but not the nave, and post-war considerations of cost changed the plans to a modern west entrance area and a lantern tower, which had to be replaced in 1998 because of structural problems. The fourth Earl of Shrewsbury, who died in 1538, gave the **Shrewsbury Chapel** in the southeast corner of the church, now used as the sanctuary of the Lady Chapel. It contains his fine tomb, on which he is represented lying in full armour and the robes of the Knights of the Garter. **St**

George's Chapel on the north is used as the Chapel of the York and Lancaster Regiment, and has a fascinating screen made from Sheffield steel swords, points uppermost to denote active service, and bayonets with their points down to signify the weapons of war at last laid aside. Whether the mixture of ancient and modern styles works harmoniously in the same building is a question of personal taste.

Opening Times and Service Times

Sheffield Cathedral Sunday to Friday 07.30–18.30; Saturday 07.45–18.30. Services Sunday 08.00, 10.00, 10.30, 18.30; Monday to Friday 07.30, 08.00, 12.00; Monday 15.30; Tuesday to Friday 17.45 in term time, otherwise 16.00; Wednesday 10.30; Thursday 13.00; Friday 12.30; Saturday 10.00, 10.30, 12.00, 15.00. Tel. 0114 2753434, Fax. 2780244.

Email enquiries@sheffield-cathedral.org.uk; http://www.sheffield-cathedral.org.uk

EPWORTH
(Lincolnshire)

The small town of **Epworth** is in the north of Lincolnshire on the A161 between Goole and Gainsborough. This is a holy place to many people because of its connection with the Wesley family and the origins of Methodism. The **Old Rectory**, where John and Charles Wesley were born, was burnt down by a mob who were opposed to their father's political views, and the infant John was rescued through the window 'as a brand snatched from the burning'. It was rebuilt, however, and Samuel, his father, lived there until he died. It has now been made into a museum, which is very evocative of the lives of the whole Wesley family. **St Andrew's Church** in Epworth, where Samuel Wesley was Rector, is a twelfth-century building. It contains the font where all his children were baptized. When John Wesley was forbidden to preach in the church, after his father had died, he stood on his father's grave outside and preached from there. The Methodist **Wesley Memorial Church** was built in 1888–9, and contains a window including portraits of John and Charles.

Opening Times and Service Times

Old Rectory March, April, October Monday to Saturday 10.00–12.00, 14.00–16.00; Sunday 14.00–16.00; May to September Monday to Saturday 10.00–16.30; Sunday 14.00–16.30. At other times Tel. 01427 872268. Email curator@epwortholdrectory.org.uk; http://www.epwortholdrectory.org.uk
St Andrew's daily 10.00–17.00 or dusk. Services Sunday 08.00 (1, 3, 5), 10.30; Thursday 09.30. Tel. 01427 872471
Wesley Memorial Church daily 10.00–16.00. Services Sunday 09.00 (1), 10.45, 18.15.

The Wesley Family

The Reverend Samuel Wesley (1662–1735) was the Rector of Epworth and ancestor of a remarkable dynasty. His wife Susanna (1669–1742) bore him 19 children, of whom John (1703–91) was the fifteenth and Charles (1707–88) the eighteenth. As a fellow of Lincoln College, Oxford, John Wesley gathered round him a group of Christian friends who were so methodical in their practice of daily prayer and holiness of life that they were derisively called 'Methodists'.

He went as a missionary with the SPG missionary society to the American State of Georgia, preaching to the British people who had settled there but were without clergy. Preaching against slavery and gin did not make him popular and two years later he returned. Some Moravians persuaded him that he still lacked the faith that is necessary for us to be saved, and he was attending a meeting in Aldersgate Street, London, and reading Luther's Preface to his *Commentary on Romans*, when he felt his heart 'strangely warmed'. Feeling called to evangelize, and finding the churches closed to him, he became an open-air preacher, reaching large sections of the population with whom the Church had lost touch.

He arranged annual conferences for lay preachers, and the congregations were organized into class-meetings, but continued to receive communion in their parish churches. The British Government refused to appoint bishops for America, who might have claimed seats in the House of Lords, so Wesley took it upon himself to ordain ministers although he was not a bishop. He balanced mysticism and activism, and emphasized preaching, frequent Holy Communion, extempore prayer, perfection and assurance.

Charles Wesley went with his brother to Georgia from 1735 to 1736, where he served as secretary to the Governor. Like John he was influenced by the Moravians on his return to London, and converted on Whitsunday 1738. Charles then spent 17 years as a travelling preacher, before settling at the City Road Chapel in London. He wrote over 5500 hymns and knew their importance in evangelism and in teaching Christians to pray. To mention 'Jesu, lover of my soul'; 'Love divine, all loves excelling'; and 'Lo, he comes with clouds descending'; together with 'Hark how all the welkin rings' – later changed to 'Hark, the herald-angels sing' – gives some idea of his influence. He remained loyal to the Church of England and was irritated by John's ordinations. His son Samuel Wesley (1766–1837), and Samuel's son Samuel Sebastian Wesley (1810–76), were both distinguished church musicians and composers.

Tel. 01427 872319. http://www.
wesleymemorial.co.uk

STOW-IN-LINDSEY
(Lincolnshire)

On the B1241 south of
Gainsborough is the village
of Stow. In about 975
Aelfnoth, Saxon bishop of
Dorchester-on-Thames, built
a church there at the centre
of a block of estates he
owned, to administer the
Lincolnshire part of his large
diocese; he staffed it with
members of his household of
priests. There is a legend that
St Etheldreda (630–79; see p.
200) rested here on her way
from Northumbria to East
Anglia, so there may have
been a church even earlier.
The lower parts of the
transepts and the crossing
date from Aelfnoth's time,
but the rest of St Mary's was
destroyed in a fire and rebuilt
sometime between 1034 and
1050. Earl Leofric of Mercia
and his wife Lady Godiva in
1054 endowed the church to
pay priests to sing the
services 'in the same way as
they were sung in St Paul's
Cathedral in London'.
Between 1067 and 1073
Remigius, the first Norman
Bishop of Dorchester, built
the nave that we see today. In
1865 the architect John
Pearson conducted what is
considered to have been a
very sympathetic restoration.
So in the middle of a tiny
Lincolnshire village we find a
large church, basically Saxon

with Norman alterations.
The round arch supporting
the tower is very wide by
Saxon standards. The
thirteenth-century font has
carvings with pagan origins
such as a five-pointed star
and a 'Green Man'.

Service Times
St Mary's Sunday 10.45 (1, 2, 3)

BRANT BROUGHTON;
HECKINGTON; BOSTON
(Lincolnshire)

The A607 runs south from
Lincoln, and a short way to
the west on a side road lies
the village of Brant
Broughton. From there the
A17 takes you southeast, and
a few miles east of Sleaford
you pass the village of
Heckington, just south of the
road. Then you fork left to
travel 12 miles (19 km) east
to Boston, Lincolnshire. The
thirteenth-century church of
Brant Broughton (BREW-
tun) has a spire 60 metres
(198 feet) tall, which is richly
decorated with ballflowers
and fantastic figures of
people and beasts; the
interior was sympathetically
restored in the nineteenth
century, with the addition of
wrought-iron work which
has been made for centuries
by the Coldron family in
their nearby forge. It is a
perfect combination of
Medieval Gothic and
Victorian Gothic-Revival by
the architect G.F. Bodley.

Heckington has a wonderful church, all in the same Decorated style, with a pinnacled spire, and canopied buttresses either side of the delicate tracery in the windows. The fourteenth-century chancel fittings are original; there is the **tomb** of the founder, Richard de Potesgrave, and an **Easter Sepulchre** – a model of the tomb of Jesus – with finely carved figures of sleeping soldiers, faithful women and guiding angels against a background of delicately carved foliage. It was built so that the host, the wafer of bread representing the body of Christ, could be hidden inside the tomb from Good Friday to Easter morning, and is the finest example in England. On the **sedilia** opposite – the seats for the clergy – are carved a series of domestic scenes of village life.

Boston, meaning 'Botolph's town', was named after the Anglo-Saxon monk who in 645 established a monastery here. In the thirteenth century, due to the wool trade with Flanders, it became England's second largest port. Prosperous merchants began to build **St Botolph's Church** early in the fourteenth century in the Decorated style. The **tower** was started later in the fourteenth century in the Perpendicular style, and may

have been intended to hold a spire, but instead in the sixteenth century a stone lantern was added to the top of it to hold a light for guiding shipping, and also travellers across the flat fen country. The tower is therefore universally known as **'Boston Stump'**. It is 83 metres (272 feet) high and you can climb the 362 steps to the top to admire the view. The fourteenth-century **misericords** have some witty scenes depicting such things as the use of a cat as a bagpipes, a teacher punishing some schoolboys, and a hunter pursued by his wife. The **Cotton Chapel**, in the southwest of the church, is dedicated to John Cotton (1584–1652), who was vicar here in 1612 and a leading Puritan. Some of the Puritan **Pilgrim Fathers** tried to escape religious persecution from Boston to Holland, and were imprisoned in the nearby Guildhall. John Cotton then accompanied them to found the colony of Boston, Massachusetts.

Opening Times and Service Times

St Botolph's, Boston daily 08.30–16.30. Services Sunday 08.00, 08.45, 10.30, 18.30; Monday to Saturday 08.45, 16.30; Wednesday 10.30; Thursday (1) 19.30. Tel. 01205 362864. Email parishoffice@virgin.net
Brant Broughton Church

Services Sunday 09.00, 10.00, 18.00. Tel. 01400 273987
Heckington Church Monday to Saturday 09.00–17.00 or dusk. Services Sunday 08.30, 10.30; Thursday (1) 09.30. Tel. 01529 460302

GRANTHAM
(Lincolnshire)

St Wulfram, who died in 720, was Archbishop of Sens and a colleague of the English missionary St Willibrord. Some relics of Wulfram were brought to **Grantham**, and for 100 years they were venerated in the porch; then the crowd of pilgrims grew so great that the relics were moved to the fourteenth-century crypt, which has both up and down staircases. **St Wulfram's Church** in Grantham, one of England's most beautiful parish churches, is mostly Early English with original Norman pillars, and a **spire** which is one of the tallest, and arguably the finest, in Britain, 83 metres (272 feet) high, erected in the fourteenth century. It is covered in regularly spaced ballflower decorations; Ruskin is said to have swooned when he first saw it. All round the roof-line of the exterior of the church is a series of corbels with the ugliest grimacing faces imaginable. The **chained library** in the south porch, with 150 books in it, was established in 1598, though

the oldest book it holds is dated 1472. The **high altar,** like many others, had been turned sideways at the Reformation, so that the people could gather round it with the priest at the north side. In 1627 the High Church party thought it should be more prominent and turned it to face down the church; the Puritans came and turned it back again. The ensuing brawl became a *cause célèbre,* and was quoted as one of the causes of the Civil War. Grantham is where the A52 crosses the A1.

Opening Times and Service Times
St Wulfram's daily November to Easter 09.00–12.30, 14.00–17.30; Easter to October 10.00–16.00. Services Sunday 08.00, 09.30, 18.30; Monday to Saturday 08.30; Tuesday 19.00; Wednesday (2) 12.30; Thursday 11.00. Tel. 01476 563710.
Trigge Library Monday 10.00–12.00; Monday, Thursday, Friday 14.00–16.00 (summer)

CROWLAND
(Lincolnshire)

Croyland Abbey is both a romantic ruin and the well-cared-for parish church for a town whose name differs by one letter. This is all that remains of an enormous priory on a site made holy by St Guthlac (c. 673–714). Guthlac fought in the army of Mercia as a youth, but when he was 24 he became a monk at Repton. Seeking greater austerity of life, he became a hermit at Crowland, which was then an 'island' in the marshy ground of the Lincolnshire fens. His life story was written soon after his death by a monk called Felix, and in the twelfth century it was made into a series of drawings which are now in the British Library. He had a close relationship with the birds and animals, but regarded the local people who attacked him as demons. After he died, a monastery grew up around his hermitage. It was destroyed by the Danish invaders, and again in a fire in 1091; around this time Hereward the Wake, who led Saxon resistance to the Normans, is said to have been buried at Croyland Abbey. Another rebuilding began in 1113, and was destroyed by an earthquake in 1118, but this is the earliest building of which we can see significant portions today, consisting of a fine dog-toothed arch and the west front of the south aisle, with more than 20 statues of saints. Building continued until it became one of the largest Benedictine monasteries in England, funded by their success in farming the fens, and the wool trade. At the Dissolution, the nave and aisles of the Abbey church became the parish church. The central roof collapsed in 1720, leaving the ruin we see today; the south aisle was dismantled in 1743 to provide stone to shore up the north aisle, which alone forms today's vast parish church. In the museum over the porch you can see timbers from the Saxon buildings, and the skull, with a sword-gash in it, of Abbot Theodore who was killed at the high altar by the Danes in 850.

Service Times
Croyland Abbey Sunday 08.00, 10.00, 18.00. Tel. 01733 210499 or 210500

The East Midlands

The university town of Cambridge and the counties to the
north and east of it form a diverse group, with no very
striking scenery but many places worth visiting because of
their association with notable Christians from Nicholas
Ferrar to John Bunyan.

LITTLE GIDDING
(Cambridgeshire)

At Junction 16 of the A1(M) follow the B1043, which parallels the motorway to the south, and then the B660 which crosses it to the west. At Great Gidding there is a sign that directs you down a side road to the south to **Little Gidding**. This obscure little village, not even mentioned on some maps, is one of the most important places in the history of English Christianity, for here Nicholas Ferrar made an experiment in community living which influenced many people from King Charles I to the poets George Herbert – who was prebend for a while of nearby **Leighton Bromswold** and rebuilt the church there – and T.S. Eliot.

The tiny church is virtually as Ferrar left it, and it is still deeply moving, as T.S. Eliot puts it in his poem 'Little Gidding', 'to kneel where prayer has been valid'.

Opening Times and Service Times
Little Gidding Church daily 09.00–dusk. Services whenever there is a fifth Sunday in the month; for details write to Ferrar House PE28 5RJ or Tel. 01832 293383

CAMBRIDGE
(Cambridgeshire)

A tour of Cambridge on foot could start on the north edge of the town at **Magdalene College**; like the Oxford college its name is pronounced Maudlin, but here it is spelt with an extra

---

Nicholas Ferrar (1592–1637)

Leaving his Fellowship at Cambridge on account of his health, Nicholas Ferrar travelled abroad for some years. On returning to his native London he worked for six years as Deputy Treasurer of the Virginia Company before being elected to Parliament. The possibility of a brilliant career was given up, however, when he decided to settle at Little Gidding in what was then Huntingdonshire and form a new type of religious community. He was ordained deacon but never priest; he invited his brother and brother-in-law with their families to live with him a life of prayer. Some 30 people took it in turns to recite the Psalms and read the Gospels every hour in the Chapel, and Nicholas himself frequently sat up all night continuing the vigil. King Charles I visited Little Gidding and was impressed by the life of the community; but the Puritans attacked it and after Ferrar's death destroyed most of his papers and ended the community.

'e' on the end. It was founded by the Benedictines as a hostel for monks who were studying here, and has been a university college since 1542. In the second courtyard is the Pepys Building (pronounced Peeps), where the entire 3000-volume library of Samuel Pepys (1633–1703), a former student, including his famous diary written in shorthand, is displayed in the original red oak bookshelves he designed himself. Across Magdalene Bridge in Bridge Street is the **Round Church**, built by crusader monks in 1130, based on the pattern of the Church of the Holy Sepulchre in Jerusalem, one of only five circular Norman churches in England. It is now used as the Christian Heritage Centre; walking tours of Cambridge start from here, and prayers are said regularly for peace and reconciliation. Opposite is **St John's College**, founded by Lady Margaret Beaufort and given its charter in 1511, two years after her death. The turreted Tudor gatehouse bears her coat of arms. The first three courts are Tudor, beyond the third court is a bridge over the River Cam, dating from 1831 and called after the bridge in Venice that inspired it, the Bridge of Sighs. This leads to the fantastic New Court, known from its wealth of Gothic pinnacles as the Wedding Cake. Beyond that is the

thirteenth-century stone School of Pythagoras, the oldest house in Cambridge.

Trinity College, next to St John's, the largest Cambridge college, was given its charter in 1546 by Henry VIII, whose statue – holding a chair leg – adorns the gatehouse, though both the 1432 King Edward's Tower and the 1535 Great Gate are older. The true story of the Christian athlete Eric Liddell told in the movie *Chariots of Fire* begins with the race around the Great Court of Trinity. The Wren Library of 1695, designed by Sir Christopher Wren with woodcarving by Grinling Gibbons, includes a First Folio of Shakespeare. Queen Mary paid for the building of the chapel. **Gonville & Caius College**, usually called Caius and pronounced 'Keys', has buildings of 1348, much altered since then. Through the aptly named Gates of Humility, Virtue and Honour, students can pass to the **Senate House**, built between 1722 and 1730, to receive their degrees. **Clare College** is tucked away behind the Senate House; it was founded in 1326, destroyed by fire and refounded by Lady Elizabeth de Clare in 1338. After another fire it was rebuilt between 1638 and 1715 by Robert and Thomas Grumbold. Clare Bridge of

1640 is the oldest bridge across the Cam; it has a missing segment in one of the stone balls because Thomas Grumbold vowed not to finish it until he was paid, and he never was. **Trinity Hall** nearby has an Elizabethan chained library. **Great St Mary's Church**, the university church opposite the Senate House, is fifteenth century.

King's College was founded in 1441, and is sandwiched between King's Parade and the stretch of the River Cam or Granta – famous for the punts that can be hired nearby at Silver Street Bridge – known as The Backs. Evensong in **King's College Chapel** is an unforgettable experience. Access to the chapel is from Senate House passage; it was built between 1446 and 1515 by three kings, Henry VI, VII and VIII, and is the fullest and most glorious flowering of the Perpendicular style of architecture. It has the largest single-span vaulted stone roof in the world, 29 metres (94 feet) high, 12 metres (40 feet) wide, and 88 metres (289 feet) long, soaring columns, huge windows, and delicate tracery of fan-vaulting. The Flemish stained glass, with scenes from the New Testament and Apocrypha below Old Testament portrayals, and the Italian wood carving of the choir stalls, were given by Henry VIII; the organ case is seventeenth century; the Rubens painting *The Adoration of the Magi* was acquired in the twentieth century. Visitors who consider themselves to be pilgrims will want to join in the daily Evensong in many university college chapels in term time, and in cathedrals, and are very welcome, though for some it will be a new experience of corporate prayer to realize that others, with better voices, are responsible for the singing, whereas our part is to turn that into worship by our silent prayers.

The Saxon **St Benet's Church**, in Benet Street opposite King's College, is the oldest building in the city, built in the early eleventh century. The name is short for Benedict; the parish clerk, Fabian Stedman, in 1668 wrote the first ever book on **bell-ringing** and invented the peculiarly English art of change-ringing, in which the order of the bells rung one after another follows a series of permutations in a regular mathematical order. The bells are first raised to a position with the cup uppermost, and the tradition, done to the glory of God and to call people to worship, has given us the expression 'ringing the changes'. What Oxford calls quads are known in Cambridge as

---

King Henry VI (1421–71)

Henry VI became King of England and King of France as a one-year-old baby on the death of his father Henry V in 1422. He grew into a man whose pious character and withdrawal from contact with others made him incapable of firm government, and he concentrated instead on religious observance, and the foundation of Eton College and King's College, Cambridge – of him Wordsworth wrote 'Tax not the royal saint with vain expense'. His weakness was one of the causes of the Wars of the Roses (between the Dukes of York, with a white rose as their emblem, and the Dukes of Lancaster, represented by the red rose), and of English loss of control over its French territories. He was captured in 1465 and imprisoned in the Tower of London. Although he returned to the throne briefly in 1470, the death of his son Prince Edward in the Battle of Tewkesbury in 1471 led to the triumph of his enemies, and King Henry was murdered in the Tower.

---

courts, and the oldest of them all, built in the fourteenth century, is at **Corpus Christi College**. Named for the Body of Christ, the college was founded in 1352 by the townspeople. The playwright Christopher Marlowe (1564–94) was a student here. **St Catherine's College** opposite, known as Cats, was founded in 1473. **Queens' College** is behind Cats in Silver Street, and, unlike the Oxford one, is spelt with an s-apostrophe because two queens gave the funds to build it: Margaret of Anjou, wife of Henry VI, and Elizabeth Woodville, Edward IV's spouse. Old Court was completed in 1449, three years after the first charter was granted. Desiderius

Erasmus (c.1466–1536), the Humanist Catholic scholar of Rotterdam, taught Greek here. The Mathematical Bridge over the Cam is a copy from 1904 of the original, designed in 1749 so that it would still stand if all the bolts were removed.

A 900-metre (1000 yards) walk along Silver Street and then to the end of Sidgwick Avenue brings you to **Selwyn College**, which was founded in 1881 in memory of George Augustus Selwyn (1809–78), the first Bishop of New Zealand. His son, John Richardson Selwyn (1844–98) was Bishop of Melanesia in the Pacific Ocean from 1877 to 1889, before returning to become Master of the College.

John Milton (1608–74)

While still a student at Christ's College, Cambridge, Milton wrote his acclaimed *Ode on the Morning of Christ's Nativity*; it was followed soon after by *L'Allegro* and *Il Penseroso*, and the masque of *Comus*. *Lycidas* is both a lament on the death of a friend, and a bitter attack on the corruption of the clergy, a constant theme in his writings. When his wife left him soon after their marriage he wrote a passionate pamphlet in favour of divorce, arguing that the sanctity of marriage was an invention of the clergy. When he was accused for publishing this without a licence he responded with *Areopagitica*, an argument against censorship. He rejected the established Church and joined the Presbyterians, but falling out with them he became an Independent, and having supported Oliver Cromwell disagreed with his plans for an established Presbyterian Church. By this time he was completely blind, but his greatest works were the three religious poems of these final years, *Paradise Lost*, *Paradise Regained*, and *Samson Agonistes*, in which a blind hero defies the world.

Pembroke College, on the corner of Trumpington Road and Downing Street, founded in 1347 by Valence Mary, the widowed Countess of Pembroke, has a chapel which was the first building to be completed, in 1663–65, to a design by Christopher Wren, who was a mathematician rather than an architect but did it to oblige his uncle Matthew Wren, Bishop of Ely, who had been Master of Pembroke College, in thanksgiving for his release after the Civil War. Recently a sketch by Wren to guide the builders was discovered behind the panelling in some rooms at Pembroke. Alumni include Prime Minister William Pitt the Younger, and poets Edmund Spenser, Thomas Gray and Ted Hughes. **Peterhouse**, almost opposite, is the oldest and smallest college in Cambridge, founded in 1284; the thirteenth-century hall is original but it was remodelled by William Morris in the 1870s. The baroque chapel was built in 1632. Walking up Downing Street past the University Museums to Sidney Street brings us out opposite **Emmanuel College**, popularly known as Emma. This was founded to train Protestant clergy after the Reformation in 1584, and

Charles Simeon (1759–1836)

On ordination in 1783 Simeon moved from his position as a Fellow of King's College, Cambridge, to become Vicar of Holy Trinity Church in the same town, where he remained until his death. He became a leading light in the Evangelical movement, and was a supporter of the British and Foreign Bible Society and one of the founders of the Church Missionary Society. A phrase in his writings serves as a motto for all those distressed by religious controversy: 'Truth does not lie in either extreme taken on its own, nor yet midway between them: truth lies in both extremes held together in tension.' A guest wrote that 'Mr Simeon invariably rose every morning, though it was the winter session, at four o'clock; and after lighting his fire, he devoted the first four hours of the day to private prayer, and the devotional study of Scripture'. He loved *The Book of Common Prayer*, and said of the blessing: 'In pronouncing it, I do not do it as a mere finale, but I feel that I am actually dispensing peace from God, and at God's command. I know not the individuals to whom my benediction is a blessing; but I know that I am the appointed instrument by whom God is conveying the blessing to those who are able to receive it.'

graduates of the college were among the settlers in New England, and gave its name to Cambridge, Massachusetts. The cloister gallery and the chapel are by Wren. **Christ's College**, like St John's, was founded by Lady Margaret Beaufort, whose coat of arms is on the gateway. The Fellows Building is attributed to Inigo Jones. In the first court are the rooms occupied by John Milton when he was an undergraduate. **Holy Trinity Church** in Sidney Street numbers Charles Simeon in its list of incumbents.

Sidney Sussex was founded in 1594; the Tudor brickwork was cemented over in the early nineteenth century. Oliver Cromwell was a student here, and his head is believed to be buried in the chapel. **Jesus College** was founded by the Bishop of Ely on the grounds of a Benedictine nunnery that had been suppressed in 1496. Cloister Court retains the feel of the convent, and the chapel is the chancel of the Priory church, restored with ceiling designs by William Morris and Pre-Raphaelite stained glass. Archbishop Thomas Cranmer and the

---

Miles Coverdale (1488–1568)

Miles Coverdale was a priest in the house of Augustinian friars in Cambridge when he began his Bible translation. He preached sermons attacking confession and images, and was compelled to live abroad. His translation of the Bible was printed in Zürich; many of his phrases have entered into common speech, and his version of the Psalms is included in *The Book of Common Prayer*.

---

poet Samuel Taylor Coleridge are among the former students.

Colleges' Opening Times and Service Times
In most cases the times of services given for the Cambridge colleges are in term time only. For further information consult http://www.christiancambridge. org, or http://www.cam.ac.uk/ cambuniv/colleges.html. Each college has a website with an address such as http://www. clare.cam.ac.uk, then click on 'chapel'. All Cambridge telephone numbers begin with area code 01223.

Clare Old Court, Hall and Chapel usually daily 10.00–16.30. Tel. 333200, Fax. 333219
Christ's daily 09.30–12.00. Services Sunday 09.00, 18.00; Monday to Saturday 08.30; Tuesday 22.00; Thursday 18.45. Tel. 334900
Corpus Christi daily except Christmas 14.00–1600. No groups larger than 12. Services Sunday 09.30, 18.45; Monday to Saturday 08.45. Tel. 338000
Emmanuel daily 09.00–18.00. Services Sunday 09.00, 18.00; Monday to Friday 08.30; Monday, Wednesday, Thursday,

Friday 18.00. Tel. 334200
Gonville & Caius late March to early May and mid June to September Monday to Friday mornings only. Closed early May to early June and BH. No group over 6. Services Sunday 10.00, 18.00; Tuesday, Thursday 18.30. Tel. 332400
Great St Mary's Church daily 08.00–18.15. Tower 10.00–13.30. Services Sunday 08.00, 09.30, 11.15, 18.30; Monday to Saturday 09.00; Monday to Friday 13.05; Monday, Friday 11.00. Tel. 741716, Fax. 462914. Email jb344@cam.ac.uk
Holy Trinity Church Services Sunday 10.30; 14.00 (Korean), 18.30
Jesus courts, gardens and chapel daily July to May 09.00–17.00. Services Sunday 11.00, 18.00; Monday to Saturday 08.30, 18.30. Tel. 339339
King's College and Chapel (functions permitting) term time, weekdays 09.30–15.15, Sunday 13.15–14.15, 17.00–17.30; summer vacation, weekdays 09.30–16.30, Sunday 10.00–17.00. Services Sunday 10.30, 15.30; sung Evensong term time Tuesday to Saturday 17.30. Tel. 331212 (College

tower at the crossing collapsed in 1322, destroying the choir at the same time, the architects hit on the brilliant solution of cutting off the corners of the base of the tower, creating an eight-sided space, the eight pillars of which support about 200 tonnes of wood, lead and glass in the lantern. Then they set about rebuilding the east end in the new architectural styles. The **choir** was rebuilt in the Decorated style, with choir stalls from the same period. The **presbytery** beyond is earlier, from the thirteenth century, and was built to contain the shrine of St Etheldreda, which was visited by many pilgrims; then at the east end are three **chantry chapels**, the northernmost of which was completed in 1533 in an elaborate Renaissance style. The **choir screen**, however, was built in the nineteenth century by George Gilbert Scott. The **Lady Chapel** is not in the usual position, but is a separate building approached through the north transept. The sculpture was defaced and the glass removed at the Reformation, but the **fan-vaulting** is still a superb example of the English Gothic style of architecture. There is a modern statue of a joyful Virgin Mary. In the centre of the south wall of the nave is the **Prior's Door**, which now

leads to a video presentation; over the door is a magnificent carving of Christ in Majesty from around 1135.The **southwest transept** contains some of the finest Norman and Transitional blind arcading in England; near the main entrance to the Cathedral, it houses a new exhibition on faith, and the stairs leading to the **stained-glass museum** in the south triforium. The old **monastic buildings** to the south of the Cathedral are the largest collection of medieval domestic buildings still in use in Europe. Ely is on the A10 north of Cambridge.

Opening Times and Service Times
Ely Cathedral daily April to October 07.00–19.00; November to March Monday to Saturday 07.30–18.00, Sunday 07.30–17.00. Services Sunday 08.15, 10.30, 15.45; Monday to Saturday 07.40, 08.00, 17.30; Thursday 11.30, 12.30.
Octagon tours May Day to September Monday to Saturday 10.30, 11.45, 14.15, 15.30; Sunday 12.30, 14.15. **West Tower** July and August Saturday 10.45, 12.00, 14.30, 16.00; Sunday 12.30, 14.30. **Stained-glass museum** April to September Monday to Saturday 10.30–17.00, Sunday 12.00–18.00; October to March Monday to Saturday 10.30–16.30, Sunday 12.00–16.15. Tel. 01353 667735, Fax. 665658. http://www.cathedral.ely.anglican.org

---

St Etheldreda (d. 679)

The Venerable Bede tells us that Etheldreda or Ethelreda was the daughter of King Anna of the East Angles. Although he was a Christian, he married her while she was still very young to the Prince of the Gyrvii. She was still a virgin when he died three years later. However, five years later her family arranged for her to marry King Egfrid of Northumbria, but she refused to consummate the marriage. Twelve years later she obtained Egfrid's permission to become a nun, and in about 672 she received the veil from St Wilfrid at Coldingham where her aunt Ebba was the Abbess. A year after that she founded a double monastery, with monks and nuns living in separate houses but worshipping together, at Ely, and remained the Abbess there until she died. She is the patron saint of Cambridge University. Another form of her name is Audrey, and cheap finery sold at the St Audrey fairs on her feast day gave us the word 'tawdry'.

NEWARK-ON-TRENT; SOUTHWELL (Nottinghamshire)

In **Newark** (NEW-urk), the **Church of St Mary Magdalene** is a Norman church built in 1180, with a tower added in 1220 and a spire from 1300 to 1370, 77 metres (252 feet) high, soaring above the town centre. The size of the glass windows in the transepts is breathtaking. There are two panels from a 'Dance of Death' painting, with the inscription 'As I am today, so you will be tomorrow'. The rood screen was made in 1508 by Thomas Drawsword of York, and the brightly gilded reredos by Sir Ninian Comper in 1937.

In the tiny city of Southwell (SUDH-ul), the ancient **Southwell Minster** was made the cathedral of Nottinghamshire in 1884, because there was no suitable church in the much larger county town of Nottingham. The present church is built on the site of a Saxon church, which used a **mosaic floor** from a Roman villa, and which can be seen in the south choir transept. There is also a well-preserved wall painting from a Roman bath-house in the south transept. The Saxons have left us a carved stone tympanum over a door in the north transept. The Normans completed the **towers** of the present cathedral in about 1108; it is the only cathedral in England

with three completely
Norman towers. The **north
porch** is Norman with a rare
example of barrel-vaulting.
The **nave** is also
predominantly Norman,
with dog-tooth decoration
on the arches; the **choir** is
thirteenth-century Early
English. A door from the
choir leads into the **Chapter
House**, dating from 1288,
which is large because it was
the place where the chapter
of nearly 50 canons met. The
Chapter House has no
central pillar, the first in the
world to attempt this, and is
chiefly famous for the
exquisite stone-carving, in
tough, amber grit-stone, of
foliage – buttercup,
hawthorn, hop, ivy, maple,
rose, oak and vine, so
delicate that each leaf looks
as though it has just opened
from a plant. The **screen** is
from the fourteenth century
and is highly decorated. The
east window contains
wonderful Flemish sixteenth-
century glass; the west front
has a Perpendicular seven-
light window with modern
glass from 1996 of a host of
angels. Newark is on the A1
and Southwell to the west of
it on the A612.

**Opening Times and Service
Times**
St Mary Magdalene's, Newark
Monday to Saturday
08.30–16.30; also Sunday
afternoons (summer). Closed 1
hr at lunchtime. Services Sunday
08.00, 09.30, 18.00; Wednesday
10.15. Tel. 01636 706473 or
704513
Southwell Minster daily
08.00–19.00 (dusk in winter).
Services Sunday 08.00, 09.30,
11.00, 15.15; Monday, Saturday
08.30; Tuesday to Friday 08.00;
Monday to Saturday 17.45. Tel.
01636 812649, Fax. 815904.
http://www.southwellminster.
org.uk

STAUNTON HAROLD;
MOUNT SAINT
BERNARD;
LUTTERWORTH
(Leicestershire)

Staunton Harold Church
stands in a picturesque
setting beside a lake in a park
and next to Staunton Harold
Hall. It was built during the
Commonwealth by a
royalist, who died in the
Tower of London three years
later. It is therefore in the
style of Charles I's reign,
with a Gothic exterior, and a
carved, wooden double-
decker pulpit, box-pews,
panelling and screens; the
pulpit and altar have their
original purple velvet
hangings. The organ, on the
gallery over the door, is one
of the earliest English organs
to survive in its original
form. The painted ceiling
represents creation, moving
from chaos into reasoned
order; only two other similar
ceilings are known, and may
refer obliquely to the chaos
of the Civil War. The reason
why many pilgrims keep

returning to this little church is to read again the inscription over the west door:

'In the year 1653 when all things sacred were throughout ye nation either demolisht or profaned, Sir Robert Shirley, Barronet, Founded this church; Whose singular praise it is to have done the best things in the worst times, and hoped them in the most callamitous. The righteous shall be had in everlasting remembrance.'

To reach the church follow the signs from the junction of the B587 with the A42 northeast of Ashby-de-la-Zouch (pronounced Zootch) towards the Ferrers Centre (or simply follow the sign of an anvil), and continue past the centre following signs to the Sue Ryder Centre in the old hall; the church is on the far side of this.

Mount Saint Bernard, on a side road in the Charnwood Forest area near Whitwick, is a living Roman Catholic Cistercian community, giving an impression of what the Yorkshire Abbeys must have been like before the Dissolution. In 1835 a small community was founded here, mostly of monks who had been members of a short-lived community at Lulworth or who had joined that community in its temporary home in France. They farmed the land and built a small monastery; many famous people came to visit them, and the sixteenth Earl of Shrewsbury paid for Augustus Pugin to build a new monastery, in simple Cistercian style, which was opened in 1844. They have always been active in promoting Christian unity, and many non-Catholics were among the visitors. The number of poor Irish immigrants, fleeing the great potato famine of the 1840s, when added to the existing rural poverty in Leicestershire, meant that the community were feeding tens of thousands of needy people each year, a service that has never been forgotten. Trappist silence is at the heart of their contemplative life, but modified to suit modern conditions. Visitors can attend the public end of the church during monastic services, and visit the shop and the calvary in the garden. The Guest Master can also arrange for days of prayer and retreat.

Lutterworth Parish Church was restored in the nineteenth century but still has two fifteenth-century wall paintings. It is close to Junction 20 of the M1. There is a monument to John Wyclif who was the parish priest here.

John Wyclif or Wycliffe (c. 1329–84)

'The Morning Star of the Reformation', as he is sometimes called, was the son of the Lord of the Manor of Wycliffe-on-Tees near Richmond in Yorkshire. He was educated at Oxford, and was Master of Balliol College by about 1360. In 1374 he was appointed Vicar of Lutterworth, and held the position until he died on 31 December 1384, though much of his time was spent teaching at Oxford. Wyclif attacked traditional medieval philosophy, and argued that the substance of the bread and wine remained after the consecration. He protested against the corruptions in the church of his time, maintaining that the Pope's claims were ill-founded in Scripture, that his salvation was no more certain than that of any other man, and that his authority depended on his conformity to the gospel. He also attacked the worldliness of monks, the worship of saints, clergy who drew the income of parishes without living in them, money-making pilgrimages, and other abuses. He taught that the Bible is the only criterion for Christian action and belief, and he began to translate it into English, so that every humble and holy man was to be free to read and interpret the Scriptures for himself. His followers, who became known as Lollards, continued and completed this work by producing the first complete Bible in the English language. Wyclif's teachings were condemned by successive Popes, and after his death, in 1415, the Council of Constance ordered his writings to be burned and his bones to be dug up. But in protesting against the abuses of the medieval church he was an important influence in a movement that later led to the Protestant Reformation.

Opening Times and Service Times
Staunton Harold Church (National Trust) April to September Wednesday to Sunday, October Saturday to Sunday, 13.00–17.00 or sunset if earlier. Tel. 01332 863822, Fax. 865272, clergy 864845. Email stauntonharold@ntrust.org.uk; http://www.benefice.org.uk
Mount Saint Bernard daily 07.00–19.30. Monastic Services daily 07.00, 12.15, 14.15, 17.30. Mass Sunday 08.00, 09.00; Monday to Saturday 08.00. Tel. 01530 832298 or 832022
Lutterworth Church Services Sunday 08.00, 10.30, 18.15 (1, 3); Thursday 10.30. Tel. 01455 552669. Email rector.stmarys. lutterworth@care4free.net; http://www.stmarys.lutterworth. care4free.net

KING'S CLIFFE
(Northamptonshire)

The Parish Church of **All Saints and St James**, King's Cliffe, is mostly fifteenth century with a twelfth-century tower and a thirteenth-century spire. On the left inside the churchyard gate is the tomb of William Law, who wrote his *Serious Call* here; on the right, outside the gate, is a new map showing the site of his birthplace, next to the Cross Keys Inn, and the library that he founded; over the door of the library is inscribed: 'Books of Piety are here lent to any Persons of this or ye neighbouring towns.' King's Cliffe is between the A43 and A47, west of Peterborough.

Service Times
All Saints and St James
Sunday 08.00 (1), 10.00; Wednesday 10.30. Tel. 01780 470314

NORTHAMPTON
(Northamptonshire)

The county town of Northamptonshire is known as a centre for shoe-making. **St Peter's Church** has a fine display of Norman blind arcading on the exterior, and a row of carved monsters. It was built in 1170 by Simon de St Liz, the first Norman Earl of Northampton, on the site of the church of the early Saxon settlement of Hampton, a royal estate that grew into a Danish town and by about 900 was the largest town in the area. St Peter's Church is no longer used for services. Keys are available from the Old Black Lion pub next door. The **Church of the Holy Sepulchre** in Sheep Street is one of only five Norman round churches in England. It has a circular nave and ambulatory, and a rectangular chancel that has been extended into a second nave and sanctuary. It was founded by Simon de Senlis

---

William Law (1686–61)

William Law was a fellow of Emmanuel College, Cambridge, but refused to take the oath of allegiance to George I. He became tutor at Putney to the father of Edward Gibbon (who wrote *The Decline and Fall of the Roman Empire*), then retired to King's Cliffe where he organized schools and almshouses and led a life of great simplicity and devotion. Law's *A Serious Call to a Devout and Holy Life* earnestly recommends a life of moral virtue and meditation; his later works have a more mystical tendency, emphasizing the love of God already within us.

> ### Philip Doddridge (1702–51)
>
> Doddridge was a dissenting minister in Northampton. He had a wide friendship, and believed that love of Christ is a surer test of orthodoxy than any precise formulation of words. His hymns are all pervaded by joy: 'Hark! the glad sound'; 'O happy day!'; and 'My God, and is thy table spread'.

in imitation of the Church of the Holy Sepulchre in Jerusalem when he came back from the crusades. **All Saints Church** in the Drapery was built after the fire of 1675 by Sir Edward Goudge, a colleague of Sir Christopher Wren, in the characteristic buff Northamptonshire ironstone.

Opening Times and Service Times

Church of the Holy Sepulchre
May to September Wednesday 12.00–16.00, Saturday 14.00–16.00. Services Sunday 10.30, 16.30; Wednesday 10.30. Tel. 01604 627988. Email holysepulchre@waitrose.com
All Saints daily 09.00–15.00; also Monday, Tuesday, Thursday, Friday 17.00–18.30. Services Sunday 08.00, 10.30 (and 18.30 during school terms)

BRIXWORTH; EARLS BARTON (Northamptonshire)

North of Northampton on the A508 is the village of **Brixworth**, with the largest completely Saxon church in the land. A monastery, probably of wood, was built

in around 690 by monks from Lindisfarne. It has been suggested that this was the important monastery of Cloveshoe where a synod was held in 746. Between 750 and 850 a stone church was built, using Roman tiles and distinctive Saxon arches in the nave and chancel, then rebuilt after being sacked by the Danes in the ninth century. Originally the arches in the nave led to a row of chambers, possibly side-chapels or monastic cells, and the clerestory windows were added to give light to the nave; but these chambers were abandoned in the thirteenth century. Originally there was a narthex the full width of the building; in the eleventh century it was replaced by the tower and the round stair turret; the spire was added in the fifteenth century. At the east end was a round apse, with an ambulatory round it for pilgrims to pass close to the relics of a saint; the ambulatory has been blocked off, but a much later reliquary was found which may have contained relics of

St Boniface (see p. 74). In the thirteenth century a Lady Chapel was built in the southeast corner, and a wooden screen which had been placed across the Saxon chancel arch in the fifteenth century was later moved to the Lady Chapel.

On the A45 there is another Saxon church, at **Earl's Barton**, with a tower built during the reign of Edgar the Peaceful (959–95), decorated with stones in a pattern copying the construction of timber houses. The tower door and the west door are Norman. The screen, restored in the 1930s, shows saints in modern dress.

Opening Times and Service Times

All Saints, Brixworth daily all year 10.00–18.00 (or dusk in winter). Services Sunday 07.45 (1), 10.00, 18.00 (or 16.30 November to February); Tuesday 09.30; Friday 07.30
All Saints, Earls Barton Monday to Saturday 10.30–12.30, 14.00–16.00. Services Sunday 08.30 (2), 10.00, 18.00; Wednesday 09.30. Tel. and Fax. 01604 810447

BEDFORD (Bedfordshire)

John Bunyan was born just to the south of Bedford in the village of **Elstow**, between the A6 and the A421, and although the house where he was born no longer exists, **Elstow Abbey church** contains the font in which he was christened. The Abbey was founded in 1078 by the niece of William the Conqueror, and became one of the richest Benedictine nunneries in the land. In the fourteenth century the Abbey church was twice its present length; six Norman arches remain to remind us of the glories of the past. John Bunyan repented that he had enjoyed bell-ringing in this church. There are windows illustrating his *The Pilgrim's Progress* and *The Holy War*. In Bedford, **St John's Rectory** is where John Gifford, the pastor of the Independent congregation, explained the faith to him, and has become 'The House of the Interpreter' in the allegory of *The Pilgrim's Progress*. For a while during the Commonwealth, the Independents were allowed to use St John's as their place of worship. The **Meeting House** was built in 1849 on the site of the barn where he preached from 1672. Next to it is the **Bunyan Museum** with a moving display of personal items. Bunyan was imprisoned in Bedford county gaol, which stood at the corner of High Street and Silver Street. He preached in many local villages; the village cross in **Stevington**, to the northwest of Bedford, has been identified as the

John Bunyan (1628–88)

The tinker of Bedford – actually he inherited his father's trade of working in brass and other metals – seems to have read no books other than the Bible, *The Book of Common Prayer*, Foxe's *Book of Martyrs*, and two or three more. He joined an Independent congregation and became a popular preacher. After the Restoration of the Monarchy he was imprisoned for refusing to conform to the established Church, and *Grace Abounding to the Chief of Sinners* was written while he was in Bedford gaol between 1660 and 1672. He was imprisoned again in 1676 and during that six months' confinement he wrote the first version of *The Pilgrim's Progress*. The simple parable and direct imagery have encouraged millions to see their progress in Christ as a pilgrimage, and many of the phrases have passed into the heart of the English language. 'He who would valiant be' and 'He that is down need fear no fall' are in many hymn books. After his release from prison he enlarged the book, wrote *The Holy War*, and continued to preach.

model for the place where Christian's burden rolled from his back. There is a holy well behind the parish church where formerly a group of nuns provided a hospice for pilgrims seeking healing. **Houghton House**, off the B530 from Bedford to Ampthill, was built by Inigo Jones for the Dowager Countess of Pembroke; the accounts include payments to 'the tinker', presumably Bunyan, who visited there often. The house is now ruined, but is thought to have been the basis of 'The House Beautiful', and the **Chiltern Hills** feature as 'The Delectable Mountains'. The familiar scenery of Bedfordshire formed the topography of the world's most famous allegory of life as a pilgrimage, and reminds us that every pilgrim can begin his or her journey to paradise by starting where they are.

Opening Times and Service Times
John Bunyan Museum March to October Tuesday to Saturday 11.00–16.00.
Bunyan Meeting Free Church, worshipping in Bunyan Meeting House, Services Sunday 11.00, 18.30. Tel. 01234 213722.
http://www.museums.bedfordshire.gov.uk/sites/bunyan/museum.html
St John's Church Monday, Tuesday, Friday 09.00–13.00. Services Sunday 10.30, 18.30. Tel. 01234 354818.

St John's Rectory by arrangement with Bedford St John Ambulance, Tel. first 01234 216200

Elstow Abbey Key at Vicarage or caretaker's house nearby. Services Sunday 08.00 (2, 4, 5), 09.30 (1, 3, 4), 11.00 (all), 18.30 (all). Tel. 01234 261477

Houghton House (English Heritage) always open

Stevington Church Keys from 25 Church Road or Tel. 01234 825743. Services Sunday 09.30 (1, 3), 10.00 (4), 18.00 (2)

BARNACK; CASTOR (Cambridgeshire)

The village of **Barnack** is on the B1443 northwest of Peterborough. **St John's Church** has a Saxon tower, with a short spire from about 1200 which may have been the first in England. The interior is full of carving. In the north aisle is a carving of Christ in Majesty, discovered under the floor in 1931, a masterpiece of Saxon art.

Near the A47 on the outskirts of Peterborough is the village of **Castor**, founded in Roman times. The Roman praetorium, built in about 250, was the second largest building in Roman Britain; it supervised an industrial area in the Nene river valley, where pottery known as Castor Ware was made. In 650 St Kyneburgha, a daughter of King Penda of Mercia, established a double monastery of women and men among the ruins of the Roman town. This was sacked by the Danish invaders, after which a college of priests occupied it as a minster, ministering to a wide area. Some of the stones from the Saxon church have been incorporated in the Norman building, including an eighth-century carving of an apostle, part of the shrine of St Kyneburgha, which attracted hundreds of pilgrims. There are wonderful carvings on the capitals at the crossing, of fights with wild beasts, and of two men fighting over a woman, possibly St Kyneburgha; they date from 1120–24. The tower is covered with marvellous Norman decoration. There is a fourteenth-century wall painting showing St Catherine with her wheel. The fifteenth-century oak roof of the nave has brightly coloured carvings of angels. There is also a delightful modern wood-carving of Kyneburgha as a young girl.

Service Times
St John's Church, Barnack
Sunday 08.00 (2), 10.00; Wednesday 07.30; Thursday 19.00. Tel. 01780 740234. http://www.parishnews-online.co.uk
Castor Church Sunday 10.15, 15.00; Monday to Saturday 07.30, 18.00. Tel. 01733 380244

PETERBOROUGH (Cambridgeshire)

Peterborough, near Junction 17 of the A1(M), began as a village of people serving the Saxon monastery, founded in about 655. This was sacked by the Danes in 870, and in the tenth century another Saxon church was built as the minster of a Benedictine abbey. This building was destroyed in a fire in 1116, and the present building was started two years later and completed in 1238. In 1643 Cromwell's soldiers smashed the stained glass, the statues, the high altar and the cloisters, but what remains is a superb **cathedral** with an interior that is one of the greatest examples of Norman architectural style. Then again in 2001 there was a fire that was put out with about 15 minutes to spare before it would have destroyed the Cathedral completely. Little was in fact destroyed, but much was damaged by smoke; restoration will take several more years.

From the outside, the thirteenth-century Early English **west front** makes a bold statement with three great recessed Gothic arches, and in the middle is a fourteenth-century porch in the Perpendicular style. Before the fire, the Norman **nave, transepts** and **choir** gave a view the full length of the building, uninterrupted except for the striking modern **hanging crucifix** from 1975. The **nave ceiling** is from about 1228 and is decorated with painted figures of mythical beasts, saints and bishops; it is one of the finest examples of medieval art in Europe and will need patient cleaning. The **ceiling of the sanctuary** is fifteenth century, and the **east end**, dating from the end of that century, has Perpendicular fan-vaulting, and seventeenth-century **Flemish tapestries** in the apse. There is a **Saxon sculpture** from the eighth century, known as the Monks' Stone or Hedda Stone, in the east end, and **St Oswald's Chapel** was reputed to contain an arm of the saint; there is a watchtower for a monk to keep guard over this precious relic. In the north choir aisle is the **tomb of Catherine of Aragon**, Henry VIII's first queen. Mary Queen of Scots was first buried here in 1587, but her remains were moved to Westminster Abbey in 1612.

Opening Times and Service Times
Peterborough Cathedral
Monday to Saturday 08.30–17.15, Sunday 12.00–17.15. Services Sunday 08.00, 08.15, 09.30, 10.30, 15.30; Monday to Saturday 07.40, 08.00, 17.30 (or 15.30 on Saturday); Wednesday 11.00; Friday 13.00.

Oliver Cromwell (1599–1658)

The most vehement advocate of applying Puritan principles to national life was Oliver Cromwell, Member of Parliament for his birthplace of Huntingdon, then for Cambridge where he had graduated, and cavalry commander at the Battle of Edgehill. As leader of the Independents who would make no compromise with King Charles I, Cromwell led his New Model Army which defeated the King at Naseby. At first contented merely to strip the King of some of his powers, royalist plots and rebellions persuaded Cromwell to press for the prosecution and eventual execution of the King. He was the chairman of the Council of State in the new Commonwealth, and he defeated the Scots royalists at the Battle of Worcester, which effectively ended the Civil War. As Lord Protector he reorganized the Church of England on Calvinist lines, but with a limited degree of toleration.

Tel. 01733 453342, Fax. 552465.
http://www.peterborough-cathedral.org.uk

HUNTINGDON (Cambridgeshire)

Huntingdon, on the A14, is where Oliver Cromwell was born; he was baptized in the fifteenth-century **All Saints Church**, opposite which there is a museum with Cromwellian relics in what remains of a medieval hospital, and was later the local grammar school, in the High Street.

Opening Times and Service Times

Cromwell Museum April to October Tuesday to Friday 11.00–13.00, 14.00–17.00; Saturday, Sunday 11.00–13.00, 14.00–16.00; November to March Tuesday to Friday 13.00–16.00; Saturday 11.00–13.00, 14.00–16.00; Sunday 14.00–16.00; closed BH

All Saints Services Sunday 09.30, 18.30 (1, 3); Wednesday 10.00.
Tel. 01480 434463

East Anglia

The bulge of land on the east coast of England between The
Wash and the River Thames and consisting of the counties of
Norfolk and Suffolk, settled by people of the Angle tribe, is
known as East Anglia. Mostly flat, the barren fens were
drained by the heroic labours of Dutch settlers and turned
into fertile land. Many great churches lift their towers above
quite small villages, giving evidence of former prosperity.
Benjamin Britten's settings of the prose of George Crabbe,
performed at the annual Festival at Aldeburgh, where each of
them lived, give an impression of one side of life on the coast
of Suffolk. Many holiday-makers go boating on the Norfolk
Broads. Walsingham has for long been a destination for
pilgrimage; Norwich is one of the finest of English cathedrals.

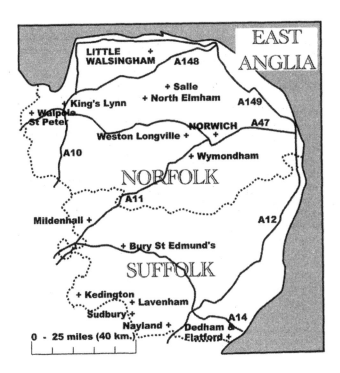

WALSINGHAM (Norfolk)

Walsingham received more pilgrims in the Middle Ages even than Canterbury, and has become a centre for the modern pilgrimage movement in England. In the reign of Edward the Confessor, Richeldis, the widow of the Lord of the manor of Little Walsingham, said that she had had a vision of the Virgin Mary, who took her in spirit to Nazareth and showed her the house where the angel Gabriel had appeared to her. Mary called Richeldis to measure this house and build a replica of it in Walsingham. This she did, and later a stone building was erected around it. Thousands of pilgrims, including the rich and famous and most of the kings of England, came to visit it, many of them removing their shoes at what came to be known as the Slipper Chapel and walking the last mile barefoot. All that remains of the large **Abbey** that grew up next to the shrine is a solitary arch and the shell of the refectory. The site is entered from the Information Centre and **Museum** at the corner of Holt Road and High Street. In 1896 the Roman Catholic Church re-purchased the **Slipper Chapel**, on the road to West Barsham, and some pilgrims still walk the last mile from there to the shrine, though not necessarily

Abbey arch, Shrine of Our Lady of Walsingham

barefoot. Next to it is the large **Chapel of Reconciliation**. When Revd Albert Hope Patten became the Anglican priest in 1921, he had the idea of rebuilding the **Holy House**, this time in brick, which he did at a site at the corner of Holt Road and Knight Street. It is surrounded by a large shrine church, during the construction of which a **well** was found; pilgrims can now drink the water or be sprinkled with it, with prayer for healing. Nearby is the tiny chapel of **St Michael and All Souls**, where pilgrims remember those who have died, and in 1927 the **Hospice of Our Lady Queen of the Sea** was opened, where

Pilgrimage Yesterday and Today

A fourth-century Spanish nun named Egeria described her pilgrimage to the Holy Land, and it was obviously already considered helpful to devotion to see the places where the events described in the Bible actually happened. To visit Rome where the apostles were martyred, and Compostela where the remains of St James were believed to have been found, later became equally important. In England the place of the martyrdom of St Thomas à Becket in Canterbury approached these in importance, and Walsingham was even more popular. Motives for pilgrimage were mixed. For some it was a means of bringing the biblical stories alive; for others an expression of penitence and an opportunity to ask for the intercessions of the saints, for forgiveness, healing and blessing. Today it has re-emerged as a means of deepening Christian fellowship in a parish or between a group of Christians, and of Christian adult education. The shrine at Walsingham, as well as offering the inspiration of large annual festivals, also provides an education centre that may be used by individuals and groups.

pilgrims may stay. The **Anglican Parish Church** is in Church Street, and the **Roman Catholic Church** is between the High Street and Back Lane. A group of **Russian Orthodox** have converted the old railway station, in Station Road, into a church where they celebrate the liturgy and paint icons. There is excellent ecumenical cooperation. Little Walsingham is between the A148 and A149; you may pass through Great and Little Snoring on the way.

Opening Times and Service Times
Anglican Parish Church
Services Sunday 11.00; Monday, Friday, Saturday 09.30; Tuesday 11.00; Thursday 19.30. Tel. 01328 821316
Anglican Shrine Services Sunday 07.30, 14.30, 16.00, 17.30, 18.00; Monday to Friday 07.30, 14.30, 17.00, 17.30, 18.00; Saturday 07.30, 12.00, 14.30, 16.15, 17.00, 18.00, 20.15. Tel. 01328 820255. http://www.walsingham.org.uk
St Michael and All Souls Chapel Mass daily 10.30; festivals 09.00
Museum and Abbey Grounds daily 10.00–16.30. Tourist Information Centre Tel. 01328 820510
Roman Catholic Church Services Sunday 10.30; Monday to Saturday 16.30
Russian Orthodox Services Sunday 10.30; Saturday 18.00
Slipper Chapel Services weekends 11.00–11.45, 12.00,

14.00, 15.00 (Sunday only); weekdays 11.00–11.45, 12.00, 14.30, 15.00, 16.00. Tel. 01328 820217, Fax. 821087. Email RCNatShrne@aol.com; http://www.walsingham.org.uk

NORWICH
(Norfolk)

Norwich (NORR-itch), the county town of Norfolk, is one of England's best preserved medieval cities. It enjoyed great prosperity in the Middle Ages, when it was the centre of the East Anglian wool trade, and many churches were built among the half-timbered houses and cobbled streets that nestle around the Cathedral. Some 30 flint churches still remain in the city, though many of them have passed their usefulness and been made redundant. Admiral Horatio Nelson was a pupil at Norwich School; John Sell Cotman was one of many talented Norfolk artists; Sir Thomas Browne was a physician in Norwich.

Norwich Cathedral was begun in 1096 and consecrated in 1278; two of the original **spiral pillars** in the nave mark the end of the first phase of building in 1119. The **transepts** and **tower** are solid Norman workmanship, and on the tower stands the fifteenth-century spire, replacing an earlier one which was blown down in a gale in 1362; at 96 metres (315 feet) it is the second highest in England after Salisbury. The **exterior** is faced with stone brought across the Channel from Caen in Normandy and up the river Wensum; the **east end** has fine flying buttresses and **ambulatory** chapels, unusual in an English cathedral. High over the **nave** and **transepts**, the fan-vaulted **roof** is marked by carved and painted bosses, which portray the whole story of God's dealings with the human race from Creation to Last Judgement. The **misericords** in the **choir** are worthy of note; behind the altar is the modern **Bishop's Throne**, with two pieces of carved stone underneath it which are believed to come from the Saxon Bishop's Throne which preceded it. The **Jesus Chapel** has an *Adoration of the Magi* painted in the 1480s by Martin Schwartz; and in **St Luke's Chapel**, at the east end of the ambulatory, is the famous *Despenser Reredos*, an anonymous masterpiece painted to commemorate the bishop who crushed the Peasants' Revolt in 1381. In the south aisle of the nave, the **Prior's Door**, in Decorated style, has on the exterior tympanum a carved and painted figure of Christ flanked by angels, bishops and monks, two of each. It

Sir Thomas Browne (1605–82)

Sir Thomas Browne studied medicine at Oxford, Montpellier and Padua, and received a doctorate from Leyden. He settled in Norwich and practised as a physician there for the rest of his life. Because of his travels he was much more broad-minded than most Englishmen of his day. He wrote *Hydriotaphia*, or Urn-Burial, an account of funeral practices in many countries, favouring cremation and opposing elaborate memorials. But his most famous work was his earliest, *Religio Medici*, a confession of the faith of a doctor. His was a tolerant faith, which he thought required that we should use our intellects, and he said he would make salvation no narrower than Christ did.

leads into the two-storey cloisters, the largest in England, where the roof bosses are lower and easier to see than those in the nave. The cloisters were rebuilt between about 1297 and 1430.

Among the many beautiful churches in the city, **St Peter Mancroft** is justifiably famous for its long and graceful Perpendicular nave and hammerbeam roof leading to a massive **tower** with a spire like a spike on the top of it. The great **east window** contains medieval glass; the **font** is from the fifteenth century.

East of Norwich Castle is King Street, turning off which, St Julian's alley leads to **St Julian's Church**, rebuilt after bomb damage; in the adjoining cell Dame Julian wrote her *Revelations of*

Divine Love, the first book by a woman to achieve a wide circulation in England.

Opening Times and Service Times

Norwich Cathedral daily May to September 07.30–19.00; September to May 07.30–18.00. Services Sunday 07.30, 08.00, 09.15 (1, 2), 10.30, 15.30, 18.30; Monday to Saturday 07.30, 08.00, 17.15 (except Saturday); Tuesday, Thursday 11.00; Monday, Wednesday, Friday 12.30; Saturday 15.30. Tel. 01603 218321, Fax. 766032. http://www.cathedral.org.uk
St Peter Mancroft Monday to Friday 10.00–15.30 (winter); 10.00–16.00 (summer); Saturday 10.00–12.30. Services Sunday 08.00, 10.00, 11.15 (3), 18.30; Tuesday 13.10; Wednesday 07.15; Thursday 10.50. Tel. 01603 627816 or 610443
The Julian Centre April to September Monday to Saturday 11.00–16.00; October to March 11.00–15.00. Church daily April

> ## *Mother Julian of Norwich (c. 1342–1420)*
>
> Mother Julian lived as a recluse at Norwich, yet many people came to learn about prayer from her. In a series of visions or 'showings', Julian sees that the whole universe is no greater, compared to the greatness of God, than a hazelnut, yet God loves his creation with a mother's care. We should pray even when we do not feel like it, because it is God who is praying in us. She wrote: 'He said not: Thou shalt not be tempested, thou shalt not be travailed, thou shalt not be afflicted; but he said: Thou shalt not be overcome. . . . Wouldst thou learn thy Lord's meaning in this thing? Learn it well. Love was his meaning. Who shewed it thee? Love. What shewed he thee? Love. Wherefore shewed it he? For Love. Hold thee therein and thou shalt learn and know more in the same. But thou shalt never know nor learn therein other thing without end. Thus was I learned that Love was our Lord's meaning.'

to September 07.30–17.30; October to March 07.30–16.00. Services Sunday 08.00, 18.30 (1); Monday 07.30; Wednesday 19.30; Friday 07.30. Tel. 01603 767380. Email TheJulianCentre@ ukgateway.net; http://www. home.clara.net/frmartinsmith/ julian/

WALPOLE ST PETER (Norfolk)

West of King's Lynn, between the A17 and the A47, signs point to the villages of Walpole St Andrew and Walpole St Peter. **St Peter's Church** is called by its proud parishioners 'The Queen of the Marshlands' and 'The Cathedral of the Fens'. There was a church on the site in 1021. The present tower was built in around 1300, but a sea-flood in 1337 destroyed everything else. The present nave was built in 1360, and the chancel in 1425. The vast size of this Perpendicular-style building, with its large windows filling it with light, was made possible by the earnings of local sheep-farmers; two shepherds' crooks are laid up against the north wall. A set of pews is placed sideways on in the south aisle, with wonderful carved pew ends from the fifteenth century; the pews in the nave, and the long western wooden screen, are from about 1630. The choir screen has painted panels from about 1450. The altar is at the top of a flight of steps, and a right-of-way passes underneath in a tunnel, locally known as

Margery Kempe (c.1373–after 1433)

Margery Kempe was a contemporary of Julian of Norwich, and visited her in her cell. She was born at King's Lynn, married John Kempe and bore him 14 children. After a period of madness she received a number of visions, and with her husband made a pilgrimage to Canterbury. Later, leaving her husband behind, she went on pilgrimage to the Holy Land and the shrine of St James at Compostela. Without fearing anyone she condemned sin wherever she saw it. Her enemies then ensured that she was herself formally condemned; undoubtedly she was psychologically disturbed, but she laid all her troubles before God in prayer, and wrote the prayers in her book. *The Book of Margery Kempe* was the first autobiography in English. In it she writes about the gift of tears: she regarded the ability to cry frequently as a blessing which God had given her, for her own benefit and for the benefit of those for whom she wept. She was also given a strong awareness of the presence of Jesus, and his love for herself and for the world. At the end of her life she devoted her time to nursing her invalid husband.

'The Bolt Hole'. A sign by the door warns those entering the church to remove their 'pattens' first, and a pair of wooden sandals hangs by it to explain the meaning of the word.

Opening Times and Service Times
St Peter's daily 09.30–16.00. Services Sunday 09.30 (1), 10.30; Wednesday 10.30. Tel. 01945 780252.
http://www.ely.anglican.org/parishes/walpole-st-peter/

KING'S LYNN (Norfolk)

Known in the Middle Ages as Bishop's Lynn, this was a bustling sea port and a member of the Hanseatic league. The **Priory Church of St Margaret, St Mary Magdalene and All the Virgin Saints** was founded in 1101 by the first Bishop of Norwich. When the Pope discovered that the Bishop had paid to be appointed, he compelled him to build this and other abbeys as penance. For its first 400 years it was a Benedictine priory; the carved choir stalls are from 1376. Two memorial brasses from 1349 and 1364 are the largest in England. In 1741 a storm demolished the steeple, so the Georgian nave was built in 1744. One of the clock faces in the west front shows, not the time, but the state of the tides, and markings by the door show the flood levels. The organ was commissioned by Dr Charles Burney from Johannes Snetzler in 1754. King's Lynn is at the junction of the A47 and A10.

Opening Times and Service Times

St Margaret's Monday to Saturday 07.45–17.45; Sunday 07.45–19.45. Services Sunday 08.00, 10.00, 18.30; Monday, Wednesday, Thursday 08.00; Tuesday 19.15; Friday 10.30. Tel. 01553 772858. http://www.stmargaretskingslynn.org.uk

NORTH ELMHAM; SALLE; WESTON LONGVILLE (Norfolk)

The Saxon Cathedral for Norfolk was at **North Elmham**. Such was the simplicity of the Saxon Christians that it was only a small wooden building. In 1071 the see was moved to Thetford, and in 1094 to Norwich. The Norman bishops, however, built a stone chapel next to their palace here, and in 1388 Bishop Despenser turned it into a fortress. Only the ruins of this survive, cared for by English Heritage and the parishioners. It is open until 20.00 in summer, or till dusk in winter. The parish church next to it was built by Bishop Herbert de Losinga in about 1096. It is on the B1110 north of Dereham.

The tiny hamlet of **Salle**, pronounced 'Saul', has one of the largest and most beautiful parish churches in Norfolk. Rebuilt in the early fifteenth century by families made rich from the wool trade, its spire standing high above the fields, its interior is full of light. You are met as you enter the west door by the loud ticking of the clock, and a font showing carvings of the seven sacraments, with a tall cover suspended by a bracket from the bell-ringers' gallery. The chancel roof is supported by a multitude of carved angels; there are medieval carved choir stalls and stained glass, and there is a three-decker pulpit in the nave. It is reached by a country road from the B1145, east of North Elmham.

Turning off the A1067 at Morton you can drive down a single-track road to the village of **Weston Longville**, where Parson Woodforde wrote his diary. Parson is an old English word meaning the 'person' of a parish. The Rectory has been rebuilt since his day, but the **Church of All Saints** still has its thirteenth-century tower, fourteenth-century Tree of Jesse painting and fifteenth-century rood screen which he knew. There is a painting of

James Woodforde (1740–1802)

James Woodforde became Rector of Weston Longville in 1776, and wrote *The Diary of a Country Parson* describing his life from 1759 until the year of his death. It gives a rare insight into the life of the Church in the eighteenth century, but what astonishes many readers is his description of the enormous meals that he and his companions ate. If to enjoy the good gifts of God's creation is a form of worship, then James Woodforde was a devout believer.

James Woodforde and a memorial. An American flag reminds us that US airmen were stationed here in 1945.

Service Times
North Elmham church see http://www.norfolkcoast.co.uk/churches/ch_northelmham.htm
Salle church Sunday 08.00 (1), 10.00 (2, 3, 4), combined (5). Tel. 01603 870220
Church of All Saints, Weston Longville Sunday 08.00 (2), 10.00 (1), 18.00 (4). Tel. 01603 880163

WYMONDHAM (Norfolk)

On the A11 southwest of Norwich is Wymondham, pronounced 'WIN-dum'. A Benedictine abbey was founded in 1107, where the monks in 1409 built the octagonal tower at the crossing of the Abbey church to keep an eye on the townsfolk, and a thick wall to keep them out of the monks' section. The people retaliated 50 years later by building a larger, square west tower, so that they could look down on the monks. The two towers are visible for miles, and the original Norman nave, with its two aisles, which is all that remains of the Abbey church, is still a large building. Your attention is riveted, as soon as you enter, by the glorious huge reredos, covered in gold leaf, designed by Sir Ninian Comper in 1919.

Service Times
Wymondham Abbey Sunday 08.00, 10.00, 18.30. Tel. 01953 602269. http://www.wymondham-norfolk.co.uk/abbey/

MILDENHALL (Suffolk)

On the A1101 near the crossroads with the A11 is Mildenhall. The north porch of **St Mary and St Andrew's Church** is the largest in Suffolk, and the room over it used to serve as a school. It has one of the most splendid angel roofs in England, originally painted but now plain; the angel carvings are integral to the structure and cover almost the whole surface. Small shot and arrowheads fired by Oliver Cromwell's Parliamentary forces were found embedded in the wood, and one angel still has the head of a pike embedded in it, but even so they could not destroy them. There was a church here at the time of the Domesday Book survey, but the oldest part of the present building dates from 1220, and most of it was built around 1420. · It is 51 metres (168 feet) long by 20 metres (65 feet) wide.

Service Times
St Mary and St Andrew's
Sunday 08.00 (1, 2, 4), 09.30 (3), 11.00 (1, 2, 4). Tel. 01638 718840. Key kept at the second shoe shop along the High Street, Stebbings, at number 18.

BURY ST EDMUND'S (Suffolk)

Southeast from Mildenhall along the A1101 will take you to Bury St Edmund's.

There was a monastery there from 633 onwards, and after St Edmund was tortured and beheaded by the Danes in 869, it was entrusted in 900 with his remains. Many pilgrims travelled to visit the shrine of Edmund, king and martyr. The Danish King Canute, two centuries later, as a gesture of reconciliation conferred on the monastery the status of an abbey. It was rebuilt by Benedictine monks beginning in 1065; here Archbishop Langton and 20 barons forced King John to accept the Magna Carta. Before its dissolution in 1539 St Edmund's Abbey had become one of the richest monasteries in England. There were several churches in the complex of abbey buildings; the late-Perpendicular style nave which now forms the heart of **St Edmundsbury Cathedral,** formerly the church of St James, was built on the site of one of them in 1503. There is a Flemish stained-glass Susanna

---

King Edmund the Martyr (c. 840–70)

Edmund succeeded his father as King of the East Angles in 855, when he was only 15, but ruled fairly and justly. In 870 the Danes under Inguar and Hubba invaded his kingdom and defeated his army. They offered him his life if he would share the rule of East Anglia with Inguar, but he replied that as a Christian he could not share power with a pagan. So the Danes used him as a target for archery practice and then beheaded his body. St Edmundsbury soon became a great centre of pilgrimage.

window from about 1480, and a nineteenth-century hammerbeam roof, with angels. It was made a cathedral in 1914, and is still under construction; the crossing and choir, designed by Stephen Dykes Bower, were consecrated in 1970; a gallery representing the north transept was blessed in 2002, and work will start soon on the building of the tower, making it the last English cathedral to reach completion. The thousand or so embroidered kneelers are an example of how ordinary Christians still like to involve their voluntary efforts in the decoration of their churches. The **Abbey Ruins** nearby, where in the Middle Ages thousands of pilgrims used to come to the shrine of St Edmund, has a good Visitor Centre.

Opening Times and Service Times
Abbey Ruins (English Heritage) daily dawn–dusk. **Visitor Centre** daily Easter to October 10.00–17.00. Tel. 01284 764667
St Edmundsbury Cathedral daily June to August 08.30–20.00; September to May 08.30–17.30. Services Sunday 08.00, 10.00, 11.30, 15.30; Monday, Tuesday, Thursday 07.30, 17.30; Wednesday 07.30, 13.00, 17.30; Friday 07.30, 08.45, 19.00; Saturday, BH 09.00, 17.30. Tel. 01284 754933, Fax. 768655. http://www. stedscathedral.co.uk

FLATFORD MILL; NAYLAND; SUDBURY (Suffolk)

The Stour Valley, south of Ipswich on the A12 and then left on the B1070, contains **Flatford Mill**, and many other scenes painted by John Constable (1776–1837). **St James' Church, Nayland**, on the B1087, contains Constable's painting of *The Last Supper*. Further south in the Stour Valley is **Sudbury**, on the B1508, where Constable went to school and the artist Thomas Gainsborough (1727–88) was born in the late medieval 'Gainsborough's House', which is now a museum and contains several of his paintings.

Opening Times and Service Times
Flatford Mill (National Trust) not open to the public, but the opposite bank of the river is always accessible. The Bridge Cottage contains a John Constable exhibition. January to February Saturday to Sunday 11.00–15.30; March to April Wednesday to Sunday 11.00–17.30; daily May to September 10.00–17.30; daily October 11.00–17.30; November to December Wednesday to Sunday 11.00–15.30. Tel. 01206 298260, Fax. 299193
St James', Nayland daily 09.00–16.00 but varies. Services Sunday 08.00, 09.30 (except 3), 10.00 (3), 18.30 (except 1). Tel. 01206 262316

**Gainsborough's House,
Sudbury** Tuesday to Saturday
10.00–17.00; Sunday, BH
14.00–17.00; closes 16.00
November to March. Tel. 01787
880286, Fax. 376991

LAVENHAM;
KEDINGTON
(Suffolk)

In the charming medieval
town of **Lavenham** stands the
fifteenth-century **Church of
St Peter and St Paul**, with
two tombs surrounded by
intricately carved wooden
screens, possibly the best
examples of their kind in
England. There is a detached
Lady Chapel, a most unusual
building with an ambulatory
running all round it. It is on
the A1141 west of Ipswich.

In **Kedington,** the **Church of
St Peter and St Paul** is
remarkable because neither
Cromwell nor over-
enthusiastic Victorian
'improvers' have altered the
interior. It has a triple-decker
pulpit, with a wig-stand and
a holder for an hour-timer, a
family pew opposite made
out of the original chancel-
screen, and many box pews
which now serve the useful
purpose of preventing small
children from running about.
Underneath trapdoors in the
floorboards are remains of a
Roman villa, and above the
altar is a wonderful Saxon
stone cross, with the figure of
the Crucified carved in low
relief. Kedington is off the
B1061 east of Haverhill.

**Opening Times and Service
Times
St Peter and St Paul,
Kedington** Monday to Friday
14.00–16.00; Saturday to
Sunday, BH 14.30–16.30.
Services Sunday 09.30 (1–4),
18.00 (4). Tel. 01440 710216
**St Peter and St Paul,
Lavenham** daily 08.30–17.30.
Services Sunday 08.00, 10.00,
19.30 (1); Wednesday 09.30 (1).
Tel. 01787 247244

North of London

Only two counties remain in our tour of English Holy Places, northeast and north of Greater London. Despite being in the commuter-belt they have their own distinctive character and a niche in the religious history of the land.

ST ALBAN'S (Hertfordshire)

The city of St Alban's is where English Christianity began, for it was here that the first Christian British martyr was executed. The Roman settlement of Verulamium was established here in 49, sacked by Queen Boudicca (Boadicea) in 61, and destroyed by fire in about 155. The excavations can be seen in **Verulamium Park** beside the river; many items of Roman manufacture discovered there are displayed in **Verulamium Museum** in St Michael's Street off Bluehouse Hill; and the remains of the **Roman**

Theatre are on the opposite side of Bluehouse Hill. A shrine to St Alban the martyr was erected on a hilltop where **St Alban's Cathedral** now stands, and thousands of pilgrims flocked to visit it. King Offa, the Saxon King of Mercia, established a Benedictine monastery here. The Saxons gathered together heaps of bricks from the remains of the Roman city, ready to build a larger church, but had not started by the time of the Norman Conquest. In 1077 the present building and its Norman central tower were begun, using the Roman bricks conveniently to hand,

0 - 25 miles (40 km.)

M11

A1(M)   + Thaxted

M1   HERTFORDSHIRE   ESSEX   + Copford

ST ALBAN'S +   + Hatfield   A12

M25   + Waltham Abbey

NORTH OF LONDON

by Paul of Caen, a Norman who may have been the illegitimate son of Lanfranc the Archbishop of Canterbury. Nicholas Breakspear, the only Englishman to become Pope, was born in St Alban's, and in 1156 declared the Abbot to be the premier Benedictine abbot in England. In 1217 Matthew Paris, a great historian, became a monk here.

Between 1195 and 1235 the nave was lengthened in the Early English style; it is 84 metres (275 feet) long, and when five piers collapsed on the south side the piers which replaced them were in the Decorated style. The

Fourteenth-century wall painting, St Alban's Cathedral

thirteenth-century presbytery ceiling is the oldest wooden ceiling in England. There are impressive medieval wall paintings and ceiling panels. The Lady Chapel dates to 1320, the nave screen is dated to 1350, the reredos is from 1484, and the medieval shrine of St Alban has been reassembled behind the high altar. The church became a cathedral in 1877. The west front is Victorian, from 1879, and the Chapter House and Visitors' Centre from 1982.

Opening Times and Service Times
St Alban's Cathedral daily 09.00–17.30. Services Sunday 08.00, 09.30, 11.00, 12.15 (1, 3, 5), 18.30. Tel. 01727 860780, Fax. 850944. Email mail@ stalbanscathedral.org.uk; http://www.stalbanscathedral.org.uk
Roman Theatre daily April to September 10.00–17.00; October to March 10.00–16.00. Tel. 01727 835035
Verulamium Museum Monday to Saturday 10.00–17.30; Sunday 14.00–17.30. Tel. 01727 751810 or 751817. http://www.stalbansmuseums.org.uk

THAXTED; COPFORD (Essex)

The magnificent fourteenth-century church at **Thaxted** has a 55-metre-high (180 feet) spire and a light, airy interior. It was decorated by the vicar, Conrad Noel (1869–1942), a leader of the Anglo-Catholic Revival, and

St Alban the First British Martyr (d. c. 209)

The first Christian to be killed for his faith in the British
Isles was martyred in Verulamium. The date is rather less
certain; traditionally it was said to be during the
persecution started by the Emperor Diocletian at the
beginning of the fourth century, but now it is thought that
he died rather earlier than that. The story is told by the
Venerable Bede, and a number of earlier authors as well.
Alban was a Romano-British pagan from a good family.
When the persecution broke out, Amphibalus, a Christian
priest fleeing for his life, begged him for shelter. Although
he knew the penalties for doing so, Alban allowed the
fugitive to hide in his house and asked him to explain his
religion. Alban was converted and baptized. When the
priest's pursuers came near the house, Alban said that a
teacher who could make further converts was of more use
to the Church than a newly baptized disciple, so he sent
the priest away and dressed himself in the priest's cloak.
The soldiers arrested Alban and brought him before the
magistrate, enabling the priest to get away alive, at least
for the time being. The magistrate, furious at how he had
been tricked, ordered Alban to be beheaded. The hill on
which he was executed very soon became a place of
Christian pilgrimage.

Gustav Holst composed his
Planets Suite while living in
Thaxted, and played the
organ in the church. The
room above the north porch
is a chapel dedicated to the
memory of John Ball, 'priest-
martyr' and organizer of the
Peasant Revolt in 1381. In
the south aisle is a charming
window from about 1450
telling the story of Adam and
Eve. Thaxted is on the B184
southeast of Saffron Walden.

**St Michael's Church,
Copford,** was started around
1130 and still has the
springers for a stone vault,
which appears to have been
replaced with a wooden roof
in the fifteenth century. In
the thirteenth century,
Norman arches were inserted
in the south wall and an aisle
added; one of the arches is of
brick, a material that was
only just beginning to be
made in England at the time;
they are probably mixed with
reused Roman bricks. At the
same time all the walls were
covered by paintings made
directly onto the wet plaster,
which were therefore very
durable. Whitewashed over
at the Reformation, they
were rediscovered in the

nineteenth century, and repainted with varying degrees of ruthlessness. Those in the apse at least give an idea of what most churches looked like before the Reformation; over the pulpit there is a painting of Jesus raising Jairus's daughter from death, which is almost unaltered. They form one of the best collections of medieval wall paintings in the country. Follow signs from Colchester to Copford, Copford Green and Copford Church; the church is tucked behind the cricket club.

Service Times
St Michael's Church, Copford
Sunday 08.00 (1, 3); 11.00 (1–4); 10.30 (5 in various churches). Tel. 01621 815434
Thaxted Church Sunday 08.00, 10.00; Monday, Thursday, Friday 09.30; Wednesday 10.00; Saturday 12.00. Tel. 01371 830221

WALTHAM ABBEY (Essex)

An abbey was founded here by King Sabert of the East Saxons in 610, and the first stone church on the site in 780 was built on the orders of King Offa. In about 1020 a huge stone crucifix, which had been found buried on a Somerset hilltop, was brought here, and pilgrims started coming to the **Abbey of the Holy Cross** to pray for healing. The more superstitious may have thought that the cross itself had healing powers; those who were wiser prayed to Jesus Christ who in his love gave his life for us on the cross. King Harold rebuilt the church in 1060 and came to pray here before the Battle of Hastings in 1066. After he died his body, so mutilated that only his widow, Edith Swan-Neck, could identify it, was buried here behind the high altar. Part of Henry II's penance for the murder of Thomas à Becket was to triple the Abbey's size, so that it was one of the largest abbeys in England, rivalling Canterbury. All that remains after the Dissolution is a glorious Norman nave, with spiral and chevron grooves on the pillars. The east end was splendidly decorated by William Burges in 1860, with some of Burne-Jones's earliest windows. East of the present east wall is the outline of the original apse, with a stone identifying the probable site of the high altar and where King Harold was buried. The Lady Chapel to the south of the choir has a fourteenth-century wall painting of the Last Judgement. Waltham Abbey is near Junction 26 of the M25 London orbital road.

Opening Times and Service Times
Waltham Abbey opens at 12.00 Sunday; 11.00 Wednesday; 10.00 other days; closes 16.00

Thomas Fuller (1608–61)

Successively curate of St Benet's, Cambridge, Rector of Broadwindsor, Dorset, Vicar of Waltham Abbey and Rector of Cranford, Fuller is chiefly remembered for his biographical writings. He compiled a Church history of Britain, and the book called *Worthies of England*, published posthumously and generally known as 'Fuller's Worthies'.

---

winter, 18.00 during British Summer Time. Services Sunday 08.00, 10.30, 18.30; Monday to Saturday 08.30; Monday to Friday 17.00; Tuesday 10.30; Wednesday 10.00. Tel. 01992 767897. Email abbey-po@fish.co.uk

HATFIELD HOUSE (Hertfordshire)

Leaving the M25 at Junction 24 takes you onto the A1000 north to Hatfield House. The red brick **Old Palace**, built in 1485, is where Queen Elizabeth I spent her childhood, and was kept a virtual prisoner by her half-sister Queen Mary; it is said that under an oak-tree nearby she first heard that she had become Queen. The gardens in front of the Old Palace have been recreated in the seventeenth-century formal style, with a knot garden and a herb garden. During her reign it was occupied by her powerful adviser Lord Burleigh, and after her death between 1607 and 1611, his son Lord Robert Cecil, first Earl of Salisbury, partially

demolished it and built the stately **Hatfield House** beside it. The Marble Hall has a richly carved Jacobean oak ceiling, screen, minstrels' gallery and panels; the huge seventeenth-century allegorical tapestry came from Brussels; the 'Ermine Portrait' of Queen Elizabeth I is attributed to Nicholas Hilliard, and there is one of her cousin Mary Queen of Scots believed to be by Rowland Lockey. The Grand Staircase is of oak and a superb example of Jacobean carving; it is guarded by heraldic beasts, and there is a relief of John Tradescant, the gardener to King Charles I, on one of the newels at the top; the portrait of Elizabeth I here is known as 'The Rainbow Portrait'. The Long Gallery has a gold-leaf ceiling; crystal by Cellini is displayed at one end, and Queen Elizabeth's silk stockings, hat and gloves at the other. The library of 10,000 books contains a mosaic portrait of Robert Cecil, a letter from Mary Queen of Scots and her

227

Queen Elizabeth I (1533–1603)

The Virgin Queen cared strongly about the unity of her nation; she disliked Catholicism because the Catholics had declared her illegitimate, and feared that the Calvinists, with their desire to abolish bishops, would before long threaten the monarchy. So she tried to steer a middle course, and at the beginning of her reign the Catholic Mass and the 1552 *Book of Common Prayer* were used side by side. But when Pope Pius V excommunicated Elizabeth and told her subjects they need no longer obey her, Elizabeth was afraid that a Catholic revolt would join the Spanish Armada which threatened to invade, and ordered the execution of Mary Queen of Scots. Tired of fruitless theological disputes about what Jesus meant when he said of the communion bread, 'This is my body', she wrote a verse which though appalling poetry is sound religious common sense:

> The Word it was that spake it;
> He took the bread and brake it;
> And what his word does make it,
> That I believe and take it.

execution warrant signed by Lord Burleigh. The chapel has Flemish stained glass with biblical scenes. Visitors today can be taken on midweek conducted tours of the New Palace, or explore it for themselves at weekends. Follow signs to Old Hatfield and Hatfield Railway Station.

Opening Times
Hatfield House Park daily 11.00–17.30; New Palace daily 12.00–16.00. Tel. 01707 287010, Fax. 287033.
http://www.hatfield-house.co.uk

Further Reading

Donald Attwater with Catherine Rachel John, *The Penguin Dictionary of Saints*, Penguin Books, London 1995 (3rd edition).

Ronald Blythe, *Divine Landscapes*, Canterbury Press, Norwich 1998 (2nd edition).

Janet and Colin Bord, *Sacred Waters, Holy Wells and Water Lore in Britain and Ireland*, Paladin Grafton Books, Collins Publishing Group, London 1986.

F.L. Cross and E.A. Livingstone, *The Oxford Dictionary of the Christian Church*, Oxford University Press, London, New York, Toronto 1997 (3rd edition).

John Gordon Davies, *Pilgrimage Yesterday and Today, Why? Where? How?*, SCM Press, London 1988.

David Edwards, *The Cathedrals of Britain*, Pitkin Unichrome Ltd, Andover, Hants 1989.

David Hugh Farmer, *The Oxford Dictionary of Saints*, Oxford University Press, Oxford 1997 (4th edition).

William Golding, *The Spire*, Faber & Faber, London; Harcourt, Brace & World, New York 1964.

Simon Jenkins, *England's 1000 Best Churches*, Alan Lane/Penguin Press 1999.

Andrew Jones, *Every Pilgrim's Guide to Celtic Britain*, Canterbury Press, Norwich; Liguori Publications, Liguori, Missouri 2002.

Ellis Peters (Edith Pargeter), *A Morbid Taste for Bones*, Macmillan 1977; and another 18 novels in the 'Brother Cadfael' series; the first 13 published by Macmillan, the rest by Headline in hardback, and all by Futura in paperback.

Robin Whiteman, *The Cadfael Companion*, Macdonald, London 1991.

Glossary

abbot (Aramaic 'abba' = father) the ruler of a religious community called an abbey

aisle (French = wing) the section at the side of the nave or choir

ambulatory a passage for processions around the east end of a church (see Norwich Cathedral)

apse the section at the east end, either semicircular or polygonal (see Wreay)

arcade series of arches, resting on columns or piers

baldachin canopy supported by pillars over an altar or throne

Baroque architectural style modelled on Classical style but with extravagant features (see Great Witley)

barrel vaulting roof with the same semicircular section from end to end (see St Martin-in-the-Fields)

basilica a church modelled on a Roman judgement hall, usually with an apse (see Wing)

battlements roof edging with depressions ('embrasures') through which a weapon could be fired

bays the vertical section of a building defined by one arch width

blind arcade series of arches raised on a wall surface (see Lincoln Cathedral)

boss raised central point of a roof, often carved

box pews seating with wooden surrounds raised to head height to prevent draughts (see St Mary's, Whitby)

buttresses sections protruding from a wall to take the weight of a roof

Byzantine style of architecture from the Eastern Church (see Westminster Cathedral)

cathedral church containing the 'cathedra' or throne of a bishop

capital the top section of a pillar

chancel (Latin cancellus = screen) section of a church east of the crossing

chantry chapel endowed for Masses to be said for the souls of those who have died (see Winchester Cathedral)

Chapter House building for the ruling council or chapter of a monastery or cathedral (see Wells Cathedral)

choir part of the chancel where the choir sing

Classical 17th–18th-century style of architecture based on Greek and Roman models (see St Paul's Cathedral)

clerestory (pronounced clear-story) the top storey of a three-storey wall, with windows to admit light

cloisters (Latin claustrum = enclosed space) square area, with corridors where monks sat to write

close the area around a cathedral occupied by houses for the clergy (see Salisbury Cathedral)

colonnade a series of columns

corbel projecting stone to support a beam, or point from which ribs spring to support a roof

crossing the centre of a cross-shaped church

crypt room underneath a church, also called undercroft (see Ripon Cathedral; Hexham Abbey)

Decorated style of Gothic architecture with elaborate tracery about 1250–1340 (see Ely Cathedral)

diocese or **see** area where a bishop rules the church

dog-tooth zigzag decoration of a Norman arch

Early English style of Gothic architecture with tall slim lancet windows, slim pillars of Purbeck marble, and ribbed vaults, about 1175–1250 (see Salisbury Cathedral)

east end the end of a church with the main altar

fan-vault decorated roof, almost horizontal, with ribs spreading out in a fan pattern (see King's College, Cambridge)

flying buttresses buttresses with the centre cut away to form half an arch (see Norwich Cathedral)

gargoyle carving of an ugly face, often used as a water-spout

Gothic style of architecture characterized by pointed arches

Gothic-Revival nineteenth-century imitation of Gothic (see Truro Cathedral)

Green man a face peering through some leaves, which may have been an attempt to Christianize an old fertility symbol, and show that our God, too, is at the heart of nature (see Evesham Abbey)

hall church with aisle roofs the same height as the nave

hammerbeam wooden roof with horizontal beams projecting a short way from the walls, on which a central arch rests (see Westminster Hall). Earlier wooden roofs had tie-beams right the way across, or may be waggon roofs

hatchments boards with the family coat of arms, put up at the time of a funeral

jamb the vertical side of a doorway

Jesse Tree based on Isaiah 11.1, Matthew 1.6–17: 'there shall come a shoot from the stump of Jesse', a family tree with King David's father Jesse as the first member and Jesus Christ as the last (see Norwich Cathedral)

Lady Chapel chapel dedicated to the Blessed Virgin Mary (see Gloucester Cathedral)

lancet a tall slender section of a window, with a pointed top

lantern the highest point of a roof when it has windows to let light in or out (see Ely Cathedral)

liernes ribs in a roof vault that link the main ribs to each other, but are decorative rather than structural

lintel horizontal beam at the top of a rectangular doorway or window

long and short work alternating strips of stone at corners of a Saxon building (see All Saints', Earl's Barton)

minster (Latin monasterium) church from which missionary priests travelled out to minister to the area around

misericord (Latin = mercy) projection on a folding seat, monks could rest on this while standing, but not sit (see Exeter Cathedral)

nave (Latin navis = ship) the western part of a church where the congregation gather; the church is often compared to Noah's ark, and the inside of a church looks like a ship turned upside down

Norman the English name for Romanesque architecture, from around 1050–1200 (see Durham Cathedral)

Palladian a style of neo-Classical architecture based on the writings of Palladio (see Banqueting House, Whitehall)

pediment triangular area above a series of pillars (see St Paul's Cathedral)

pendants hanging section in fan-vaulting from which the ribs appear to fan out (see Henry VII chapel, Westminster Abbey)

Perpendicular uniquely English style of architecture characterized by vertical ribs running up the pillars into the almost horizontal ceiling, and windows with many rectangular panels separated by vertical mullions and horizontal transoms, approx. 1340–1530 (see King's College Chapel, Cambridge)

pier free-standing pillar or group of pillars that support an arch

piscina place for washing the communion vessels; it may be the only evidence of an earlier altar

pre-Raphaelite highly stylized and decorated artistic style, by the 'Arts and Crafts' movement of William Morris (see Birmingham Cathedral)

presbytery (Greek presbyteros = elder) or sanctuary, part of the chancel where the priests conduct services

prior the ruler of a priory, which is a less important religious community than an abbey

portico porch supported by pillars (see St Martin-in-the-Fields)

pulpit place from which sermons are preached. A double-decker pulpit has a sounding board to reflect the sound above it (see John Wesley's Chapel, Bristol); and a triple-decker pulpit has another small pulpit below it for the parish clerk to read or sing the service from (see St Mary's, Whitby)

pulpitum screen

rector formerly one who had the right to the Great Tithes of a parish, i.e. one-tenth of wheat, hay, wood and fruit

Renaissance the rebirth of knowledge about and imitation of classical Greece and Rome

reredos (REER-doss) a vertical panel or panels behind an altar

ribs strips of stone that support a roof. The main ribs run from the corbel to the boss, the ridge rib links the corbels, and the liernes, or tiercerons, link the main ribs to each other

Rococo architectural style in pastel colours with ogee (S-shaped) curves (see St John's Church, Shobdon)

Romanesque style of architecture typified by round arches, drum-like pillars, and zigzag decoration

rood screen screen that supports a rood or cross

Rose Window circular stained-glass window (see York Minster)

Saxon style of architecture characterized by irregular stone lengths, herring-bone patterns, long and short work at the corners, triangular and roundheaded openings to very small windows, c. 700–1066 (see p. 41)

screen structure separating two areas of a church, typically the crossing from the choir

sedilia seats for the clergy near the altar, built into the wall

spandrel triangular area between the curve of an arch and the horizontal and vertical wall edges (see Lincoln Cathedral)

springer the lowest point at the side of an arch which supports the weight. For a roof arch this is called the corbel

squint slit through wall giving a view of the altar. There are four possible explanations: (1) for lepers; (2) for those who had been excommunicated; (3) for those who only wanted to enter the church to see the elevation of the consecrated wafer; (4) so that a priest in a side chapel can synchronize his movements with those of the principal celebrant

tracery the stonework separating the panes of a window, or similar patterns elsewhere.

transept the arms projecting north and south from a church, at right angles to nave and choir

Transitional architecture that is between two styles, e.g. 1145–89 between Norman and Early English (see Ripon Cathedral)

tribune gallery roof space over an aisle

triforium the middle storey of a three-storey wall (clerestory, triforium and arcade)

Tudor Gothic style that is transitional between Perpendicular and Classical

tympanum the carved area over a doorway (see Kilpeck Church, Kilpeck)

vault a stone roof

vicar formerly one appointed by the Rector to take services, living off the lesser tithes and farming the Glebe land.

Vikings invaders from Scandinavia and Denmark, and the patterns of carving that they brought (see Kilpeck Church, Kilpeck)

west front the exterior at the west end of a church (see Ripon Cathedral)

zigzags decorations in Norman architecture, including chevrons, dogtooth and lozenges

Index

(References to people are in *italics*; place names are in normal type).

à Becket, St Thomas, 33
Abbey Dore (Herefords.), 114
Abingdon (Oxon.), 110
Aidan, St, 168
Alban, the First British Martyr, 223
Aldhelm, St, 57
Alfred the Great, King, 48
Alpha Courses, 13
Alfege, St, 25
Altarnun (Cornwall), 77
Andrewes, Lancelot, 49
Anselm, St, 33
Arthur, King, 83
Arundel (W. Sussex), 43
Ashbourne (Derbys.), 137
Augustine of Canterbury, St, 31
Augustinian Canons, 86
Austen, Jane, 54
Aylesford Priory (Kent), 37

Banqueting House, Whitehall, London, 16
Barfreston (Kent), 40
Barnack (Cambs.), 208
Bath (Somerset), 84
Battle Abbey (E. Sussex), 42
Baxter, Richard, 124
Becket, Thomas, St, 33
Bede, the Venerable, 171
Bedford (Beds.), 206
bell-ringing, 192
Bell, Bishop George Kennedy Allen, 38
Bemerton (Wilts.), 52
Benedict Biscop, 170

Bere Regis (Dorset), 62
Betjeman, Sir John, 82
Beverley Minster (E.R. Yorks.), 177
Birinus or Birinius, St, 100
Birmingham (W. Mids.), 129
Blake, William, 70
Bodleian Library, Oxford, 95
Bodmin (Cornwall), 79
Boniface, St, 74
Booth, William, 25
Boston (Lincs.), 186
Bournemouth (Dorset), 60
Bradford-on-Avon (Wilts.), 58
Brant Broughton (Lincs.), 185
Bridlington Priory (E.R. Yorks.), 176
Bristol (County Borough), 86
Brixworth (Northamptons.), 205
Brompton Oratory, London, 12
Brontë Sisters, 181
Browne, Sir Thomas, 215
Browning, Robert, 8
Buckfast Abbey (Devon), 67
Buckland Abbey (Devon), 75
Bunhill Fields, London, 21
Bunyan, John, 207
Burne-Jones, Sir Edward, 130
Burrington Combe (Somerset), 84

Bury St Edmund's (Suffolk), 220
Butler, Josephine, 167
Byrd, William, 162

Cadfael, Brother, 133
Caedmon, 174
Cambridge (Cambs.), 190
Campion, Thomas, 91
Campion, St Edmund, 14
Canterbury (Kent), 30
Carlisle Cathedral (Cumbria), 151
Cartmel Priory (Cumbria), 147
Castor (Cambs.), 208
Catherine of Aragon, 26
Chad, St, 122
Chalfont St Giles (Bucks), 108
Charing Cross, London, 16
Charles I, King, 18
Chaucer, Geoffrey, 35
Chawton (Hants.), 54
Cheadle (Staffs.), 136
Chelsea, London, 12
Chester (Cheshire), 144
Chichester (W. Sussex), 37
Christchurch Priory (Dorset), 60
circular churches, 19
Cirencester (Gloucs.), 112
City of London, 19
City Road, London, 20
Clapham, London, 22
Clitherow, Margaret, 162
Constable, John, 221
Cookham (Berks.), 106
Copford (Essex), 225
Corbridge (Northumbria), 166
Corfe Castle (Dorset), 62
Cornish Saints, 80
Cosin, John, 156
Covent Garden, London, 14
Coventry (W. Mids.), 118

Coverdale, Miles, 196
Cowper, William, 107
Cranmer, Thomas, 94
Crediton (Devon), 74
Cromwell, Oliver, 210
Crowland (Lincs.), 187
Cuthbert, St, 169

Deerhurst (Gloucs.), 113
Didling (W.Sussex), 45
Dissolution of the Monasteries, 43
Ditchling (E. Sussex), 42
Doddridge, Philip, 205
Donne, John, 9
Dorchester (Dorset), 64
Dorchester-on-Thames (Oxon.), 99
Dover (Kent), 40
Drake, Sir Francis, 76
Dunstan, St, 71
Durham (Co. Durham), 153

Earl of Shaftesbury, 15
Earls Barton (Northamptons.), 205
EAST ANGLIA, 211
EAST MIDLANDS, 189
Ebbsfleet (Kent), 30
Edgbaston (W. Mids.), 131
Edington (Wilts.), 58
Editha, St, 129
Edmund, King, 220
Edmund Rich, St, 111
Edward the Confessor, King, 7
Edward the Martyr, King, 63
Eliot, Thomas Stearnes, 190
Elizabeth I, Queen, 228
Ely (Cambs.), 197
Epstein, Jacob, 94, 119
Epworth (Lincs.), 183
Escomb (Co. Durham), 171
Etheldreda, St, 200
Eton (Berks.), 90
Evensong, 192

Evesham (Worcs.), 162
Execution of King Charles I,
  18
Exeter (Devon), 66
Eyam (Derbys.), 136

Faber, Father Frederick
  William, 13
Fairford (Gloucs.), 111
Ferrar, Nicholas, 190
Fisher, St John, 36
Flatford Mill (Sussex), 221
Fleet Street, London, 19
Fountains Abbey (N.
  Yorks.), 157
Fox, George, 149
Frideswide, St, 91
Fuller, Thomas, 227
Furness Abbey (Cumbria),
  149
Further Reading, 229

Gainsborough, Thomas,
  221
Gill, Eric, 42
Glastonbury (Somerset), 69
Glossary, 230
Gloucester (Gloucs.), 101
Grantham (Lincs.), 187
Great Malvern (Worcs.),
  125
Great Witley (Worcs.), 124
Green Man, 231
Greenwich, London, 25
Grey, Lady Jane, 23
Grosseteste, Robert, 164
Guildford (Surrey), 52

Hadrian's Wall
  (Northumbria), 166
Hailes Abbey (Gloucs.), 112
Hampton Court Palace,
  London, 10
Hardy, Thomas, 64
Hatfield House (Herts.),
  227

Hawksmoor, Nicholas, 6,
  22, 25, 95, 96, 177
Haworth (W. Yorks.), 180
Heckington (Lincs.), 186
Henry VI, 193
Henry VIII, 26
Herbert, George, 53
Hereford (Herefords.), 103
Hexham (Northumbria), 166
Heysham (Lancs.), 146
Hilda, St, 174
Hoar Cross (Staffs.), 135
Holborn, London, 17
Holy Island (Lindisfarne;
  Northumbria), 168
Holy Trinity, Brompton,
  London, 13
Hopkins, Gerard Manley,
  146
Howard, St Philip, 44
Hugh of Lincoln, St, 163
Hull (E.R. Yorks.), 178
Huntingdon (Cambs.), 210
Hyde Park, London, 13

Inns of Court, London, 19
Isle of Wight (Hants.), 54
Isle Abbots (Somerset), 84

Jarrow (Tyne and Wear),
  170
Johnson, Dr Samuel, 123
Jordans (Bucks.), 108
Joseph of Arimathea, 70
Julian of Norwich, Mother,
  216

Keble, John, 96
Kedington (Suffolk), 222
Kempe, Margery, 217
Ken, Bishop Thomas, 73
Keswick (Cumbria), 151
Kidderminster (Salop.), 123
Kilpeck (Herefords.), 105
King, Edward, Bishop of
  Lincoln, 165

King's Cliffe (Northants.), 204
King's College Chapel, Cambridge, 192
King's Lynn (Norfolk), 217
Kingston-upon-Hull (E. Yorks.), 178
Kirkstall Abbey (W. Yorks.), 180

Lancaster (Lancs.), 146
Latimer, Hugh, 93
Laud, William, 23
Lavenham (Suffolk), 222
Law, William, 204
Leeds (W. Yorks.), 179
Leighton Bromswold (Cambs.), 190
Lewis, Clive Staples, 99
Lichfield (Staffs.), 120
Lincoln (Lincs.), 162
Lindisfarne (Northumbria), 168
Little Gidding (Cambs.), 190
Littlemore (Oxon.), 110
Liverpool (Merseyside), 139
LONDON, 6
Lord Mayor's Chapel, Bristol, 87
Ludlow (Salop.), 133
Lullingstone Roman Villa (Kent), 39
Lutterworth (Leics.), 202

Malmesbury (Wilts.), 57
Manchester (Greater Manchester), 145
Martyn, Henry, 81
Mary I, Tudor Queen, 8
Mary, Queen of Scots, 227–8
'The Mayflower', 75
Melbourne (Derbys.), 138
Metropolitan Tabernacle (Spurgeons), London, 22
Mildenhall (Suffolk), 219

Milton Abbas (Dorset), 63
Milton, John, 108, 194
Minster-in-Thanet (Kent), 40
Montgomery, James, 182
More, Sir Thomas, 12
Morris, William, 130
Mount Saint Bernard (Leics.), 202
Mount Grace Priory (N. Yorks.), 174
Mow Cop (Cheshire), 143
Mystery Plays, 119

Nayland (Suffolk), 221
Newark-on-Trent (Notts.), 200
Newman, Cardinal John Henry, 110, 131
Newton, John, 107
Nightingale, Florence, 55
North Elmham (Norfolk), 218
North Marston (Bucks.), 108
NORTH OF LONDON, 223
NORTH-EAST, 153
NORTH-WEST, 139
Northampton (Northants.), 204
Norwich (Norfolk), 214

Old Sarum (Wilts.), 50
Olney (Bucks.), 106
Osborne House (IOW), 54
Osmund, St, 51
Oswald, St, 135
Oswestry (Salop.), 134
Oxford (Oxon.), 91
Oxford Movement, 98

Parracombe (Devon), 76
Paulinus, St, 160
Penn, William, 109
Pershore (Worcs.), 126

Peterborough (Cambs.), 209
Piccadilly, London, 15
Pilgrim Fathers, 75
pilgrimage, 213
Pilgrims' Way (Kent), 35
Plymouth (Devon), 74
Polesworth (W. Mids.), 129
Poore, Richard, 51
Prinknash Abbey (Gloucs.), 113
Prior John of Bridlington (E. Yorks.), 177
Pusey, Edward Bouverie, 97

Quakers' Friars, Bristol, 87
Quarr Abbey, (IOW), 55
Queens and Poets, 8

Raleigh, Sir Walter, 17
Retreat Movement, 37
Rich, St Edmund, 111
Richard of Chichester, St, 38
Ridley, Nicholas, 95
Rievaulx Abbey (N. Yorks.), 174
Ripon (N. Yorks.), 175
Rochester (Kent), 35
'Rock of Ages', 84
Roman Britain, Christians in, 40
Ryle, Bishop John Charles, 141

St Alban's (Herts.), 223
St Alfege, Greenwich Parish Church, London, 25
St Andrew's, Holborn, London, 17
St Augustine's Abbey (Kent), 30
St Bartholomew the Great, London, 20
St Bees (Cumbria), 150
St Benet's Welsh Anglican Church, London, 19

St Benet's Church, Cambridge (Cambs.), 192
St Botolph's without Bishopsgate, London, 21
St Bride's, Fleet Street, London, 19
St Chad's Cathedral, Birmingham (W. Mids.), 130
St Clement Danes, London, 18
St Clether (Cornwall), 77
St Cross Hospital, Winchester (Hants), 48
St Dunstan-in-the-West, London, 19
St Edmund, Lombard Street, London, 22
St Enodoc (Cornwall), 81
St Ethelburga's, Bishopsgate, London, 21
St Etheldreda's, Ely Place, London, 17
St George's Chapel, Windsor (Berks.), 89
St Helen's, Bishopsgate, London, 21
St John's Chapel, Tower of London, 22
St Julian's Church, Norwich (Norfolk), 215
St Laurence Church, Bradford on Avon (Wilts.), 58
St Martin's Church, Canterbury (Kent), 30
St Martin-in-the-Fields, London, 16
St Mary Redcliffe, Bristol, 87
St Mary, Woolnoth, London, 22
St Mary-le-Bow, London, 20
St Mary-le-Strand, London, 18
St Michael's Mount (Cornwall), 68

St Neot (Cornwall), 78
St Paul's Cathedral, London, 8
St Paul's, Covent Garden, London, 15
St Peter Mancroft, Norwich (Norfolk), 215
St Peter ad Vincula, Tower of London, 22
St Stephen, Walbrook, London, 19
Salisbury (Wilts.), 50
Salle (Norfolk), 218
Salvation Army College, London, 25
sanctuary knockers, 128
'Sarum Rite', 51
Saxon Churches, 41
Selwyn, George Augustus and John Richardson, 193
Shaftesbury, The Earl of, 15
Shaftesbury Abbey (Dorset), 59
Shakespeare, William, 127
Sheffield (S. Yorks), 181
Shepherd's Church, Didling (W. Sussex), 45
Sherborne (Dorset), 59
Shobdon (Herefords.), 115
Shrewsbury (Salop.), 132
Simeon, Charles, 195
slave trade, 142
South London, 22
SOUTH COAST, 46
SOUTH-EAST, 30
Southwark Cathedral, London, 23
Southwell (Notts.), 200
Southwell, Robert, 14
Spencer, Stanley, 106
'Spring Harvest', 151
Spurgeon, Charles Haddon, 24
Staunton Harold (Leics.), 201
Stoke Poges (Bucks.), 109

Stone, near Dartford (Kent), 39
Stonyhurst College (Lancs.), 145
Stow (Lincs.), 185
Strand, London, 18
Stratford-upon-Avon (Warwks.), 127
Studley Royal (N. Yorks.), 158
Sudbury (Suffolk), 221
Swarthmoor Hall (Cumbria), 148
Swithin, St, 49
Synod of Whitby (N. Yorks.), 173

Tallis, Thomas, 25
Temple of Mithras, London, 20
Temple Church, London, 19
Temple, Archbishop William, 34
Tennyson Down (IOW), 56
Tennyson, Alfred Lord, 56
Tewkesbury (Gloucs.), 101
Thanet, Isle of (Kent), 30
Thaxted (Essex), 224
Theodore of Tarsus, 33
Thomas de Cantelupe of Hereford, 104
Thomas à Becket, St, 33
Time Line of English History, 4
Tintagel (Cornwall), 82
Tissington (Derbys.), 137
Tower of London, 22
Trafalgar Square, London, 15
Trebetherick (Cornwall), 81
Trewint (Cornwall), 78
Trollope, Anthony, 50
Truro (Cornwall), 79
Tyburn, London, 13

Venerable Bede, 171

Venn, Henry and John, 24
Verulamium (Herts.), 223
Victoria, Queen, 54–55
Vindolanda (Northumbria), 166

Walpole St Peter (Norfolk), 216
Walsingham (Norfolk), 212
Waltham Abbey (Essex), 226
Wareham (Dorset), 61
Warwick (Warwks.), 128
Wellow, (Hants.), 54
Wells (Somerset), 71
Wesley, Charles, 184
Wesley, John, 79, 183
Wesley's Chapel, Bristol, 87
Wesley's House, City Road, London, 20
WEST COUNTRY, 66
WESTERN MIDLANDS, 116
WEST OF LONDON, 89
Westminster Abbey, London, 6
Westminster Cathedral, London, 13
Weston Longville (Norfolk), 218

Whippingham (IOW), 55
Whitby (N. Yorks.), 172
Whitchurch Canonicorum (Dorset), 64
Whitehall, London, 16
Whitefield, George, 102
Wight, Isle of, 54
Wilberforce, William, 179
Wilfrid, St, 161
William of Wykeham, 49
Wimborne (Dorset), 61
Winchelsea (E. Sussex), 41
Winchester (Hants.), 46
Windsor (Berks.), 89
Wing (Bucks.), 107
Wolsey, Cardinal Thomas, 11
Woodforde, Parson James, 219
Worcester (Worcs.), 116
Wreay (Cumbria), 152
Wren, Sir Christopher, 10
Wulfstan, St, 117
Wyche, St Richard of, 38
Wyclif, John, 203
Wymondham (Norfolk), 219

York (N. Yorks.), 159

Ingram Content Group UK Ltd.
Milton Keynes UK
UKHW022213050523
421320UK00009B/105

9 781853 115226